Las Vegas Blackjack Diary

Stuart Perry

ConJelCo titles:

Books

Winning Low-Limit Hold'em
by Lee Jones

Las Vegas Blackjack Diary
by Stuart Perry

Software

Blackjack Trainer for the Macintosh

Blackjack Trainer for Windows

Ken Elliott's CrapSim Professional for DOS

Ken Elliott's CrapSim Interactive for DOS

Percentage Hold'em for DOS

Sozobon Poker for Windows

Las Vegas Blackjack Diary

Stuart Perry

ConJelCo
Pittsburgh, Pennsylvania

Las Vegas Blackjack Diary
Copyright © 1997 by Stuart Perry

Library of Congress Catalog Card Number: 96-72324

Third Edition
1 3 5 7 9 0 8 6 4 2

Cover design by Cheri Soriano

ConJelCo
132 Radcliff Drive
Pittsburgh, PA 15237
[412] 492-9210

Table of Contents

Foreword by Don Schlesinger

E very once in a while, a new blackjack book arrives on the scene that is destined to become a classic—a work so different from any other before it that it must be read by all who are fascinated by the game of casino twenty-one. Such is the case with Stuart Perry's wonderfully compelling *Las Vegas Blackjack Diary.*

Not a professional, by any means, Perry studied the Hi-Opt I counting system, read everything he could from the "experts," took a $20,000 stake, and headed west to attack the Las Vegas blackjack tables. Now, this is not the first time that an aspiring card counter has taken such an approach to the game. What makes Perry's saga unique is that he had decided, before leaving, to chronicle *every session* of blackjack that he would play during his two-month adventure! And document it, he did! We are caught up in the intrigue of the "cat-and-mouse" game, played by every counter who tries to avoid detection and, ultimately, barring; we suffer with Perry as he endures the inevitable downswings inherent in the nature of the exercise; we rejoice after the big wins; and most of all, vicariously, we *live* the life of a card-counter going up against the "big boys" in this gripping real-life account.

Along the way, we learn a tremendous amount about the game of blackjack, for Perry, although not a published "authority," is nonetheless, extremely knowledgeable when it comes to blackjack matters. A true expert in the field of sports wagering, Perry has a great mind for numbers, odds, and probabilities, and thus has a deep understanding of the complexities of the game. As we move from casino to casino with him, Perry is never shy to impart a blackjack lesson or two along the way. Thus, we learn painlessly, effortlessly, and almost in spite of ourselves. And always we are eager to "turn the page" to see what awaits Stuart in his ongoing battle with the Las Vegas Strip and downtown casinos.

Some time ago, I wrote an article for Arnold Snyder's *Blackjack Forum*, entitled "A Day in the Life of a Table-Hopper." In it, I tried to convey the atmosphere of a daytripping, Atlantic City card-counter (me!), as he moved up and down the boardwalk, trying to win money playing blackjack. Perry has expanded upon this theme in the grandest of styles, baring his soul, and leaving no stone unturned in an effort to bring to life the *true* lessons that over 230 hours of grueling play taught him. And this is a major highlight of Perry's work, for although it reads very much like a novel, every word in the diary is true.

In short, this is a book destined to become a classic on the blackjack scene. Perhaps most valuable to the aspiring counter just setting out to tackle the tables, there is much in *Las Vegas Blackjack Diary* for the more experienced player, as well. For, in addition to having a pleasant, engaging writing style, Perry is an excellent *teacher.*

I don't wax ecstatic about too many blackjack books that come down the pike, but trust me on this one: you're about to embark on an exciting journey, and you're going to love reading *Las Vegas Blackjack Diary.*

Don Schlesinger
November 27, 1996

Foreword by Arnold Snyder

About a year ago, Stuart Perry called me and told me about a journal he'd kept throughout an 8-week blackjack marathon in Las Vegas. He asked me if I'd like to read it. Sure, I said, more out of politeness than genuine interest. Eight weeks of blackjack table results scribbled into a notepad sounded to me about as interesting as reading logarithm charts. But I sensed it was important to him, a big piece of his life, and I didn't want to hurt his feelings by telling him not to bother sending it.

After I received the manuscript, it laid around my office for a month, six weeks, maybe two months!, with Stuart calling me once or twice a week to ask me what I thought of it. Finally, more to get him to stop pestering me than anything else, I decided to give it a quick read, skim it over so I could make a few apropos comments, so he would at least know I'd looked at it. Then I could send it back to him so it would stop collecting dust on top of my filing cabinet.

Not twenty minutes into my "quick read," I was immersed into his adventure. My heart was following his ups and downs, his "random fluctuations" at the tables. Here, in this crude diary, was everything that computer simulations can't tell you about the roller coaster ride of trying to beat the casinos at blackjack. The hopes. The dreams. The enormous swings. The victories. The defeats. The long, boring sessions of nothingness. The fears of being cheated, of questioning your own abilities, of trusting the "experts" whose books and systems you'd taken on faith.

Stuart had put his heart into this journal. No bullshit. No padding. No bragging. No pretensions. Just a man with a dream to beat the casinos, and the guts to tell the world where it led him.

This is a phenomenal book. It would bore the hell out of anyone who never dreamed of being a professional gambler. It will fascinate and enlighten the true aficionados of the game. That the original manuscript spent weeks collecting dust in my office is today more of an embarrassment to me than anything else. And when I think back to the irritation I'd felt each time Stuart had called me to ask me if I'd looked at it yet, I'm ashamed of myself.

I don't think I've ever properly thanked Stuart Perry for sharing his manuscript with me, for his honesty, his guts, and his dogged persistence. So, thanks, Stuart. Thanks for writing it. Thanks for sending it to me. And thanks for bugging my ass for weeks on end to get me to read it. I discovered a treasure in your words, and I'm sure thousands of players will likewise feel the same gratitude I feel that you've had the courage to tell it like it is.

Arnold Snyder
December 15, 1996

Preface

For 30 years, the book market has been inundated with publications that tell you how to make fortunes in casinos by playing blackjack and counting cards. The majority of these books tell of almost continuous winning experiences and give winning examples of all pointers. Many of them brush aside losses and negative fluctuations, or worse yet, use these as "proof" that blackjack dealer cheating still exists. *Las Vegas Blackjack Diary* is not such a book.

The heart of this book covers the eight-week period in which a former successful sports bettor with a good mathematical mind and a strong background in the wagering field played casino blackjack in Nevada for serious stakes for the first time. The author's eight-week diary relates the day-to-day, session-to-session experiences covering two months and more than 230 hours of decent money blackjack play. In this period of play, the author won—though at a rate much less than he expected.

The introduction of *Las Vegas Blackjack Diary* relates the events and previous blackjack experience that led to the two-month period of his serious blackjack play in Nevada.

In the diary portion of the book, the author reveals the monetary results and other details of every blackjack session (one of which lasted just one hand before a barring!) he played in the casinos between February 28 and April 22, 1994. He relates details about the camouflage and *acts* used to keep casino personnel from recognizing him as a pro and discusses how he received and reacted to the inevitable "heat" casinos heap on winning card counters.

During this eventful spring of 1994, the author faced many different dealers. Some of them tried, at varying risks to themselves, to help him; others acted squarely in the interests of casino management. He also met, observed, and interacted with other players— some decent but most not—and talks about those encounters.

Unlike most accounts of blackjack play, the diary tells of the wild up-and-down financial fluctuations of actual casino play and pays particular attention to the grinding emotional experiences that occur as a result of these swings, an element missing from many other books.

Uniquely, the author takes a long-hard look at the mistakes he made, criticizes them, and notes the adjustments he had to make in his play, his act, and his overall playing style in order to win, discovering—as do all successful blackjack players—that winning at blackjack is a never-ending learning experience.

Every serious blackjack player must be concerned about two relevant playing issues—dealer cheating and player barring. They are covered as part of the diary.

As further aids for readers who have various degrees of blackjack knowledge, the Appendices cover the rules of the game, basic strategy, and the count system and play indices of the Hi-Opt I card-counting system (used by the author) respectively. Also included in the Appendices is a brief history of card counting and why it has the potential to be successful for the player, as well as the basics of shuffle tracking, a technique used by some serious blackjack players in shoe games.

On February 24, 1994, the author began surveying Nevada's casinos, looking for the games best suited to his bankroll before jumping into action. Then on the 28th, the real work commenced.

Hop on board, put yourself in the author's shoes, and find out the truth about the real world of blackjack counting.

One final note. In this book, the author makes general references to the third person singular as "he." Obviously, he could be "he" or "she" since both men and women are members of every part of the blackjack world. For brevity and to avoid possible confusion, "he" is used throughout this book.

Acknowledgments

I wish to thank 13 people, who were a major direct or indirect help to me in this project.

First is Frank, a long-time counter I spoke with many times. Frank started my blackjack education before I ever played a hand in the casinos. I used several techniques and camouflages he taught me.

Second is Lance Humble, whose Hi-Opt I count fulfilled my need for a simple, but effective count system. In my play, I used Humble's High-Opt I indexes from -6 to +6. These were published in his *World's Greatest Blackjack Book*.

Third is Arnold Snyder, whose many books and publications, such as *Blackjack for Profit*, *Beat the X Deck Game* series, *Blackbelt in Blackjack*, and *Blackjack Forum* (for which I have contributed a few articles) were an invaluable aid in helping me locate and exploit the best games. Snyder's works also helped me calculate my expected win rates and probable fluctuations in various games. Snyder also wrote a foreword for this edition of the *Las Vegas Blackjack Diary*.

Fourth is Stanford Wong, whose book *Blackjack Secrets* was a tremendous help in my Diary play and whose *Basic Blackjack* made me ready for any strange rule or situation that may pop up in a blackjack game. Wong understands, probably better than anyone, the financial as well as the emotional fluctuations of the game of blackjack. (Wong also contributed to this book since the index numbers I used for the Hi-Opt I count system in Appendix C were derived using his *Blackjack Count Analyzer* computer software.)

Fifth is the late Paul Keen, formerly of the Gamblers Book Club. I knew Paul, through the GBC, for several years before my blackjack play. Thanks, Paul, for all the answers you gave me to my blackjack questions. Thanks again for providing me with the Hi-Opt I indexes for the over +6 and under -6 counts that I used in my play. Every time I win by standing on a 13 versus a ten or by hitting a 16 versus a six, I think of you, even as the other players at my table swear and curse at how "lucky" I was with my "stupid" play! I hope all of your hands are winners and all of your games are hassle-free now, Paul.

Sixth is Peter Griffin, author of *The Theory of Blackjack*. I used the tables from his book in my calculations of the effects of various rules, the value of deck penetration, as well as the off-the-top-edge of the casino in all of the blackjack games that I played in Las Vegas and Laughlin.

Seventh is Norm Young, an up and coming East Coast blackjack counter and a vastly underrated computer expert. Norm, I've enjoyed our long blackjack conversations on topics like fluctuations, risk of ruin, computer simulations, the stupidity of some casino employees, and many other blackjack-related topics. Thanks also, for the help you gave me with my computer on this project. And a very special thanks for the computer simulations you tirelessly ran for me on streaks and the effects of fairly extensive bet camouflage; they weren't perfect, only excellent!

Eighth is Dwight Burdette, a Michigan computer expert and the only non-blackjack person on this list. Thanks, Dwight, for answering all of my questions about my computer and its operation. Thanks for tolerating my computer illiteracy in our conversations. Without your patience, I have doubts that my 486 computer would have finished this job. Instead, it probably would have been thrown through my office window by now!

Ninth is Don Schlesinger, noted blackjack author, theoretician, and player. Don painstakingly helped me to edit earlier editions of *Las Vegas Blackjack Diary*, and wrote a foreword to this edition of the book.

There are three characteristics that I would like to share with readers concerning Don Schlesinger. First is his tremendous knowledge of the game of blackjack and his attention to its details. I greatly respect any professional who pays attention to detail. In our fast-paced, corner-cutting, and largely phony world, true and competent professionals like Don Schlesinger are becoming exceedingly rare. Happily, they are not yet extinct. I will always treasure the conversations I had with Don and the insights I gained from them.

Second is Don Schlesinger's true passion for the game of blackjack. As someone who also brings strong passion to activities and work I take part in—including the game of blackjack—I really respect this part of him. It is too bad that more people in our world can't bring Don's passion of blackjack to their own activities.

And, third, is Don Schlesinger's patience. In my talks and get-togethers with Don on this book, I came to know how much about the game of blackjack I still have to learn. As a 20-year veteran of the game, Don has patiently—and never condescendingly—imparted some of his knowledge of the game to me.

Very often when I speak to players about the game of blackjack, I, in an exasperated way, ask myself, "Why are you wasting your time talking to this dope, Stuart?" With Don, I sometimes wondered why he wasted his time talking with "a dope" like me. And, this was a first in my blackjack experience!

Thanks again for your editing help on this book, Don. I hope your prediction that it is a "landmark" book for counters who want to play for extended time comes true.

Tenth is Bart, a knowledgeable blackjack player who found mistakes not seen by either myself or Don Schlesinger in the first edition. Thanks for your help, Bart. You have shown me that a writer can never receive too much quality help in a project like this.

The next three contributors were most helpful for the ConJelCo edition of *Las Vegas Blackjack Diary*. Chuck Weinstock, of ConJelCo, the publisher believed in this book enough to become its publisher. Thanks for greatly raising the quality of the printing, layout and binding of the book. Let's hope that your belief in *Las Vegas Blackjack Diary* makes it a winner for both of us.

Maryann Guberman edited the book for ConJelCo. Thanks for improving the readability of the book.

Lastly, I wish to thank someone on the other side of the blackjack tables—Bill Zender of the Aladdin Hotel and Casino. Bill graciously provided a quote for the cover of this edition. While we are enemies at the tables, Bill, your quotes show that you have respect for someone that makes a serious effort to beat the game of blackjack. I have deep respect for how you work in the interests of the casino in the game of blackjack, as you will see in the chapter on "Player Barrings" beginning on page 150.

Anyone who thinks that I made any mistakes or has any other comments about *Las Vegas Blackjack Diary* can get in touch with me either on-line at sdperry@aol.com or can write me at:

Stuart Perry
PO Box #262
Yonkers, NY 10704

I n casino betting there are only two games in which a bettor has a long-term opportunity to profit via skillful play. One of these games is poker. If a player is better than the other players at the table and the fee paid to the casino to play isn't high, he should make a profit. The long-term odds are in this player's favor in such a game.

The other casino game in which a skilled player has the potential to enjoy a long-term edge is blackjack.

The key to winning at blackjack is counting or keeping track of the cards. As we show later, this does not mean that the player knows every single card that comes out of the deck or shoe. All counting systems keep track of high cards (tens and aces) versus low cards (usually threes through sixes, though some systems also use twos and sevens). When the deck is rich in tens and aces, the game is favorable and the counter bets more. Because the deck or shoe is almost never shuffled after every hand, the cards that come out on one hand (or round) have a relation to the cards not yet played. In other words, if a lot of low cards have been played and the deck or shoe is still being dealt, the probabilities are that a higher than normal percentage of tens and aces—cards good for the player—will be dealt.

In other casino games, like craps, roulette, keno, or slot machines, each event is independent of every other event. Thus the odds of rolling a 12 in craps are always 1 chance in 36. This is true whether the last two rolls were 12's or if 12 hasn't come up in 75 rolls. The dice have no memory. In blackjack, the cards do. That is why this game has the potential to be beaten by a competent player.

Unlike in poker, the blackjack player isn't competing against other players. His job, and the task of every other player at the table, is to try to beat the dealer. If a player is able to keep an accurate count in a game with good conditions (more on this later) and makes correct plays and correct betting decisions, the long-term odds are in his favor. Sufficient size bankrolls are needed for both the professional poker and the card-counting blackjack player, just as adequate capitalization is needed for every other business.

Another major difference between casino poker and blackjack is the casino's attitude towards winning players. The casino has no qualms with professional poker players; these players are winning the money of other players at the table. The casino gets its profit regardless of the table results. Blackjack is very different. The player is trying to win against the dealer—someone who is an employee of the casino. Any win that a blackjack player enjoys is a financial loss to the casino. If the casino thinks the player has an edge via card counting or even if the player is a high roller (by this, I usually mean a poor player betting a lot of money) who is having a lucky run that poses an immediate financial threat to it, the casino may bar him or prohibit his play. As I have seen, different casinos have different tolerance levels in this regard.

The only casinos that are not permitted to bar card counters are those in Atlantic City. As I quickly came to realize, the Atlantic City casinos have other ways of making life miserable for card counters. These are shown in the chapter "Player Barrings" beginning on page 150.

Thus expert blackjack players must have a different approach to casino play than expert poker players. Poker players can always use the best play and bet strategy to their advantage; they have no fear of being kicked out of the casino because of expertise and wins (or potential winnings). However, a blackjack player who always bets correctly on every hand according to the count will have a very short blackjack playing career if he plays successfully and for any real money (playing mostly at $25 and up minimum tables). Thus, camouflage and "putting on an act" are paramount to survival because virtually every casino has employees who know that blackjack can be beaten by a skilled count player playing under good conditions.

My Start In Blackjack

For many years I had been heavily involved, financially, in one of the other wagering enterprises that can give the skilled bettor a long-range edge: sports betting. Though I was well ahead lifetime in that field, I had decided in December of 1992 to look for other financial pursuits. The last serious sports wager I made was on the final game of the 1993 NBA playoffs. By this time I was much more involved with blackjack than with sports.

My study of blackjack began with the reading of several books: Ed Thorp's *Beat the Dealer*; Lance Humble's *The World's Greatest Blackjack Book*; and Lawrence Revere's *Playing Blackjack as a*

Business, provided good starting points. Later, books and publications by Stanford Wong, Arnold Snyder and the late Ken Uston were helpful.

From Humble's book, I picked up and still use the Hi-Opt I count system. In this count system, threes through sixes are low cards (bad for the player) and tens (tens, jacks, queens and kings) are the high cards (good for the player). The other cards of the deck: the twos, sevens, eights, nines, and aces are considered neutral cards. Fairly early in my play I found it very helpful to keep a side count of aces; in my opinion, Humble underestimates the importance of the ace side count in his book.

As I read blackjack books, I started practicing blackjack at home. First, I learned the basic strategy. Basic strategy shows the correct way to play every hand assuming that the player knows only his cards and the dealer's up-card. In other words, this is the correct way to play blackjack without counting or tracking the cards. In about a week I knew basic strategy cold to the point of total boredom.

Then, I started counting. First, I practiced with two decks. I practiced a running count, which told me how many extra high or low cards—in comparison to each other—were remaining. Since there were 32 of each (16 in each deck), the count at the end was supposed to be even or zero. At first, counting cards gave me a headache! It seemed hard to master and I seemed to be dealing to myself too fast. But, I eventually got the hang of it.

Then I started to practice playing hands and varying my bets. Finally I learned how to adjust my playing strategy according to the running count. I continued doing this with two decks. My two deck running count practice lasted for about a month.

Finally, I graduated to the true count. The true count is the running count divided by the number of decks (or fraction of remaining decks) to be dealt. Being able to compute and make correct play and bet decisions based on the true count is mandatory if one wants to become a professional-level blackjack player. Most card counters make serious mistakes in this area. Either they estimate the remaining deck or decks incorrectly or they make mistakes in the division, which causes incorrect bet or play decisions. These mistakes with the true count are one of the reasons that most counters lose money in their blackjack careers.

When I started to practice the true count, I started playing with six decks. This practicing and mastering of the true count took me another month and a half.

I now decided I was ready to seek my blackjack fortunes in the Atlantic City casinos. On paper, I had done well with a 1-8 spread in the six-deck game over a 10,000-hand span. However, I was to see that playing blackjack at home and playing it in the casino were very different. I did not really fully understand blackjack factors such as fluctuation and good play conditions at this time.

As is typical of many rookie blackjack counters, I had decided far too soon to play for big stakes in the casinos. I learned my lesson quickly. In late February of 1993, I drove to Atlantic City and played for about seven hours at the Trump Plaza. I played mostly in head-on games and mostly at the $25 minimum tables—tables at which mid-shoe entry was prohibited (a rule specifically made to frustrate back-counters [Wongers] who try to play only in favorable shoes). During my play I varied my bets from $25-$200 a hand and always played just one hand. I never increased my bet by more than $25 a hand and did so only after a win.

And, I got my ass kicked losing slightly over $3,000. Part of the reason for my loss was that I struggled to keep the true count at casino speed (though when I lost track of it, I left the table). Another part of the reason I lost was that I didn't yet realize that a six-deck game in which just four decks are dealt (as was the case at Trump Plaza) is not beatable with a 1-8 spread. As I was to read a month later in Arnold Snyder's excellent *Beat the X Deck Game* series (volumes covering one-, two-, four-, six-, and eight-deck games in detail are featured in this series), a six-deck game with the bet spread I was using yields only a.25% to.33% edge assuming perfect play and bet spreading. I was thus playing in a poor expectation game: a game with poor playing conditions (counters should try to play in conditions that yield at least a one percent edge).

However, probably the main reason that I lost was that I experienced what blackjack pros call a negative fluctuation. These negative runs are ignored by almost every blackjack author (Stanford Wong, Arnold Snyder, and the late Ken Uston are the major exceptions) and media promoters who claim that card counting in blackjack is a quick road to wealth. I had endured losing streaks at home; however, in the casino, with real money at stake, it felt different. I decided I needed more practice. I also saw that I still had much to learn about the game of blackjack.

In retrospect what I probably should have done was to learn the game more slowly in stages, then play for small stakes after each stage. First, I should have—as I did—learn basic strategy cold. Then I should have played for small stakes in the Atlantic City casinos. Then I should have gradually mastered each part of card counting—the running count and varying the bets, the running count and varying my play from basic strategy, and then finally varying bets and then playing strategy with the true count. Trying to master everything before a trip to the casino made matters more difficult.

However, this book is about my experience in blackjack play, so it is appropriate that it is told truthfully. Perhaps, readers can learn from my mistakes.

After my Atlantic City debacle, I practiced harder at home. I now incorporated an advanced technique: an ace side count for betting purposes, which I had not done prior to my first casino play (yet another possible contributing factor to my losses). In later chapters I will discuss why this technique is important.

In April of 1993, I decided to go to Las Vegas for a couple of months. I'd bet small stakes in blackjack until I could count at casino speed in my sleep. Since I was still following professional basketball, I also decided to bet the NBA playoffs on this trip. Because I would be playing for small stakes, I doubted that anyone would bar me.

On this Vegas trip, I varied my bets from $5-$40, then $10-$80 and finally, $5-$80. I always played one hand, virtually never more than doubled my previous bet and never bet over $20 unless I had won the previous hand and the count was high enough. The true count had to be +3 or more for me to make my maximum bets.

I played a variety of blackjack games in Vegas mostly two-deck games; later in the trip I played a fair number of one-deck games. I played four-deck games occasionally at Circus Circus and Palace Station (the only Vegas casinos with four-deckers then) and very occasionally played six-deck games. In the second month in Vegas, I sometimes played in games in which the dealer hit soft 17 (a rule that harms the player to the tune of about 0.2 percent).

In these two months I played about 110 hours in about 20 casinos. Only once was I badly hassled. Outside of this incident, I got only a few glares from pit bosses and a few shuffle-ups. (The pit boss can order the cards to be reshuffled at any time. This is usually done to frustrate counters and eliminate positive situations.)

The time I got severely hassled was in my third graveyard shift visit to the Pioneer Club casino in downtown Vegas. In my first graveyard visit to the Pioneer Club I was the only player in the casino. I played against a very friendly female dealer from mainland China. Since I was now fairly good at counting at casino speed, I could easily talk and play at casino speed in the two-deck game. The dealer and I talked about China (a subject I have always found fascinating) during my play session. During this session one of the pit bosses was practically sitting on the table as I was winning about $150. During my 45-minute play, this boss took two phone calls from upstairs (from the "eye in the sky").

When I quit my play, I wished the dealer and the pit boss a nice night; the dealer responded in a friendly way and the pit boss sneered, "Well, you have a nice night, too, *sir!*"

A week or so later I again played on the graveyard shift at the Pioneer Club. On this visit, there were about ten other blackjack players present. I got ahead about $300 in about 15 minutes (a very lucky positive fluctuation considering my betting level) when a new dealer came to my table. I lost five of six hands—and about $60—to this new dealer (winning only on a blackjack). Since I felt a little (probably unjustifiably) paranoid, I left.

Two nights later, I again returned to the Pioneer Club on the graveyard shift. Only one other player was playing blackjack in the casino. As soon as I reached the table, the pit boss crept up to my dealer and whispered to him. For two straight decks, the dealer dealt only six hands—1/3 of the two-decks—and shuffled. A 1/3-dealt two-deck game is a waste of time. I left—ahead $10 for the session—and have never played at the Pioneer Club since. Later, a sports-betting friend of mine (one of the few that know I play blackjack) informed me that the Pioneer Club is known as a "sweat joint" meaning they hate to have anyone win at all. This friend told me, just half-jokingly, that he was surprised I wasn't arrested.

Over the 110 hours of 1993 Vegas blackjack play, I won slightly over $1,000. However, these profits did not come without some wild fluctuations. I sometimes won or lost over $800 in a day. Considering that my biggest bet was $80—a level I very seldom reached—I was starting to understand how much of a financial roller coaster blackjack was. Most importantly, I was now able to count at casino speed.

After another month of constant practice at home, I took a trip to Michigan to visit some friends and also play blackjack in the Indian casinos. The Michigan blackjack games I played were four-deckers, in which three decks plus were dealt—good penetration. I was able to get away with a $5-$160 bet range on one hand with very little casino hassle in my 25 hours of play.

I ended up a few hundred dollars ahead playing blackjack in Michigan; but, more importantly, I also learned two more lessons about the game.

First, I learned even more how severe fluctuations can be in blackjack. At one time, I was behind over $1,800 for the trip. Very soon after, in three hours of play, I won $1,500, which was the key to my winning for the trip.

Second, and even more important, I finally came to realize that different games with differing rules meant that I had to use different true counts to raise my bets. Using Las Vegas examples, a bettor playing a double-deck game at the Golden Nugget—a downtown casino in which the dealer hits soft 17 and the player may not double after a split—faces a .52% disadvantage off the top of the deck. In such a game, a bettor like myself needs a true count of +1.75 to have any real reason to raise his wager. At the Excalibur, the double-deck game has much better rules for the player; in this game he may double after a split and the dealer stands on soft 17. With these rules, the player has only a .175% disadvantage off the top, and may profitably raise his bet when the true count reaches +1. (Bankroll considerations are very critical in bet-raising decisions.)

Before the latter part of my Michigan play, I was always raising my bet on a true count of +1 no matter what number of decks and rules I played. I wondered how I had won in Las Vegas playing so stupidly.

Getting Ready For Las Vegas

During the Autumn of 1993, I planned another blackjack trip to Las Vegas. As yet, I didn't know when this would occur. But I knew that on this trip I would play for serious money. I planned to vary my bets from $25 on one hand to as high as $200 on two hands.

I planned to use various camouflages. I might ask pit bosses for advice on hands in which there was a close play decision; thus, no matter what they advised, I couldn't be badly hurt on long-range expectations. I'd make a few mistakes that were not costly (such as sometimes not doubling on soft totals of 16 or less). On bets in which I had a total of $100 or more risked on a round, I would not increase after losses. Sometimes—particularly in single-decks—I'd start with big bets off the top, especially if I was winning.

I figured I would still be barred in some clubs despite my camouflage. I would avoid places in which big action brought undue attention.

Meanwhile, I used the lousy games of Atlantic City to practice my bet and play camouflages and also to add the final weapon to my playing arsenal: keeping a side count of aces for playing decisions. For example, when doubling down on a nine or a ten, the more aces left in the deck, the better for the player, and the more likely I am to double. When deciding to double on an 11, extra aces left in the deck make it more likely that doubling down should be avoided, especially when the dealer has a nine showing (an ace in the hole gives the dealer a 20). In insurance decisions, the more aces (which act as small cards for this decision) left in the deck, the less likely I am to take insurance. This is a good camouflage since some pit bosses realize that counters are likely to insure when big bets are on the table. When the deck is rich in aces, I am likely to bet big—since aces are good for me—but less likely to insure. Conversely, on some small bets, which I may make when the deck is lean in aces, I am more likely to insure since extra aces—or small cards for this decision-have been played).

In November and December of 1993, I took seven trips to Atlantic City and played about eight to ten hours on each trip. I varied my bets from $5-$100 a round and occasionally jumped my bets radically (as from $5 on one hand to two hands of $20) since Atlantic City casinos can't bar counters. I also practiced my act on dealers, pit bosses, and players. I told jokes, sometimes made deliberately stupid comments, and tried out different deportments to see which ones would bring the least attention to me.

I played the six-deck games at the Trump Plaza and Trop World and won about $650 on these trips. These winnings were more than my expected win rate, thus I had been lucky. Fluctuations of $1,500 and more occurred—part of the game.

In between these Atlantic City trips, I played about another 100,000 hands at home in simulated Las Vegas casinos with one, two, and six-deck rules. I practiced in one and two-deck games with various rules with about a 65% shuffle point and in six-deck games (with double after split but no surrender allowed) with a 75% shuffle point. I practiced various types of bet camouflage—especially in the one and two-deck games.

Though I won at over a 1% rate, I saw that the fluctuations would be strong. I had one negative swing of $13,000, and two negative swings of about $9,000 in my 100,000 hand marathon. Since I figured that I would play between 200 and 250 hours in Las Vegas (and probably play about 25,000 hands), I knew I would probably have one downswing of at least $9,000. With a $20,000 bankroll, I expected that I could handle such a loss.

By mid-February of 1994, I felt confident that I was finally ready to play blackjack for real. I would go to Las Vegas with my $20,000 and play from about March 1 through May 1. In 200 hours plus of play, I believed I was a favorite to win at least $10,000 or $40-$50 an hour. I would be very disappointed if I won less. I thought that a win in the $15-$20,000 range was very possible. If I was very lucky (had more positive fluctuations than negative ones), I could win over $20,000.

I knew that all sorts of experiences—some expected, some not—awaited me in the Las Vegas casinos as I tried to win serious money in them as a professional card counter. These experiences are related in the upcoming diary.

Before reading my diary, readers should be able to understand and see through several myths concerning blackjack and card counting. Seeing through these myths will not only help readers to understand this diary better, but will also help them harbor realistic financial expectations about the game of blackjack. After reading this section, the reader will also have insights into the many authors in the blackjack field; he will be able to judge correctly if an author has genuine knowledge of the game or is a phony trying to sell a get-rich pipe dream.

Myth: Counters always make money playing blackjack.
Pit bosses and shift supervisors often spout this myth as an excuse to bar count players. However, upper management in almost every casino knows that most counters lose money in the long run. How do they know this? Because the vast majority of their colleagues who sit in the eye in the sky are former card counters. Almost to a man, these former counters are those who made just enough mistakes to lose. Even under good playing conditions, which sometimes are hard to find, a card counter's edge seldom exceeds 1 percent for the long run. Just a few key mistakes can wipe out a card counter's financial edge and put him into the red.

Myth: Counters can significantly beat any blackjack game.
Even assuming that a card counter always raises his bets at the right time and makes perfect playing decisions, he may still be an underdog to win money in the long run in some blackjack games. Deck penetration, the rules of the game, the number of other players in the game, his ability to see the cards of other players (in the face down games) for play decisions, and the betting spread he uses are all factors in whether a counter has the long-range potential to win money in a given game. Deck penetration is the most important factor and the bet spread of the counter is probably the next most important factor of those mentioned above.

For example, if a card counter uses a 1-4 bet spread in a 2/3 dealt six-deck game in which he plays every hand (unlike table hoppers, or Wongers, who almost always play in just positive decks), he virtually will never have a long-range edge of over 1/4 percent. This counter probably will have to play over a million hands and play perfectly (which is something no counter does) to have a statistically significant edge. This represents about ten years of full-time playing, with all sorts of mean negative fluctuations thrown in. With bad game rules, such as the dealer hitting soft 17 and the player being allowed to double only on ten or 11 on his first two cards, even a 1-8 bet spread and perfect play would lose money in a 2/3 dealt six-deck game in which every hand was played.

On the other hand, a 1-4 bet spread would win money in most one-deck games over the long haul. The main exception to this would be a one-deck game with an off-the-top disadvantage in which the dealer shuffles after every hand (which sometimes does happen). With good play, a 1-6 bet spread in a single-deck game with decent rules and 50 percent or more penetration would garner a professional a better than 1 percent win rate.

Arnold Snyder's *Beat the X Deck Game* series shows a player's short and long-range financial expectations in one-, two-, four-, six-, and eight-deck games. Examples showing the effects of 50, 65, 75 and 85 percent penetration with various bet strategies are shown for each of the games. There are numerous bet strategies for various games in which Snyder shows that even a perfect counter is playing at a long-range disadvantage.

Myth: When the count is high,
the counter wins a majority of his bets.

Most counters believe this myth. Even the late Lawrence Revere in his book, *Playing Blackjack as a Business*, stated that the player will win the majority of his high-count bets.

When some counters go on a losing streak in high-count situations, which, as I'll show, is as likely as when the count is negative, they whine that they were cheated and sometimes quit playing. The reality of blackjack is that a professional player will, in the long run, win between 47 and 48 percent of his non-tied hands in virtually any deck and count situation. Before the cards are dealt, the player is virtually always a favorite to lose that hand.

The reason that decks rich in tens and aces favor the player is not that he'll win more hands in such decks, but that four positive financial events are more likely to occur in such decks than in negative (low-count) decks. These events will not only wipe out his surplus losses, but will also give the professional a long term edge—assuming, of course, that he is playing in a profitable situation to begin with. These four events are as follows:

1. The player is more likely to get a blackjack dealt to him.
This is by far the most important player edge in a high-count deck. Of course, the dealer is also more likely to get a blackjack. However, the player gets paid 3-2, or 50% over his original investment, on a winning blackjack while he loses just even money to a winning dealer blackjack. The 3-2 blackjack payout for a player blackjack versus an even money loss to a dealer blackjack represents a 25 percent edge to the player in hands in which a blackjack is dealt. Since a count player tries to bet more money when the deck is rich in tens and aces, this 25 percent edge is vital.

The ace's place in a blackjack (and it being only 1/4th as likely to be dealt as a ten value card) is the reason that the ace is such a key card in betting decisions.

The insurance decision is also related to the higher instance of blackjacks in a high-count deck. When the dealer has an ace up, the player can make a side bet at 2-1 odds that the dealer has blackjack (the player can bet up to 1/2 his original bet). In a high-count deck, the count player is likely to take insurance; correct use of this option increases the above-mentioned 25 percent player edge over the house on blackjacks since he will use insurance to cut down his losses to dealer blackjacks.

2. The player will profit more heavily when he doubles down.
When a correct double down play is made, the player is always the favorite to win that hand. Doubling down exploits these favorable situations by giving the player the opportunity to invest more money when the odds of winning are most in his favor. When a player doubles down in a high-count deck (a deck with extra tens, especially), he not only tends to have more money on the table, but also has his best chances of winning.

One drawback to high-count decks in terms of doubling down is that a player will be doubling down less than he would in lower count decks. This is because there are fewer of the small cards needed to create nine, ten, and 11 player totals: the totals a player is most likely to double down on.

3. In a high-count deck, the player is more likely to split pairs
Unlike doubling down, which should always be done to make more money, pair splitting is often a defensive gesture in which the player is trying not to make more money but to cut losses. The concept behind most pair splits—wagering more money in a fi-

nancially losing situation—seems contradictory. That is, a player is doubling his investment in order to lose less money on two hands than he would on one.

If you watch somewhat knowledgeable but amateur blackjack players, you will often see them make poor pair split decisions; this is because they remember losing money in pair splits (especially twos, threes, sixes, and eights—particularly eights versus tens and aces). What these players never comprehend is that they lose more money by not splitting those pairs at the right time.

There are some times when pair splitting is an offensive decision, a decision in which the player is favored to win money. Splitting aces (except versus an ace), and nines (versus a two through six and an eight) are two major categories of offensive pair split decisions. Splitting eights versus a three through a seven is an offensive split with a tremendous gain: the player now is a favorite to win money on the round by playing two hands rather than lose money on one (on a 16, the worst total a player can get). For a card counter, splitting tens versus a four, five or six in a positive deck provides a huge gain. Instead of being a favorite to win one hand, he now is a long-range favorite to win more than one bet (though sometimes a counter should not split tens since this play can be a giveaway that the player is counting). Ten splits are also an economic gain in a high-count deck because a counter is more likely to be dealt two tens in a deck that is rich with them.

In a high-count deck, the counter tends to have a big bet out. Cutting losses, which pair splitting usually tries to accomplish, is extremely important on these bets.

4. A number of casinos allow surrender.

When a player surrenders a hand, he does so after receiving the first two cards. Assuming the dealer does not have a blackjack, the player gets back half of his bet on a surrendered hand. (This assumes that early surrender—an almost obsolete rule—is not in force.) In a high-count deck, surrender is more likely to be a correct play. Like most pair splitting decisions, surrender cuts down losses and in the long run preserves more winnings. The correct use of the surrender option can be worth 1/4 percent or more to a card counter using a large bet spread.

Another important factor concerning surrender is that the hands a player is most likely to take this option on—15's and 16's versus a dealer ten—are more likely to appear in high-count decks. If surrender was not allowed, the player would be more likely to lose these bad (or stiff) hands than he would in a more neutral deck.

Thus, surrender not only cuts down losses more strongly in high-count decks, with the counter having his biggest bets out, and not only is the player more likely to surrender in a high-count deck, but the player is also more likely to be dealt a surrenderable hand as well in a ten-rich deck.

Myth: Counters win every time they play.

The late Ken Uston had teams of blackjack players that allegedly made millions of dollars in casinos around the world (though I have heard differing reports about the success of these teams). Before the practice was outlawed, some of Uston's teams used hidden computers in casino blackjack play. With these computers (which kept track of every card played), Uston's teams won at a supposed 80 percent rate in one-hour play sessions: and always playing in favorable games. Thus, even in great conditions and with perfect play, a counter will lose at least 20 percent of the time.

Without the use of a computer in the casino (a felony in virtually all jurisdictions), a good player is only a slight favorite to win money in a one hour or so session: the amount of time my sessions will be. I hope to be able to win in about 55 percent of my play sessions. Uston's teams were very happy if a 60 percent winning rate was attained in their sessions.

Thus, even with expert play in good games and good conditions, even the best counter will lose money at least four out of every ten hours he plays. For counters, losing sessions, days, weeks, and even months are inevitable. Wild fluctuations in blackjack are unavoidable. My two months of play in Las Vegas would show that once again.

When I watch someone play, the least important factor in how I judge that person's play is how he does financially. I realize that the 15 minutes to half hour I may be watching represents a very short run in which almost anything can and often does happen, financially. Casinos that have pit employees who get alarmed over a player solely because he is on a short-term hot streak, represent the epitome of financial stupidity.

I flew to Las Vegas the night of February 23 happy to get away from the New York winter: its worst in over a hundred years. I decided to spend the next four days scouting the casinos to see what kinds of blackjack games were being offered. I would also use Arnold Snyder's *Blackjack Forum*, and Stanford Wong's *Current Blackjack News*, as guides. Both list every Vegas casino and provide the reader information about each casino game in terms of deck penetration, rules, and how casinos react to big money being bet. However, I used these guides primarily as a backup because blackjack conditions in the Vegas casinos can change literally overnight.

Though I visited virtually every casino, there were a few that I knew would not be playable for my purposes. I skipped Caesars Palace because they never deal more than four decks out of six and some times they deal as few as three. I need a six-deck game that is dealt at least 4-1/2 decks through. I skipped the El Cortez (a downtown casino in which pit bosses go on high alert if a player bets $10 or more on a round). And I skipped the Barbary Coast (considered by many players to be the burn joint of all burn joints). During my experience in Las Vegas, I was to hear nothing but bad reports about the Barbary Coast. Pit bosses even get paranoid when a basic strategist plays well. Counters using even a $5-$15 bet spread have been barred. In addition, dealers I spoke to often mentioned how Barbary Coast dealers are badly hassled by the pit when a table is losing, regardless of circumstances. Lastly, the games dealt at the Barbary Coast are terrible from a counter's perspective. Often less then 50 percent of the two decks are dealt: an unacceptable game to play in. And I have another, personal, reason to avoid the Barbary Coast. A fellow who I used to allow to pick my brains on sports betting is employed in their sportsbook. When I stopped giving him freebies, this "oddsmaker" got very angry towards me. I am sure he would like nothing better to get me barred from the tables of this and any other casino that he has influence in.

If all goes well, I'll start play on Monday morning, February 28. I will be staying in a quiet off-Strip apartment complex in which I have rented a room during two other Vegas stays. I will keep my money in a box at one of the Vegas casinos in which I have a good give-and-take relationship with the sportsbook director. I won't be playing at this casino; the games there are not as bad as the three casinos mentioned above, but are not up to my playing standards.

After my four-day casino tour, I decided that there were 24 casinos in which I would be able to play on a somewhat consistent basis. I decided that I would play in these 24 casinos on a rotating basis. I would play in virtually none of them more than two of the eight weeks that I would be playing here. I also would virtually never play more than three sessions on any one shift in any casino in any one week.

I also made some money management decisions. I would limit sessions to an absolute maximum $2,000 loss (usually my limit would be about $1,000; however, if the game conditions were excellent, I would play further into a loss) and would virtually never play more than one hour at a time. If I got ahead in the session by $1,000 or more, I would, for the most part, set a stop-loss limit at 1/2 of the profits. Each of these money management decisions was made so that I would limit losses, but not wins. Playing this way also gave me psychological, if not mathematical, comfort. If I get $1,000 ahead in a session, it is nice to know that no matter what happens, I'll be leaving with at least a $500 profit. Suffering a loss after getting $1,000 ahead is a depressing and mind-draining experience that could affect my play in the next session. Also, I would usually quit a session after about a $1,000 losing streak; for instance, if I got $600 ahead and then fell $400 behind, I'd stop.

I also made decisions on how much to play on each hand. In single-deck games, I would keep my betting between $25 on one hand to two hands of $100. I'd often play over the minimum off the top. On other games I'd go from one hand of $25 to two of $200, or whatever I could get away with. I would never progress past two hands of $50 unless I was coming off a win of some kind.

Though some players might consider these huge and waiting-to-be-barred bet spreads, I decided to use them for two reasons. First, I wished to have over a 1 percent edge in games I played. Use of a smaller spread would not give me such an edge. And second, if I used a smaller spread, bet camouflage (such as betting big off-the-top in single-deck) would take away much of my edge. I think a player who uses a small bet spread with no camouflage is much easier to spot as a counter than one who uses a larger spread with camouflage.

Though I wish to give as honest an account as possible, I must change some names, times, and, occasionally, casinos. I am doing this to protect not only myself for future Vegas visits, but, more often, dealers, who sometimes gave me much better games (usually in terms of deck penetration) than was the norm of the casino employing them.

Unlike some counters, I do sometimes tip dealers. The main reason I do so is to get better deck penetration in key situations. I virtually always tip by betting for the dealer on hands I play. If I have a very strong session I may tip an extra dollar or two at the end of it, particularly if the dealer has been friendly. On average, my tipping will probably be between $6-8 an hour, and, hopefully, I'll get value that exceeds that. If not, I may have to revise this policy.

Before I write my observations of the playable casinos, I should mention what criteria I use for evaluating a casino for potential blackjack play. There are five factors that I consider.

1. How a casino reacts to the bet sizes I want to make.

To make blackjack a worthwhile occupation, a player needs to be betting enough so his long-range expectation is to earn at least $40-$50 per hour in casino play. If a player isn't going to be earning that much, blackjack should be just a vacational pastime, not a present or potential occupation.

To make decent money, a player has to bet decent money. And, to do that over any long run, a player must be able to make decent-sized bets without drawing excessive attention. Being the biggest bettor in a casino is not a good way to guarantee long-term play.

I wanted to be able to progress to as high as $100 on two hands in a single-deck game and as high as $200 on two hands in multiple-deck games. I figured that these high bets were needed to be able to earn at least $40-$50 an hour over the long haul. I would mostly steer clear of casinos in which I couldn't reach these high bets, at least occasionally.

2. Deck penetration.

As any serious blackjack player knows, the most important factor in the game is how far into the deck a dealer goes before shuffling. The deeper the penetration, the more likely a player will obtain a high true count (running count divided by the remaining deck(s)). More high-counts mean greater long-range profits.

Stanford Wong mentions a routine example of the importance of deck penetration on page 82 of his *Blackjack Secrets*. In a two-deck game a player has a true count high enough to give him a 4.8 percent edge (a true count of at least +7 or +8 is needed for this edge).7 percent of the time with 50 percent (52 card) penetration, 3 percent of the time with 73 percent (76 card) penetration, and 4 percent of the time with 79 percent (82 card) penetration.

Another factor concerning deck penetration is that the less the penetration, the higher the percentage of hands a player bets off the top with a disadvantage. Conversely, the deeper the penetration, the smaller the percentage of hands off the top the player bets with a disadvantage. A crowded table hurts a counter in the same way presenting him with a larger percentage of hands with a disadvantage off the top.

Yet another critical factor regarding deck penetration is the vanishing casino advantage at various points of deck penetration. This is covered thoroughly in Don Schlesinger's *Floating Advantage*.

Thus deeply penetrated games not only will give the player a greater percentage of good counts, but these good counts also are worth more than earlier in the deck or the shoe. This floating advantage comes into play more strongly in single and double-deck than in shoe games.

What constitutes good deck penetration? In single-deck, 60 percent dealt is a good game and a player should try to avoid play in a game when less than 50 percent of the cards are dealt. In double-deck, 2/3 penetration is good; 75 percent or more is great, and a player should try to avoid games with less than 60 percent penetration. In four- or six-deck play, a player should never settle for less than 75 percent penetration. Over 80 percent (3.2 decks dealt) constitutes a good four-deck game and over five decks dealt (83 percent) makes a good six-deck game.

I very seldom play eight-deck games. If I had to play eight deckers, I would play either as a table-hopper (playing only in plus true counts) or in games in which at least seven of the eight decks were dealt. In my two months of Las Vegas play, I did not participate in any eight-deck games.

3. Crowd conditions.
I wanted to play head-on as much as possible. Head-on games let me play more hands and bet more money per hour. Also, as stated

earlier, they yield the fewest percentage of hands bet in non-profitable, off-the-top situations. All of these factors mean more long-range profit.

In face down games, which all one-, two- and four-deck games in Vegas are, head-on play would mean that I would know all the cards for my play decisions. After my third week of playing in Vegas, I almost always avoided face down games in which more than two other players were present.

4. Rules of the game.
The number of decks and the rules used determine the house edge off the top of the deck or shoe. The number of decks, rules and some simple mathematics would tell me when it was profitable to raise my bets, and by how much, under optimal conditions.

Good playing rules for the player include double after split (DAS), which is worth about 0.14 percent, and surrender, which is worth at least 0.06 percent. Bad rules for the player include a dealer hitting soft 17, which is worth around 0.2 percent for the house, and no doubling on soft totals or nine totals, each worth about 0.13 percent or less for the house. The more decks used, the less these last two particular rules hurt the player.

The more decks in play, the bigger the house advantage off the top of the deck. The use of two decks is worth about 0.32 percent for the house. The use of four decks is worth about 0.48 percent for the house. The use of the eight-deck monsters gives the house a 0.57 percent edge off the top.

I nearly always avoid games in which the house edge is much over 0.5 percent. Only once on this trip, because of a unique rule and great deck penetration, did I play in a game with much over a 0.5 percent casino edge off the top.

In the charts that follow this chapter, I show the exact casino off-the-top advantages in various games and how the rules used can effect these advantages. In these charts, I also show the counter's advantage, or disadvantage, in each of these blackjack games for each full plus true count up to plus eight.

5. Casino treatment of counters.
When I started my play on this trip I had limited knowledge in this area. My experience was limited to my 1993 Las Vegas blackjack play, articles I read in Snyder's *Blackjack Forum* (his September

1993 Cheesies award article was informative and humorous), talks I had with two dealers I got to know during my 1993 visit, and my conversations with Frank, a long-time Vegas card counter I had been introduced to by a mutual acquaintance.

I wanted to be very sensitive to overplaying in any given casino. With extensive time, any intelligent pit person (and most casinos have some) can tell if a player is not only a card counter, but also a competent one. Thus the reason for my time limits.

If I had total freedom, I'd choose only nine Vegas casinos in which I would play blackjack. These casinos were: the Aladdin, Desert Inn, Excalibur, Golden Nugget, Harrahs, Imperial Palace, The Mirage, Palace Station and Treasure Island. In each of these casinos, there were profitable games in which I could probably bet decent money. However, if I played in just these nine casinos in my 200 plus playing hours, I might wear out my welcome in any or all of them. This is why I need to and am willing to play in 15 other casinos in which the games are somewhat less tolerable.

Below are my observations of the 24 casinos that I considered playable.

Aladdin: Has probably the best blackjack penetration in Las Vegas. One and a half decks or more are dealt in their two-deckers and at least five (usually 5-1/2) from their six-deckers. Surrender and DAS are allowed in all games and the dealer hits soft 17 in all games. The excellent deck penetration is the biggest plus here. Another plus is that heavy action is not discouraged.

However, the biggest minus of the Aladdin games is that their pit crew, eye-in-the-sky, and the head man, Bill Zender, all have the reputation of being very sharp—they spot counters, and bar only the real threats in terms of competent and big play. Counters who never go past $100 a round virtually never get barred from the Aladdin. Some professional players, who have never been barred in other casinos, have been barred at the Aladdin.

I'll definitely play at the Aladdin, but not until my fourth week in Vegas when my play act has improved. I'll keep almost all Aladdin sessions under one hour.

Circus Circus: This casino has great penetration on most games: up to 3/4 dealt on the two-deckers and at least 3/4 on the four-deckers. No DAS will keep me away from their six-deck games.

The single-deck rules (no DAS but dealer stands on all 17's) give even a non-counting basic strategist a small edge (.02 percent) in the game. Only the Frontier (a place I won't play in because of their long unsettled strike) matches Circus's single-deck game.

Circus's biggest minus is that it caters to the smaller bettors, they have just one $25 minimum two-deck game. The one-deck game may be very hard to play for any real money. Still the great penetration here will get some, though not a great deal, of my action.

Desert Inn: This casino has just six-deck games. Next to the Aladdin, the Desert Inn has the best six-deck games in Vegas; in fact, their total package might be better. DAS and surrender are allowed and the dealer stands on all 17's. At least 4-1/2 and often close to five decks out of six (some dealers go still further) are dealt. Big action is not sweat by the pit, and the uncrowded conditions often allow heads-up play.

The Desert Inn also has a reputation of tolerance towards counters. They'll certainly get a lot of my shoe play.

Excalibur: One-, two-, and six-deck games are offered in this casino. There are several pluses to playing here. First, two huge and separate game areas permit a player to move around a lot and not stand out (though I am sure that the "eye" can and has followed players around). Second, penetration is excellent in the single- and double-deck games: 60 percent in single-deck and sometimes close to 75 percent in double-deck. Third, the double-deck rules are as good as almost any in Vegas: the dealer stands on all 17's and DAS is allowed. These rules give the casino under a .2 percent edge off the top. Fourth, when I played here last year—though then it was for small stakes—I got little heat in spreading my bets. Still, since this is one of the few casinos in which Frank, the longtime counter I know, is allowed to play. That says something about the tolerance of the Excalibur.

The two major minuses of the Excalibur are that the $25 minimum tables—the tables I figure to play most at—are six-deck games. These games give the player at a .4 percent disadvantage off the top, by far the biggest off-the-top player disadvantage in this casino. And, second, it is hard, but not impossible, to find 75%+ penetration in these games, the minimum to settle for in six-deckers.

However, there is a good deal of green ($25) action in the single and especially double-deck games. I have even seen occasional black ($100) action on these tables. I imagine I'll play six decks the majority of the time at the Excalibur, but I'll be sneaking into the one- and two-deck games if I sense that my action is not sticking out.

Flamingo Hilton: This casino offers two- and six-deck games in which the dealer stands on all 17's and DAS is allowed. According to both Snyder and Wong, the penetration here is great. However, my scouting trip proved quite otherwise; the deck penetration here now stinks. A player is lucky to get over 50 percent penetration in the two-deckers and 2/3 in the six-deckers. These penetration changes must have occurred recently since Snyder's four time a year *Blackjack Forum* and Wong's monthly *Current Blackjack News* have competent reporters.

The one plus here is that big action doesn't bother the bosses. There are lots of $25 tables. However, I imagine that I'll play here only a little and only because I need to spread myself around as a counter. I'll probably play just the two-deckers and try to get the best penetration I can.

Fremont: I still have nightmares about the $800 plus loss I had in this casino in under two total hours of play at the $10 minimum table during my small stakes play last year. This loss was over ten top bets ($80)! I did not think that I would be able to play here this year, but my scouting trip revealed that the Fremont now has a $25 minimum table. So, I'll give at least some play to this casino. The major minus is the bad two-deck rules (all their games are two-decks). The dealer hits soft 17 and DAS is not permitted. This gives the house slightly over a .5 percent edge off the top. However, penetration seemed good—in the 2/3 area. And deck penetration is the most important factor for a counter in a blackjack game.

Gold Coast: This casino got bad grades from both the Snyder and Wong reporters. However, my observations showed otherwise in this all-two-deck blackjack casino. In every game I observed, I noted 2/3 deck penetration and that will bring me to this casino. A few $25 tables seem to indicate that some players bet decent amounts. The rules are mixed: DAS is allowed, but the dealer hits soft 17. Often crowded conditions seem a minus. Still, the blackjack at the Gold Coast seems highly beatable.

Golden Nugget: This is probably the best place for me, or practically anyone else, to play blackjack in Las Vegas. (For small stakes players the Aladdin might be better, though not by much.)

The Nugget has, in my opinion, everything going for it. First, when I played here last year, I spread from $5-$80 on one hand and never got any heat doing so. Second, according to Frank, the Nugget doesn't consider counters like me ($25 on one hand to two hands of $200) a financial threat and thus is willing to put up with a player like me for "a long time." This opinion was corroborated by a dealer named Steve that I got to know a little here last year (who has since moved away).

In addition, and very importantly, the Nugget offers very beatable games. Though they hit soft 17 and don't offer DAS in their single- and double-deck games, the penetration is often great. Over 50 percent and up to 2/3 and beyond can be found in single decks and at least 2/3, and up to 75 percent, can be found in double decks. The six-deck Nugget games allow DAS and surrender and the dealers stand on all 17's. Between 4-1/2 and five decks are dealt in the six-deckers.

Lastly, the Nugget buffet has excellent and healthy food. I'm sure that I'll play at the Nugget more than any place else and I may be willing to play over an hour at a time and over three hours on a shift per week in this casino.

Harrahs: This looks like a very good place to play mostly because the games are deeply dealt—up to 1-1/2 decks in the two-deck games and often over five decks are dealt in the six-deck games.

The rules are a mixed bag. Surrender is allowed in both games, but DAS is allowed only in the six-deck games. The dealer hits soft 17 in both games. Thus, the casino's off-the-top edge is over .4 percent in the two-deck games and over .5 percent in the six-deck games (the great penetration more than compensates). Strangely, in many of the Harrah six-deck games, the cards are dealt face down, while most casinos deal face up in six-deck games.

Another minus is that the only $25 tables are in the six-deck games and there don't seem to be many players in my financial league in this casino.

Still, the superb penetration will get my play here. How much I will play the two-deck game versus the six-deck game will depend on how my action is accepted.

Horseshoe: Virtually every game in this wild (Damon Runyon must be crying in his grave over the characters he missed in this joint) downtown casino is single deck. The rules are typical downtown Vegas: the dealer hits soft 17 and no DAS is allowed; the player however can re-split aces and thus starts with a 0.14 percentage disadvantage off the top. $25 tables are easy to find and big action seems plentiful and, seemingly, is not sweat too much.

However, there are three major minuses in Horseshoe blackjack. First, Frank, my major counter information source, and others have told me that the Horseshoe is very fast to "flat bet" counters (forcing them to bet the same on every hand of a deck, thus destroying their edge). Second, I did not like the way their dealers held the deck very close to their chests when dealing. Though it seems unlikely to happen, dealers could deal seconds, undetected, holding the cards this way. I did find out later that the dealers dealt this way at the Horseshoe because of casino policy. It seems that some dealers found ways of stealing chips when the cards were dealt lower down; this way of dealing supposedly makes stealing less likely. The third major minus of the Horseshoe is the crowd conditions. This place always seems to be jammed, even at three in the morning! In single decks, I almost never play with more than two other players at the table and that could be a hard find here.

I'll play at the Horseshoe but will probably leave if conditions are too crowded, I feel any real heat, or I feel at all suspicious about the dealer. My average session here will probably be in the 30-40 minute range.

Imperial Palace: Though I certainly don't agree with the publicized purported pro-Nazi shenanigans of the owner, I'll play in this casino. Winning will thus provide two rewards for me: I'll make money and make a purported Nazi-lover poorer.

Politics aside, this is one of the best places to play in Vegas. The rules and deck penetration are good; DAS is allowed in both games; the dealer stands on all 17's; and in terms of penetration, up to 75 percent is dealt in the two-deck games and five of six-decks are dealt in the shoes.

Even though I saw just a couple of $25 minimum two-deck games and no $25 six- deck games, green and even black chip action is not at all unusual in what a sports-betting friend of mine calls "The Hitler Joint."

Las Vegas Hilton: This is another casino in which Wong and Snyder need to provide their readers with a negative update. Deck penetration has been recently flushed down the toilet. Players are lucky to get over 50 percent penetration in the two-deck games and 75 percent in the six-deckers. The DAS and surrender rules as well as the very relaxed attitude towards big action are small pluses. Like its sister casino, the Flamingo Hilton, I'll play in this casino only because I have to spread my action around.

Luxor: This casino has all six-deck games with DAS, but no surrender, allowed. The best penetration I saw available was 75 percent, and that was hard to find. This is yet another spread-myself-around casino, which I'll play in only because they don't seem to sweat big action that much. The Luxor will probably provide me with an occasional break from the far superior Excalibur games, which are right next door.

Maxim: Before I scouted this casino, I didn't think it would make my play list. Not only is the Maxim allegedly the home of the Griffin Detective Agency (an agency that, among other things, hassles counters), but also they were reported to have lousy games.

Well, their games seemed halfway decent when I observed them. I saw up to 2/3 of the two-deck games being dealt and some decent money being bet in them. The six-deck games had lousy (2/3) penetration, so I'll probably avoid them. The DAS and surrender rules are also pluses. I'll play in the Maxim games with caution and be on the lookout for any scrutiny by plainclothes cops!

MGM: This is the second of the three newer Las Vegas casinos. Four-, six- and eight-deck games are offered. I'll pass on the eight-deckers and I'm not nearly rich enough to play in the $500 minimum four-deck games. That leaves the six-deck games.

I mostly liked what I saw in the six-deck games. Between 4-1/2 and five decks were dealt to players, who mostly, especially at the $25 tables, enjoyed fairly uncrowded conditions. DAS, but no surrender, is allowed. The Wizard of Oz theme of the casino seems friendly. I'll probably go to the MGM theme park during some blackjack break.

Mirage: Last year, the high ($25 was big blackjack money for me then) two-deck table minimums kept me away from their blackjack tables. This year I'll play the two- and six-deck blackjack games in the fancy Mirage.

I've received good reports about the Mirage and its tolerance of counters. It's supposed to be as good as the Nugget's. Though I have to see (actually feel) this tolerance to believe it, I did see abundant black-chip action as I scouted the games. Several play pits and areas are a plus: I will have room to roam.

The two-deck Mirage games are excellent. The dealer stands on all 17's and DAS is allowed. 2/3 deck penetration seems normal.

The penetration seems so-so in the six-deck games—few dealers go past the 3/4 mark. Surrender is permitted in the six-deck games.

I'll mostly play the two-deck games and play the six-deckers only if the two-deckers get too crowded

Palace Station: They offer two-, four-, and six-deck games. In all of them the dealer hits soft 17 and the player can DAS.

Before I made my observation trip here, I did not know if this casino would be playable for me. Last year, I experienced some heat from the pit and I was not very happy with the dealing depth.

However, unlike casinos such as the Las Vegas and Flamingo Hiltons, the Palace Station provided me with a pleasant surprise; penetration is much better than in 1993. Now 75 percent or more is dealt in the two-deck games and about 80 percent (3.2 decks out of four) is dealt in the four-deck games. The six-deckers seemed to have barely 3/4 penetration, so I'll probably avoid those games because of the hit soft 17 rule.

Only one $25 minimum table and little overall big action were the minuses. I also remember Frank's tale of being backroomed (not only barred, but interrogated in a backroom) in this casino a few years ago. But, it seems that times and policies may have changed here for the better. My own Palace Station blackjack experiences will provide the answer.

Plaza: If this casino was in an-out-of-the-way place, I would not have even checked out its blackjack games. I well remember the intense scrutiny I received in this casino last year whenever I bet over $20-$25. The Plaza is also known as a small-bettor place.

However, I was happy to see a $25 minimum one-deck game with 60 percent or more penetration. The dealer hits soft 17, but unlike other downtown one-deck games the player can DAS. Thus the player has a dead-even game off the top. This will make it easy for me to throw in all sorts of bet camouflage off the top.

Though I won't spend large amounts of play time in the Plaza, I will come here to play, probably when the heat chases me out of the Horseshoe up the street!

Rio: This was another casino that I was surprised to put on my play list. But, that is what scouting trips are for.

Though the one-deck rules are of the bad Reno variety (no DAS, no doubling except on 10 or 11, dealer hits soft 17), I saw some decent action being tolerated and some good deck penetration. The two-deck games sometimes had 2/3 penetration (one could double on any first two cards in this game) and also had some heavy green action. I wasn't impressed with the six-deck games; 2/3 seemed the normal dealing depth.

The Rio is another casino that I am willing to play in, if sparingly.

Riviera: This was my most played casino last spring. I liked the two-deck rules (DAS) and the consistent 2/3 penetration. Even better, dealers often went further in if they were tipped at the right time. However, Riviera blackjack has gone downhill in 1994. The rules are the same, but the penetration now is almost never 2/3. Hopefully, tipping will still get me good penetration.

One plus concerning the Riviera. When a player plays two spots in most casinos, he must bet at least double the table minimum on each hand. At the Riviera, a player can play the table minimum on each. Other casinos allowing this are the Mirage ($25 or higher tables), the Las Vegas Hilton, Treasure Island ($25 or higher), and the Gold Coast.

I noticed that head-on play was often available at the $25 two-deck Riviera games. That may be a big help.

Sands: Two- and six-deck games are available in this casino, which is now undergoing construction. Assuming that I can see and breathe through the sawdust, the games may be profitable. $25 minimum games with good penetration are available in the two and six-deck games. Two-deck games had 2/3 penetration available and the six-deck games had up to five decks dealt.

In the two-deck games, the dealer hit soft 17 and DAS was not allowed. The reverse are the Sands rules in the six-deck blackjack games. [Editor's note: Since this book was written, the Sands has closed its doors.]

San Remo: I was surprised to see a fair amount of heavy action in the two-deck games in this casino. In $5 minimum games at that! The penetration was about 2/3 and DAS was allowed. I won't play here that much, but the San Remo deserves at least a try.

Stardust: This is another casino that I'll play in a little, but would avoid if blackjack and card counting existed in a perfect world. The only reason I'll play here at all is that large action and decent bet spreads are tolerated in the two-deck games. This may compensate slightly for the lousy penetration (hard to get over 55 percent) and no DAS being allowed.

Treasure Island: This is Las Vegas's third new casino and Steve Wynn's third in Vegas (the Golden Nugget and the Mirage are the other two). Hopefully, the pit is as tolerant of counters as the Nugget and the Mirage are said to be.

The Treasure Island rules are the same as the Mirage in both the two and six-deck games. DAS is allowed in both games and surrender is permitted in the six-deck action.

The bet action seems much smaller than the Nugget and the Mirage. However, the deck penetration seems good: 2/3 in the two-deck games and 4-1/2 to 5 decks dealt in the six-deck games.

I've heard that the Treasure Island has very liberal comp policies. I plan to use comps a lot, especially for meals. There are two reasons for this: First, using comps makes me appear to be a "normal" gambler out to get bargains; and second, I'll save time and money on food. The money I can always use for other items (can't we all?) and the time saved I hope to use winning more money playing blackjack.

One huge mistake I made when I first started to play blackjack was to raise my bet at the same true count—usually plus one—in every game I played. This is a mistake that I know is made by many counters I have spoken to. Unbeknownst to them (and me, at one time) they are sometimes raising their bets when they have negative financial expectations. I was fortunate to spot my mistake in this area (during my July 1993 Michigan play) before huge monetary damage occurred. To raise bets in an optimal way, a professional blackjack player needs to have not only a full understanding of how the rules and number of decks in play create various percentages for and against him at various times of play, but also realize how any advantage relates to his betting bankroll.

A blackjack player must play according to his available betting bankroll. For example, the player who often makes a $50 bet with a $1,000 bankroll when he has just a 1 percent edge on a round will eventually go broke even if he plays perfectly. Thus, different players with different bankrolls must approach the same blackjack games differently in terms of how much to wager at various times.

I can not speak financially for any blackjack player except myself. However, what I can mention here are the percentage advantages that a player enjoys in various blackjack games at various counts. These listings can help all card counters decide what their optimal bets should be at various true counts. These listings can be particularly helpful for table-hopping players who can use them to determine the exact right time to enter a game (depending on how much of an edge they want) and the exact amount to wager. Despite casino scrutiny and heat, which makes some bet camouflage a necessity for most counters, this guide can still be helpful to all counting blackjack players.

The calculations shown below are done with the following assumptions:

1. The basic rules of the game are the following: a) the dealer stands on all 17's; b) the player may double down on any first two cards; c) the player may not double after a pair split (or no DAS); and d) the player may not surrender his hand.

2. These rules are commonly referred to as "Las Vegas Strip" rules. For each game, I state what the variations from these rules mean to a player's expectation in percentage advantage gained or

lost. The plus and minus effects of various rules (figured to two decimal places) are from Peter Griffin's *Theory of Blackjack* (1988 edition).

3. For each true count (going from plus one to plus eight), I add .5 percent to the player's expectation. This is an appropriate figure for a level-one count such as the Hi-Opt I or the commonly used High-Low. This .5 percent figure is used by Arnold Snyder in his *Beat the X Deck Game* Series. Arnold also recommended that I use this figure in this section.

In negative counts, the player expectation does not always decrease by .5% for a count player who plays perfectly. Correct play decisions and variations from basic strategy can lessen the disadvantage. Nonetheless, I don't list negative counts in the tables since a player will always be at a disadvantage with these counts. The only comment I'll make about negative counts is that they are a good time to either leave the table to find another game, go to the bathroom, or make the smallest bets you can get away with.

4. In each section the effect of deck penetration on player advantage is mentioned. In deeply penetrated games, the player not only has a better chance of seeing high true counts, but these counts give the player a greater financial expectation than would the same true count earlier in the deck.

One Deck

Table 1: One Deck Player Edge at True Count

True Count	Players Edge	True Count	Players Edge
1	0.52%	5	2.52%
2	1.02%	6	3.06%
3	1.52%	7	3.52%
4	2.02%	8	4.02%
Off-the-top casino edge: -0.02% (player has 0.02% edge)			

Table 1 shows how the player's advantage changes when the true count changes in a single-deck game. Table 2 shows the effects of various rule changes on the player's advantage in single-deck games.

Table 2: Effects of Common Rules on Single Deck Play

Rule	Effect on player's edge
No soft doubling	-0.13%
No doubling on nine	-0.13%
Dealer hits soft 17	-0.19%
Re-split of aces allowed	+0.03%
Double after split allowed	+0.14%

Let's see how the player advantage—or disadvantage can be calculated for a couple of common single deck games. In the Plaza single-deck games, the dealer hits soft 17 (a .19% player disadvantage), but the player may re-split aces (+.03%) and also DAS (+.14%). Adding in the .02% player edge with the Las Vegas Strip rules we assumed, a player is playing a dead-even game at the Union Plaza. The above table shows that when a counter has any advantage, he is playing with at least a 1/2 percent edge.

And, better yet, if the count player has rounds dealt with under a half deck to play, he gains—because of the value of this deck penetration—an additional 1/2 percent edge. In other words, in a neutral (zero count) deck at the under 1/2 deck level, the count player actually has a 1/2 percent edge! With a +2 true count at this level, the counter's edge jumps up to 1.5%!

Going away from downtown and off the strip, we come to the Rio. Their one deck rules give the player a tougher game than the Plaza's. At the Rio, the player may not double on soft totals (-.13%), or on nine (-.13%), and the dealer hits soft 17 (-.19%). In this game, the player has—adding in the .02% for the basic rules—a .43% disadvantage off the top. If the player has a true count of +1, he has a much smaller edge (.07%) than he would at the Plaza (.5%). Still, if a round is dealt with under a half deck to play, a neutral count would give the counter a minuscule .07% edge: adding .5% to -.43%.

Two Decks

Table 3: Two Deck Player Edge at True Count

True Count	Players Edge	True Count	Players Edge
1	0.18%	5	2.18%
2	0.68%	6	2.68%
3	1.18%	7	3.18%
4	1.68%	8	3.68%
Off-the top casino edge: 0.32%			

Table 3 shows how the player's advantage changes when the true count changes in a two-deck game. Table 4 shows the effects of various rule changes on the player's advantage in two-deck games.

Table 4: Effects of Common Rules on Two Deck Play

Rule	Effect on player's edge
Double after split allowed	+0.14%
Dealer hits soft 17	-0.21%
Surrender allowed	+0.03%
No soft doubling	-0.11%
No doubling on nine	-0.1%
Re-split of aces allowed	+0.05%

Let's look at how rule variations effected my two-deck play in two Las Vegas casinos: The Golden Nugget and the Las Vegas Hilton.

At the Golden Nugget my off-the-top disadvantage was .53 percent in their two-deck games. In addition to the disadvantage of playing two decks (.32 percent), I also was playing in a game in which the dealer hit soft 17's (another .21 percent disadvantage). In this game, I had a slight disadvantage with a true count of +1 (.03 percent: obtained by adding .5% to -.53%). Thus, it was to my advantage to be making small bets until the true count reached the neighborhood of +2 (when I would have a .47 percent edge).

At the Las Vegas Hilton, the rules were as good as in any two-deck game in Las Vegas. The player could DAS (+.14%) and also surrender (+.03%). These .17 percent bonuses cut down the house off-the-top edge to .15 percent. In this game a true count of +1 gave me a .35 percent advantage, as opposed to the .03 percent disadvantage I was going against at the Golden Nugget.

However, I still played the two-deck games at the Golden Nugget more because of their excellent penetration, which often exceeded 2/3. At over 2/3 penetration in a two-deck game, a counter's edge goes up .5 percent. Thus, in an neutral deck at 2/3 penetration, my disadvantage was just .03 percent. In addition, the potential for getting high true counts was much greater in the Golden Nugget's excellent penetration game than it was in the poor (seldom exceeding 55 percent, and virtually never exceeding the magic 2/3 point) penetration game of the Las Vegas Hilton.

Four Decks

Table 5: Four Deck Player Edge at True Count

True Count	Players Edge	True Count	Players Edge
1	0.02%	5	2.02%
2	0.52%	6	2.52%
3	1.02%	7	3.02%
4	1.52%	8	3.52%
Off-the top casino edge: 0.48%			

Table 5 shows how the player's advantage changes with the true count in a four-deck game. Table 6 shows the effects of various rule changes on the player's advantage in four-deck games.

Table 6: Effects of Common Rules on Four Deck Play

Rule	Effect on player's edge
Double after split allowed	+0.14%
Dealer hits soft 17	-0.21%
Re-split of aces allowed	+0.07%

The four-deck game is becoming a rarity. Most casinos that offer shoe games in Las Vegas have six-deck games. A few have eight-deck games, which I have almost never played (except for a little Atlantic City practice). The only four-deck games I was to encounter in Las Vegas were at Circus Circus and Palace Station.

Circus Circus had Las Vegas Strip rules, which puts the player at a .48 percent disadvantage. Even with a true count of +1, the player is only about even (actually a .02 percent edge) with the casino. At the Palace Station, the dealer hits soft 17 but permits the DAS option—a net loss of .07 percent for the player from the Las Vegas Strip rules, and thus a .55 percent disadvantage off-the-top. Thus, a true count of over +1 is needed for a counter to have an edge in the Palace Station four-deck game.

In order for deck penetration to play a role in a four-deck game a round must be dealt out after the 80 percent (or 3.2 decks) penetration level. This seldom happened in these games.

Six Decks

Table 7: Six Deck Player Edge at True Count

True Count	Players Edge	True Count	Players Edge
1	-0.04%	5	1.96%
2	0.46%	6	2.46%
3	0.96%	7	2.96%
4	1.46%	8	3.46%
Off-the top casino edge: 0.54%			

Table 7 shows how the player's advantage changes with the true count in a six-deck game. Table 8 shows the effects of various rule changes on the player's advantage in six-deck games.

Table 8: Effects of Common Rules on Six Deck Play

Rule	Effect on player's edge
Double after split allowed	+0.14%
Dealer hits soft 17	-0.22%
Surrender allowed	+0.06%
No soft doubling	-0.09%
No doubling on nine	-0.09%
Re-split of aces allowed	+0.07%

Six-deck blackjack is the most common type dealt in the world today. When one compares the player edges at various true counts in the six-deck game with the one-deck game (virtually never dealt outside of Nevada), it is easy to understand why counters wish that the clock could be turned back 30 years in order to return to the days when almost all games were single-deck. Additionaly, the rarity with which high plus counts occur in the six-deck games—as compared to the single-deck games—show why blackjack is much tougher to beat than in "the good old days."

The somewhat good news is that decent rules are more likely to be found in six-deck blackjack than in other games. Several casinos in Las Vegas allow the player to DAS (a .14 percent bonus), surrender (a .06 percent bonus), and even resplit aces (a .07 percent bonus). The Desert Inn, Mirage, Las Vegas Hilton, Treasure Island, and the Golden Nugget allowed all of these options. These options cut down the casino off-the-top edge to .27 percent.

In addition, good six-deck penetration can be found more readily than in other games. When a player is dealt a round with under one deck remaining in a six deck game, the plus of deck penetration starts to take effect. In this situation, a player can add about .5 percent to his advantage (or subtract it from his disadvantage). At the Desert Inn an even count at the under one-deck level gave me a .23 percent advantage rather than a .27 percent disadvantage. On true counts of over four, my edge would exceed two percent.

Two casinos that had excellent penetration in their six-deck games were the Aladdin and Harrahs. Both offered DAS and surrender—though not resplit of aces—but their dealers hit soft 17 (a .22 percent disadvantage). Though this created a player .56 percent disadvantage off-the-top, the deck penetration—exceeding at times 5-1/2 decks!—created not only a greater potential for high true counts, but also high true counts with greater value.

One final word of financial advice in using the tables and information in this Chapter. Because of the gigantic financial fluctuations in the game of blackjack, it is probably wise never to bet over 2 percent of your bankroll on any round no matter how much of an advantage you may have. And, as I came to see in my trip to Las Vegas, a 1 percent of the bankroll limit on the top bet is probably still wiser. A smart way to scale bets is to wager no more than 1/2 of the percent advantage you have in relation to your bankroll with a maximum of a 1 percent of the bankroll being your top bet.

When a player plays two spots, he can multiply his top bet by 1.5 to decide the total amount he can risk. If the most that a player wants to risk is $200 on a hand, he can play two spots at $150 each; in the long run the fluctuations will be about the same as for one bet of $200.

Golden Nugget, Riviera, Gold Coast, Rio, Flamingo Hilton, MGM

February 28

Session One. Golden Nugget. 8:50-9:50AM. Graveyard shift. 1 and 6 decks.

I woke up a little nervous this morning. I guess this is normal in any new venture, especially one in which everyone you are going to encounter is the enemy—the reality for a blackjack counter. As I drove to my money box to get $5,500 (the normal amount I will use as a daily backup), I reminded myself that the odds will be in my favor and that these odds meant that I am merely going into the casinos to earn some money. This pep talk calmed me down.

Unfortunately, the session was a losing one: a possibility that has an almost even-money chance of occurring. I made two bets of $50 off the top to start my single-deck play; I lost both hands to a dealer 20. Within 15 minutes I was behind close to $900.

After a small comeback, I left the single-deck when three other players joined. I played a $25 shoe game in which I won a small amount over two shoes of play despite never having a true count of over 1-1/4, which is the count I needed to raise my bet minus camouflage in this game.

I then hopped back to the now-uncrowded single-deck game and won back about $200. One dumb thing I did was not making a bet for the dealer (toking) when I had two hands of $100 on the table at a time when he could (or could not) shuffle. The dealer shuffled. I left the bets out to start the new deck (pulling back a bet is a very bad practice for counters) and split the two hands. Very soon after this, my hour was up. Like last year, I was given no heat by the Nugget pit. Hopefully, that will continue. | Lost: $443 |

Session Two. Riviera. 10:40-11:40AM. Graveyard shift. 2 decks.
The penetration was not good. The best I could get was 60 percent, which was about the worst available a year ago in the Riv's two-deck games. Compensating factors to an extent were my $25-$400 (two hands of $200) spread and lots of fast head-on play.

Unlike the Nugget, I was given some slight heat. I once had a play decision in which it was correct to split tens versus a dealer five;

before doing so, I quickly looked around the pit and saw no one watching. I then made this move and won both hands. After this, a pit boss did start to watch.

I got ahead close to $1,000 and then lost two straight $400 rounds (two hands of $200) near the end. The last deck went well, which helped ensure my maiden win of this venture. | Won: $498.50 |

After my win at the Riv, I walked across the street to the Stardust, ate a couple of hot dogs, and then spoke to Paul—a sports betting money mover I know. He has only two NBA games to concern himself with today, but lots of college tournament games are on the horizon—a good time to avoid him at this place!

Session Three. Gold Coast. 1:20-1:35PM. Day shift. 2 decks.
Incredibly, I suffered my first barring in my third play session. It was a shocking experience. When I first entered the Gold Coast, I noticed only crowded $5 tables and an empty $100 table. I asked a pit boss if a quarter ($25 minimum) table was available. The boss answered that the $100 table would be converted to a $25 one for me. After this was quickly accomplished, I sat down to play and was quickly joined by two other players. As I played, I engaged the pit boss in conversation. I asked about restaurants and other features of the Gold Coast (answers to which I already knew).

As I talked, I had a lucky run in my blackjack play. Without ever going beyond two hands of $100—and progressing to this point only off a win with two hands of $50 or one of $100—I got ahead nearly $700 within 15 minutes. At this point, the pit boss said to me, "I think that's enough."

I answered him, "What do you mean, sir?"

"You can play other games here, but you aren't allowed to play any more blackjack."

As I colored up my chips without protest (what was I supposed to say?), one of the other players commented, "What the hell is this? The guy (me) wins and they throw him out for that?"

I cashed out and left in a daze. Was my counting that obvious? Was this the first in a quick, long string of barrings?

Later, Frank, my counter source, told me that the Gold Coast and its sister casino, the Barbary Coast, often throw out anyone who is winning any real money if they suspect the player even knows basic strategy well. Frank also told me that each of these casinos has evicted him about 40 times. However, since they evict so many players, one could easily go back in, especially on another shift, and play again in a day or two! I'll see how I feel before I decide to go back to the Gold Coast.

> Won: $698

Session Four. Rio. 2:20-2:45PM. Day shift. 1 and 2 decks.
After I recovered from my Gold Coast experience, I walked across Valley View Boulevard to play at the Rio. After I crossed this mini-highway, a 40ish lady walked up to me and remarked how I looked like the "All-American Man." Maybe with my Levi jacket and new Levi jeans, I did. At first glance, the lady looked cute, and I thought of the possibility of some fun later. However, on closer look, she looked less attractive and in our quick conversation, I came to feel that she was looking for someone to stay with and sponge off of. Perhaps, the Gold Coast bosses had sent her out there to snare me!

After this diversion, I played mostly head-on in the one and two-deck games and my luck remained golden: even better than it was at the Gold Coast. I got blackjacks on several big bets (more likely in high-count decks, but I got far more than my expected share) and I won nearly every double down bet I made.

I used a little camouflage, mostly making some big bets off the top, and received no heat despite my winning. Then it got crowded and I decided that it was wise to leave.

> Won: $1,317

Session Five. Flamingo Hilton. 3:50-4:35PM. Day shift. 2 decks.
My three session winning streak came to an end. As I saw deck after deck getting reshuffled at 50 percent or so penetration, I asked myself, "Why am I playing in this crummy game?" I know the sad answer to my question. To stop myself from overplaying and getting barred from all of the very few good games in Vegas.

The Flamingo Hilton machine shuffles many of their two-deck games; the dealer then cuts. I prefer a player cutting.

Even head-on play and a decent bet spread couldn't make me a winner.

> Lost: $77

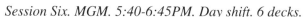

Session Six. MGM. 5:40-6:45PM. Day shift. 6 decks.
It sure is a long walk to the casino from the self-park. In the next *Blackjack Forum* cheesie awards, this casino should get the Pack Your Backpack Award. I'll lose a few pounds walking this week.

The penetration was between 4-3/4 and five decks today. I never had more than two others at my table and the true count and ace side count (see Appendix C beginning on page 188), and my method of keeping it without being obvious, caused no problems.

Though this session was not any real disaster, it was the type of session that epitomizes the frustrations of blackjack for card counters. For most of the session I was winning, a few times by around $600. On the last shoe, the true count went past 2-1/2 for the first time; I was thus a favorite to win more money. Didn't happen. I lost several $100 rounds (two hands of $50) and one $150 round (two hands of $75). Luckily, my camouflage of not increasing past two hands of $50 unless coming off a win saved me from a far worse loss since the count got very high near the end of the shoe.

| Lost: $141 |

Session Seven. Golden Nugget. 8:40-9:40PM. Swing shift. 2 decks.
I got my first meal comp here. The dinner buffet, which I actually got comped to earlier on my Graveyard play, was delicious. However, it didn't come free!

With the one-deckers crowded on the main floor, I played in a $25 two-deck game in the baccarat pit. Two or three loud high rollers from the East played at my table. One of these high rollers claimed that he had won $27,000 in one night at Foxwoods (a mostly lousy penetration, eight-deck, Connecticut casino, which I scouted but never played in). On one hand this player stood on a 15 versus a seven (in a neutral deck, though I knew he wasn't counting). This player and his friends must have gone through $5,000 each in the time I played. I also did poorly, though my losses, and bets, were for far less.

| Lost: $726.50 |

I was happy with the results of my first day of play, but realize that my results are totally insignificant from a statistical point of view.

I know well that my trip winnings will not average $200 an hour as they did today. Still, sleep came easy at my apartment. This is usual for me after a winning day.

| February 28 | Won: $1,126 | Time: 5 hr, 30 min |

March 1

Session One. Riviera. 1:15-2:15PM. Day shift. 2 decks.
I slept in late today. Most days, I'll probably start earlier.

Penetration continues to be bad here. Almost all of the few times that I had good counts, I lost. I never went past two hands of $100. No heat for me today.

| Lost: $864 |

Session Two. Golden Nugget. 3:40-4:40PM. Day shift. 1 and 6 decks.
Before I started my play, I stopped in Leroy's, my favorite sports book, across the street. I checked out the NBA lines. If I was betting, I suspect I'd bet the Knicks tonight. The Knicks have gone 0-3 on their four game West Coast trip and tonight's game in Sacramento is their last and best chance to get a win on this trip. The game opened with the Knicks a 4-1/2 point favorite and has now reached six. Thus, some big bettors feel the same way.

I realize that it would be dumb for me to bet this game since I am not following the league closely enough. I have not kept power ratings or anything else that would tell me if six—or even the opening line of 4-1/2—is too low or high. Without such an anchor, betting basketball, or any sport, is a losing proposition. It's like guessing in blackjack play, the act of a dumb gambler. My days of closely following the NBA now seem like 100 years ago.

At the Nugget, I ended my four session losing streak and also won in this casino for the first time in three tries. I played mostly single deck with two shoes mixed in. In the single deck, I was a little suspicious of how closely Lana held the cards to her body. Later, I observed her and could always see the top card coming off the deck. Though I believe that blackjack cheating by dealers in Vegas is extremely rare, I am always alert to the possibility. At the end of my session, I played a little against Lana and added about $100 to my winnings for the session.

| Won: $466.50 |

Session Three. MGM. 10:30-11:40PM. Swing shift. 6 decks.
After watching the Knicks pull away late in their covering 100-88 win, I left the Stardust and drove up the Strip to the MGM. And, no, I didn't second guess my not betting the NBA.

I had my wildest blackjack session thus far. The blackjack roller coaster was in full swing!

I fell behind by over $800 in the first 1/2 hour losing most of it in one high-count shoe in which I won very few hands. The pit observed me closely during my losing streak.

After this loss, I decided, in a bathroom trip, to risk another $1,000 plus in this decent penetration and uncrowded game. At first, I lost another couple of hundred dollars with one other player at the table. When this player left and I had head-on play, the tide turned—big time! The turnaround began with a four-bet winner on a multiple split of threes (a very lucky win since splitting threes is a defensive move in which a player is trying to cut losses) when the dealer busted. In the next shoe, the count skyrocketed to a true count of +8. On the big bets, I won nearly every hand with dealer busts and my blackjacks being the key. At the end of the shoe, after a loss and a lowering of the count, it was natural to cut back to $25 bets. Because of this cutback, I decided to play one more shoe. I often will leave a casino if I am betting very high (two hands of $200) at the end of one shoe since a small bet at the start of the next shoe is often seen as the sign of a counter. Despite this late cutback, I had over a $2,000 plus turnaround. Nothing spectacular happened in the final shoe. | Won: $1,067.50 |

Session Four. Flamingo Hilton. 12:40-1:40AM. Swing shift. 2 decks.
Crummy penetration continues to exist in this joint. I hopped around to find uncrowded conditions. | Lost: $268.50 |

Session Five. Rio. 2:20-3:05AM. Swing shift. 1 deck.
Because of my great session here yesterday, though it was on a different shift, I felt a little paranoid coming here. To give the pit bosses the "right" impression, I found some used keno tickets elsewhere in the casino before I sat down, and I bemoaned my "losses" in that sucker game.

My keno ruse and falling behind early by over $700 kept all eyes and heat away from me. I not only battled back to win, but also got a coffee shop comp from the pit boss. | Won: $90 |

Session Six. Golden Nugget. 4:10-4:45AM. Graveyard shift. 2 decks.

Just as yesterday, I got walloped in the two-deck baccarat area game. Last year, the Nugget sometimes had $10 two-deck games in this pit, and I lost every time but once. Must be a jinx! Unlike last night, I played almost the whole time by myself and thus lost faster. I don't believe I ever had over a $200 winning streak in this session. When my losses got close to $1,000 for the session, I decided to quit for the session and the day. | Lost: $966.50 |

As I well know, losing days in blackjack play are far from uncommon. I also know that I'll have days on this trip far worse than the $475 I dropped today.

March 1	Lost: $475	Time: 5 hr, 30 min
Week to date	Won: $651	Time: 11 hr

March 2

Session One. Riviera. 8:45-9:40PM. Swing shift. 2 decks.

Tipping at the right time finally got me some decent penetration at the Riv, up to 2/3rds. Larry, a new face at the Riv, went 3/4 in one high-count deck! Since there was big action as I played at the $100 minimum table, I was given very little heat. However, when I cashed out, the cashier wanted to know where my chips came from, dice or blackjack. Since I'm sure that I'm always on camera in casinos, I told her the truth. | Won: $1,071.50 |

Session Two. Rio. 10:20-11:15PM. Swing shift. 2 decks.

The penetration was lousy at the Rio tonight, not much over 50 percent. With the bad rules in force (the dealer hits soft 17 and no doubles after splits) bad penetration really hurts. Despite some hints from me and a couple of tips, the dealers never went further into the deck. One dealer, named Dan, seemed very slick with the cards. He got three or four blackjacks off the top of the deck out of six two-deck games. However, I could see nothing untoward going on.

Like my session here last night, I fell behind early and a late rally made me a small winner. I got comped to the coffee shop, which had decent food, but very slow service. | Won: $23 |

Session Three. Golden Nugget. 12:45-1:40AM. Swing shift 1 deck. In this session, I did something I had never done before. I played at $5 tables and bounced from one to another as conditions got crowded. (I virtually never play with more than two other players in single-deck.) At these tables, I used a $5-$200 (two hands of $100) spread with virtually no heat!

Obviously, I never made a jump from $5 to two hands of $100 in one bet or even in one deck. What I did was start with two hands of, for example, $50. This gave me the option of going down to one hand of $25 (normal gambler behavior after a loss and especially good counter behavior after a loss and a bad or neutral count). Or I could go up to two hands of $100 (after a win and a true count of +2-1/2 or more). If I was in a losing streak and I knew that the shuffle was imminent and if the count was lousy, I sometimes was able to decrease to one hand of $5.

As fortune had it, I had several winning streaks in this session— my best one on the trip thus far. I also tipped very liberally, about $15, which is more than twice my average. I do this when I win and get good penetration, which I got. | Won: $1328.50 |

After this session, I walked around downtown. Since the Plaza, the Horseshoe, and the Fremont are on my tentative play list for next week, I didn't want to play in them now. Instead, I went to the Lady Luck, a place not on my play list. Sometimes I may play for a short while in such places. This was a mistake.

Session Four. Lady Luck. 2:00-2:25AM. Swing shift. 2 decks. I sat at first base in a game that mostly had lousy penetration: one-deck dealt out of two. I left probably 25 minutes too late. This is the first really dumb move I've made in terms of which casino to play. | Lost: $300 |

Session Five. Flamingo Hilton. 3:20-4:05AM. Swing shift. 2 decks. I finally found a dealer who gives good penetration in this casino (2/3 plus): Sally, a cute corn colored blond from Nebraska. That was the good news. The two bits of bad news were that I lost in this casino once again and that another player really got me angry.

One play told the story. I had two hands of $100 on the table and received a 20 and a 19 versus a dealer four. I was now a favorite to win both hands. Before the dealer played her hand, the player on my left (the third baseman) busted his hand with a nine, a play I hardly noticed (especially since a nine is a neutral card in my count system). Sally then turned over a ten in the hole and drew a seven for a 21. Both of my hands and $200 were lost. Sally then remarked sympathetically to me, "You were supposed to win those hands."

I answered, "Well, tough losses happen."

Sally then said, "That's not what I mean. I was supposed to draw the nine and bust."

I then noticed that the third baseman had hit a 13 versus Sally's four—a play a non-counter should never make and a play a counter should make with a very negative deck (which certainly didn't exist now).

I was disgusted, though I fully realize that a stupid player is just as likely to turn a losing hand into a winning hand for the others at the table. This player then asked me, "Anything wrong?"

I answered, "Yeah, you just cost me $400."

"Don't be upset, nothing personal."

I quit shortly after this episode. Originally I was going to play at the MGM after this session, but I don't like to play when someone upsets me. One mistake (my play at the Lady Luck) was enough for today! Yes, I know that I shouldn't get upset at the stupid play of others. However, I think I got upset because this stupidity happened when I finally had gotten a good game in this casino. Now, I got angry that I was upset. These types of distractions make blackjack a losing proposition for a card counter. Thus, I quit for the day.

		Lost: $652
March 2	Won: $1,471	Time: 3 hr, 55 min
Week to date	Won: $2,122	Time: 14 hr, 55 min

March 3

Session One. Flamingo Hilton. 8:10-9:15AM. Graveyard shift. 2 decks.
I awoke refreshed after just two hours sleep. Now, fully recovered from last night's episode, I was ready to battle the casinos again. Early morning is the best time to get head-on games: probably the only type of game to play at a casino like the Flamingo, which usually has lousy penetration.

There were no dealers like Sally this morning. However, the session was similar to last night in that the key hand was a loss with a 19 and a 20 versus a three-card dealer 21. Unlike last night, no one else was at the table. And unlike last night, I had $400 (two hands of $200) on the table instead of $200. This round told the story. | Lost: $408 |

Session Two. Riviera. 9:40-10:40AM. Graveyard shift. 2 decks.
This was an uneventful session. Toward its conclusion, I suddenly felt tired and decided to return to my apartment for more rest: a mandatory requirement for winning play. | Lost: $69 |

Session Three. Riviera. 3:05-4:05PM. Day shift. 2 decks.
During this session I got good penetration from Lilly and especially from Mike, a dealer I knew from last year, who is one of only two dealers in Vegas (the other being Mari, who deals at Treasure Island) aware of what I am trying to accomplish. Mike consistently went 3/4 of the way into the deck, while Lilly shuffled at 2/3 depth. Unfortunately, Mike was at my table only for the last 15 minutes. This was the time during which I made most of my profit.

Last year, I did so well at Mike's table that I almost wondered if he was cheating for me! In ten or so sessions with him, I lost just once at his table. Of course, I know that Mike wasn't cheating (and he would have been nuts to have done so since he would be risking his whole gaming career for peanuts—even assuming that I was into that nonsense). However, today, like last year, I got more than my share of blackjacks and won more than my share of double downs as he dealt. These were lucky fluctuations for me (and, as I'll later relate, my playing experiences with Mari have been just the opposite): a part of the game.

Players often complain of blackjack's negative fluctuations. With Mike I get to wonder about its positive fluctuations. I quit when I saw a pit boss glaring at me. I didn't want to get myself any heat or get Mike hassled for dealing further into the deck than is Riviera policy. Besides, my hour was up. | Won: $766 |

Session Four. Golden Nugget. 5:30-6:15PM. Day shift. 1 deck.
Before I sat down to play blackjack, I watched the Knicks-Nets game in the sports book. The Nets, as they always seem to do, gave the homestanding Knicks a battle. After I left to go do my work, the Knicks did theirs in a going-away 97-86 win that also covered the seven-point spread.

Despite some rare Vegas rain, which got some strollers into the Nugget, I had head-on conditions virtually the whole time I played. I won right from the start and was given absolutely no heat over my 1-8 ($25 to two hands of $100) spread.

A few times I asked Leonard, the dealer, for advice. This was for camouflage and done at times that his advice—always followed—would not really hurt me (on close play calls, usually with small bets out). Once, when I asked Leonard what to do on a soft 13 versus a five in a neutral deck, he answered my request, "What do you need my help for? You're doing fine on your own." I doubled down and won that hand.

I tipped liberally since Leonard often went 2/3 into the deck (great in single-deck). Winning as I have this week can lead a counter to believe that blackjack counting is an easy game. I am reminding myself that I've been fairly lucky so far in my venture and have not hit anything very close to a bad run. | Won: $1,550.50 |

Session Five. MGM. 7:05-8:05PM. Day and swing shifts. 6 decks.
With my $1,000 plus win here the other night, I wondered if I would be hassled. This did not happen even when some of the swing shift crew (the crew present when I won) appeared at eight o'clock.

I played four shoes in this session. In only two of them did the count get high enough to justify anything but the $25 minimum bets (I need a true count of 1-1/2 or higher to make those bets "normally").

In the first three shoes I won about $700. In the last shoe, one in which the count got high late, I lost over $400. On the last hand, I lost two hands of $100 each. I paused a couple of times before making correct play decisions in regard to the true count. I sometimes also did so when I knew the right play; I did so to appear as if I really didn't know what I was doing. | Won: $267 |

Session Six. Rio. 10:30-11:00PM. Swing shift. 1 deck.
Again I fell behind at the Rio, this time by over $400. However, in this session, I couldn't quite fight all the way back. I quit when a third player entered the game; this player, along with Kim, the dealer, complained about my playing one and two hands seemingly at random. Sometimes my going back and forth between one and two hands has a great effect; it gets players to leave the table and gives me heads-up play. That did not happen tonight. Tonight, I left the table. Since the other tables were crowded and had lousy penetration, I decided to leave the casino. | Lost: $115 |

After the Rio session, I decided to relax back at the apartment. I ended up falling into a deep sleep. This rest would give me two more days of play this week.

One plus factor about blackjack is that a professional player has more leeway in setting his own hours than do most other businessmen.

March 3	Won: $1,991.50	Time: 5 hr, 15 min
Week to date	Won: $4,113.50	Time: 20 hr, 10 min

March 4

Session One. Golden Nugget. 1:40-2:40PM. Day shift. 2 and 6 decks.
With at least three players at every table, it was too crowded to play single-deck today. Instead, I tried the two-deck game and varied my bets from one hand of $10 to two hands of $100 using the same "crazy" betting that I did here on the night of March 2. However, there were two differences; first, I lost and second, and more important, I was given some serious scrutiny from the pit.

For the last 25 minutes of my Nugget session, I played the $25 six-deck game. I was able to win fairly significantly despite never having any very high-counts. I never progressed past two hands of $50. Thus I won for the session because I did much better in a six-deck game with a 1-4 spread than in a two-deck game with a 1-20 spread! That's known as being lucky! | Won: $202 |

Session Two. Lady Luck. 4:25-4:50PM. Day shift. 2 decks.
I didn't want to battle the Friday rush hour on the Strip, so I went to the Lady Luck. This time, the 60 percent two-deck penetration got me to play. I enjoyed an early hot streak and then left when some pit bosses started glaring. Amateur bettors would call this the "hit and run" method. I call it the "stopping myself from getting barred method."

| Won: $695 |

Session Three. Riviera. 6:00-7:00PM. Day shift. 2 decks.
Lousy penetration is the rule again in this casino. The Riviera certainly won't be the frequent play spot for me this year as it was last year.

On the last two-decks I played, Jill dealt just .6 decks, which is only 30 percent penetration. Good company girl! The Riv bosses may be very pissed off at the deck penetration and wins I received yesterday.

| Lost: $330 |

Session Four. MGM. 8:05-9:10PM. Swing shift. 6 decks.
Penetration consistently in the 3/4 area, the minimum to get in a six-deck game. I was ahead for the first three shoes I played, but lost in the last two shoes in which high counts occurred. A counter's nightmare.

| Lost: $367.50 |

I decided after this MGM session that the best time to play on Saturday (tomorrow) would be on graveyard. To be sharp for it, I needed to go to sleep now. The long walk back to the car put me in a resting frame of mine.

March 4	Won: $199.50	Time: 3 hr, 30 min
Week to date	Won: $4,313	Time: 23 hr, 40 min

March 5

Session One. Flamingo Hilton. 6:00-6:55AM. Graveyard shift. 2 decks.
I finally won in this crummy place despite lousy penetration (seldom over 50 percent); some heavy pit boss scrutiny; and falling behind by $700 early in the session. Head-on play most of the way and a decent bet spread were the pluses. I played in this casino four and a half hours this week; I'll be surprised if I play here half as much when the Flamingo is on my schedule again: probably in Week Five.

| Won: $45 |

Session Two. Rio. 7:20-8:15AM. Graveyard shift. 2 decks.
The two-deck tables varied in crowd size. The one-deck games were all much too crowded for me. I played mostly at the $10 two-deck table and spread from $10 to two hands of $100. I parlayed winnings in some early hot decks (adding the winnings to my bet) early in the session. This "money management" was applauded by other players at the table and the bosses seemed unwise. Penetration varied widely, from 50 percent to 75 percent. This is a so-so place to play. It will probably get my action again in about a month.

| Won: $618.50 |

Session Three. Golden Nugget. 9:00-10:00AM. Graveyard shift. 1 and 6 decks.
This would be about the last place I'd have suspicions of cheating, but today I couldn't help feeling a little paranoid. Ronnie, the dealer, had five straight decks in which he started with a ten or an ace as the up card: a huge player disadvantage which has less than a one percent chance of happening five straight times. But, I know that if one plays extensively, this will happen sometimes, like less than one in a hundred times! However, when Ronnie had a ten up on the fifth deck, he chose this time to start telling a story to me and the other player about a Bugs Bunny cartoon in which Bugs Bunny as the dealer cheated Yosemite Sam, his victim in a blackjack game. The proximity of this story to what had just happened got me to leave for the six-deck game in which I won a little.

Before I left, I played the single-deck some more. This time I played Christy, a very friendly and fairly attractive gal, from Colorado Springs. I played at her table for about ten minutes. Nothing bad happened with her except that I lost another $300 or so dollars!

| Lost: $717.50 |

Session Four. Lady Luck. 10:40-11:45AM. Graveyard shift. 2 decks.
I stopped for a look and to my surprise I found Paul, a dealer going 3/4 of the way on the two decks. I also got a seat next to third base, which helps since I get to see other cards of other players before I play.

Good penetration helps, but doesn't come close to guaranteeing a winning one-hour session. I lost a little to Paul and was so eager to play him that I waited and played through his break against Chindu, a dealer who gave just 50% penetration. I lost some more.

But what could I do? If I got up, my spot would be taken and I certainly couldn't hold it through a 20-minute bathroom break! Worse yet, Paul was nowhere to be found after his 20 minute break. Perhaps the shift manager fired him for dealing a good game (for counters, anyway)! | Lost: $357.50 |

Session Five. Riviera. 12:45-1:40PM. Day shift. 2 decks.
Jane gave better than average Riv penetration, about 60 percent. Mike, my favorite Riv dealer, was on the $100 table. I don't yet have the bankroll for that action; $80,000 is the minimum needed for that kind of action in two-deck play with the bet spread I use.

In the session itself, I was ahead until the last deck in which I had a high-count losing streak—something that can happen a lot in this game since a player, as I wrote in "Card Counting Myths" beginning on page 10, is always an underdog on a given hand before the cards are dealt, no matter what the count is.

I'll play at the Riv again next month. The two-deck rules (dealer stands on all 17's and DAS allowed) are good, and somehow, I'll get well-dealt games often enough to make the Riviera blackjack games worth my while. | Lost: $184 |

Session Six. Golden Nugget. 11:20PM-12:55AM. Swing shift. 2 decks.
Between my sessions at the Riv and here, almost ten hours went by. I spent some time at Leroy's with some sports betting friends—very few of whom know of my new career—and at the Circus Circus Sportsbook. I watched the end of the Warriors 17-point win over Charlotte at Circus.

Boy, the Hornets really miss Larry Johnson and Alonzo Mourning. After last season, I thought that the Hornets would be a constant 50-plus win team that would win over 80 percent of their home contests because of the very strong home support they have. But, injuries can wreak havoc with the best of NBA teams. Hopefully, the Hornet management writes off this year as a negative fluke and stays the course with few changes. Many times this does not happen and a fluke year like this causes many major, and stupid, changes to be made, which eventually destroy a team.

I got comped to the Circus buffet and drove down to the Nugget to close out my first week of blackjack play. For the rest of my trip, I'll rest on both Saturday and Sunday.

I played over my usual one hour limit because the casino was crowded, there was no scrutiny given me, and the game (a $5 two-deck game) got consistent 2/3 to 3/4 deck depth. I spread 1-40 (one hand of $5 to two of $100), though not in one jump! I won $500 plus early and then lost a little of the profits. After a little over 1-1/2 hours of play, I decided it was time to end my session and work week. I got a comp for the Nugget's late night steak and celebrated my winning first week's end there.

		Won: $371
March 5	Lost: $224.50	Time: 6 hr, 25 min
Week 1 Total	Won: $4,088.50	Time: 30 hr, 5 min

For my first week of blackjack play, I averaged winnings of over $130 an hour: an unrealistic long term rate for my trip. But I might as well enjoy the good times, because the bad times will be brutal.

On Sunday (March 6) I slept in late, did some shopping for the apartment, and went out to view a couple of movies. Since Sunshine left my life almost three years ago, I have not had much to do with women. However, it would be nice to share winning experiences like this with someone special, as well as have someone around who can lift my spirits when I lose. And, I'd like to do the same for some special woman with the good and bad times of her life.

Treasure Island, Horseshoe, Fremont, Plaza, Sands, Stardust

March 7

Session One. Treasure Island. 7:35-8:35AM. Graveyard shift. 2 decks.

This casino opened a few months ago. Treasure Island, along with the Golden Nugget and the Mirage, forms the Steve Wynn Las Vegas triad. These casinos are considered to have among the best blackjack games in Vegas and they provide the least heat for small-to-medium level counters. The Nugget fits that description and now I'll see if Treasure Island does.

Unlike the Nugget, Treasure Island has no single-deck blackjack and has no $25-minimum two-deck games open during graveyard. So I played in the $10-minimum two-deck games. My bets usually were $25 or more. Though the deck penetration was usually decent-around 2/3, I lost. I was given no heat. | Lost: $325.50 |

Session Two. Horseshoe. 9:15-10:15AM. Graveyard shift. 1 deck.
I was very careful on my bet spread here. I often started the deck with two hands of $50. I never went past two hands of $100. I watched the dealers closely to make sure, as best I could, that the top card was always being dealt. I often engaged the pit bosses and dealers in conversation so they might think, "hey, this square is no counter, he talks too much."

On my very first round of play, I insured a blackjack (and did not insure my other $50 bet). This is a play that suckers always make and to make it even better, I yelled out, "Even money!" as I insured. This one play got the pit off my back right away. It probably also got me good penetration in a rare head-on game at this usually crowded casino. Thus, my insurance "mistake" may pay dividends that overcome its long-range cost of about $4 on the hand in which I did it.

I fell behind about $500 early and was starting to make a comeback when the hour ran out. This is not a place to overstay my usual one-hour limit. I suspect my play time for most Horseshoe sessions will be much less. | Lost: $135.50 |

Session Three. Fremont. 10:40-11:40AM. Graveyard Shift. 2 Decks.

During the first 15 minutes, I felt that I was on my way to my first winning session of Week Two as I roared over $500 ahead. Then, the pit bosses started observing me and, to their delight, I started losing. This was the first real heat I've had this week. I played at the one $25 table.

| Lost: $194.50 |

Session Four. Plaza. 1:20-1:45PM. Day shift. 1 and 2 decks.

First, I played in the $25 one-deck game and then quit when a fourth player entered. I won a little in the two-deck game while conversing with Mr. Gallagher, one of the bosses. When the crowd and the heat started increasing, I decided to leave a winner for the first time in Week Two. I also wanted to say hello to the gang over at Leroy's.

| Won: $167 |

After stopping in at Leroy's, I decided to rest and play some more tonight. Before I played, I watched some NBA hoops. The Knicks-Pistons game made me happy that I'm not financially involved with the NBA. In this contest, the 10-1/2 or 11 point underdog Pistons somehow had a double figure lead late in the third quarter, which meant that they were covering by over 20 points. The Knicks then came back and outscored the Pistons by about 25 in the fourth quarter to win by 14 and cover. A loss like that seems far worse than losing with a 20 to a dealer 21 in blackjack.

Session Five. Treasure Island. 8:40-9:40PM. Swing shift. 2 decks.

I did something really stupid in my play in this session. I had two bets of $200 on the table (my max, which is seldom reached.) The dealer then shuffled. I pulled the bets back and started the new deck with two hands of $100. Pulling back bets at the end of a deck and putting out anything smaller is one of the biggest giveaways to counting. Keeping the two bets out there would have had a long-range negative expectation of under 80 cents (since my off-the-top disadvantage in this two-deck game is under .2 percent). Dumb, dumb, dumb!

To try to make up for this stupidity, I used lots of other bet camouflage and even asked the pit boss for advice on a couple of insurance bets. I still, probably deservedly, got some heat. I won big, but am still angry at myself.

| Won: $1,238.50 |

Session Six. Sands. 10:20-11:20PM. Swing shift. 2 decks.
The cards ran very well early. After this early run, I hit a bit of a
slump and then got very suspicious when Bob, the friendly dealer,
hit a hard 17 (a total never hit in any casino) with a ten card, which
was then burned. Was this a version of the peek-and-burn cheat
scam? I stayed on and saw nothing strange after this. Dealers can
also make mistakes and get tired. No real heat was given me on my
maiden Sands play. $\boxed{\text{Won: \$435}}$

Session Seven. Stardust. 12:00-1:00AM. Swing shift. 2 decks.
I fell behind by nearly $500 early on and didn't get ahead until
near the end. For camouflage, I asked Dwight, the pit manager, for
help on some close-decision hands and, of course, always followed his advice. Once, when my two nines versus a deuce
stumped Dwight I asked a passerby for help. I had a running count
of -1 with about 1-1/2 decks left, so the correct play is to split
(barely, since the index true count number for this non-DAS game
is -1). This person told me to stand, very slightly the wrong choice,
and I won the hand and thanked him with Dwight looking on with
a smile.

After I finished, I asked Dwight for his Stardust restaurant recom-
mendations and a comp. The seafood entree he suggested in the
main coffee shop ended up being better than his blackjack suggestions! Of course, I thanked him for his suggestions later, as well as
for the comp. Penetration was 50-60 percent, very so-so. Head-on
play was a plus. My act helped me get a good bet spread and avoid
heat. $\boxed{\text{Won: \$93}}$

Session Eight. Horseshoe. 2:25-2:45AM. Swing shift. 1 deck.
I decided to finish up work today on the downtown circuit. Amaz-
ingly, the Horseshoe was packed at this late weeknight hour. I
could never get any head-on play, and I even played a couple of
hands with three other players, something I virtually never do in
single-deck. The crowded conditions and some pit boss scrutiny
made me quit, though, a small winner. $\boxed{\text{Won: \$121}}$

Session Nine. Fremont. 3:00-3:40AM. Swing shift. 2 decks.
I won for a sixth straight session. When a card counter gets on a
streak like this (almost a $3,000 upswing for me in just over four
hours of play), he almost wonders how he ever lost before. In the
casino bathroom, a counter on a streak like this is wondering

where to put all of these newly acquired $100 bills—how much more to put in the shoes or in the hidden money belt, etc.

The camouflage I used at the Fremont was in asking the dealer how much money I needed to put out on a split or a double down (chips or money in the bet circle can't be touched by the player after it is bet, for obvious reasons) on some big bets. This little ploy made it seem to the bosses watching that I was not a threat. After all, how could I be if I didn't even know how much I had bet?

Financially, I got ahead $1,300 (which meant that from that point I had a $650 loss limit) and then lost nearly $400 to a cute female Asian dealer. I quit the session at that point.   Won: $916.50

Session Ten. Plaza. 4:00-4:30AM. Graveyard shift. 1 deck.
I was feeling a little tired, but I am much likelier to continue playing in a winning streak. I decided to play until I got more tired or until I had a losing session. I lost a little at the Plaza.

There were no high limit ($25) games available, so I decided to use the style I had first used at the Nugget last week (on March 2): $5 to two hands of $100 with all sorts of bet camouflage. I used much more bet camouflage here (mixing chip colors and really acting like a wild gambler needing action) than at the Nugget.

The pit bosses watched my wild betting, but did not act concerned. Unfortunately, the cards ran slightly on the bad side. After a half hour of play, I decided that it was time to quit for the session and the day.   Lost: $154

| March 7 | Won: $2,161.50 | Time: 7 hr, 55 min |

I had won more money and had put in more time than I ever had before in my Vegas blackjack play. I keep reminding myself that winning days such as today will be mostly acting as buffers against bad days. Though I hadn't been hit by any financial disasters yet, I knew that some would probably strike before my trip was finished. My home practice sessions convinced me that at least one disaster—as much as $9,000 or more on a downswing—would probably occur on this trip.

March 8th

Session One. Treasure Island. 4:05-5:05PM. Day shift. 2 and 6 decks.

My day got off to a bad start. I began by playing at Mari's table. She and Mike at the Riviera are the only two casino employees in town to whom I conveyed that I am playing blackjack as a serious counter. But unlike my sessions with Mike, I almost never win at Mari's table. She roots for me as much as Mike does (both were also rooting for my sports bets last spring, as well) and will often go far into the deck to help me, but nothing helps me at Mari's table! I not only would do badly in my own bets, but last spring it seemed that whenever I walked by Mari's table and just said hello to her, she would turn over a blackjack and beat her players. It became a sort of private joke between us. If only the bosses knew! Have no more fear, Stuart is here! Despite my adding to the casino coffers at her table, I like Mari's personality, intelligence, looks, and, most important, the game she deals me. And, yes, I fully realize, that what I've experienced at Mari's table, just as with Mike, is just a short-term negative fluctuation. If Mari were not married, I'd ask her out; she seems like my type: physically and mentally. This is one advantage I know she'll always have over Mike!

The eight-month hiatus didn't change my luck at Mari's table (the six-deck game). I lost over $300 in her 83.3 percent dealt (five decks out of six) game.

After this loss, I played in a $10 minimum two-deck game and lost another $400 plus. I got no heat in this session, and got a buffet comp from Daniel, the pit boss, who covered Mari's table. I'll use it later today. | Lost: $781.50 |

Session Two. Sands. 5:45-6:50PM. Day shift. 2 and 6 decks.

I got some severe heat here. First, I didn't get the answer I was looking for when I asked the pit boss (Andy) if I should take insurance. The running count was +2 with just under one-deck left and the ace count—four—was normal, making insurance slightly the wrong play, but not a huge mistake. Andy answered my insurance request with, "I don't know. How many tens have come out of the deck so far?" Not the answer that I wanted to hear! After this remark, the dealer then shuffled up every time I raised my bet. A couple of times I played big off the top and did OK, but the shuffle up bullshit continued.

I then moved to the six-deck pit and surprisingly the heat did not follow. I won for a while, but then lost big (over $1,000) in the last shoe, one with a high count.

| Lost: $333 |

Session Three. Stardust. 7:20-8:20PM. Swing shift. 2 decks.

My bad day continued. I played mostly with two other patrons, who were lousy players. They often stood on 14, 15, or 16 versus dealer high cards. However, these players had about 25 blackjacks between them in the one hour I played. At least six times they both got blackjacks on the same hand. Meanwhile, my blackjack total for the hour was zero! Few high-counts probably protected me from a bigger loss. One pit boss looked on but I was too pissed to make conversation. Penetration was 50-60 percent. I decided to go back to Treasure Island for some dinner. Maybe I'd feel better after eating.

| Lost: $575.50 |

Session Four. Treasure Island. 9:50-10:40PM. Swing shift. 2 and 6 decks.

Fortunes can change quickly in blackjack. Just as I believed that my first really bad streak was starting, I bounced back with a monster session. Before playing, I enjoyed the buffet (American style) through the comp Daniel had given me earlier. Long lines for the first serving was my only complaint.

After this meal, I quickly won over $400 playing the two-deck game. I noticed that the crew in the two-deck area was different from last night, so I was willing to play in that pit just one day after a big win. When the two-deck games got too crowded (I could no longer use two spots), I played at the $25 six-deck game in the baccarat pit. Unlike my experiences in the Golden Nugget baccarat pit area, I won big in the Nugget's cousin's baccarat pit.

One very lucky round was the key. On it, I had wagered two hands of $200 (the true count was around +6). Versus a dealer six, I received two aces on one hand and a hard 18 on the other. I split the aces and received another ace on the first one which I split again for another $200 (most other casinos do not allow re-splitting of aces). On my three aces, I received a five, a six, and a nine, which gave me totals of 16, 17, and 20. The five and the six I received pushed the count up still higher and made a dealer bust more likely. When the dealer turned over a five in the hole, my heart sank beneath the Treasure Island basement. A ten-card would give the dealer a 21 and me an $800 loss. And, lots of tens were still jammed into that shoe. However, the dealer, amazingly pulled a five (usually this card is the player's worst enemy) which made his total 16. The next card was a beautiful queen of clubs, a long overdue ten-value card that broke the dealer and made me $800. A switch of the ten and the five would have created a $1,600 difference against me! Luck can play a huge role in the short, and in this case the very-short, run in blackjack. My profit in this session was because of my luck on just one hand! $\boxed{\text{Won: \$1,440}}$

I played my final six sessions of the day downtown. Though I made some money, I paid the price in emotional weardown. I'm sure that all serious counters have had similar experiences.

Session Five. Plaza. 11:30-11:50PM. Swing shift. 1 deck.
The second I sat down I realized that this would not be a long session. Four pit bosses stared intently at me, and I mean *intently*. Three were in front of the table and the other was behind me. None were quite close enough for me to converse with. Though I used all sorts of bet camouflage, such as parlaying winnings even in lousy decks and often betting big off the top, the staring continued.

I also won over $250, which was way, way past my expected earnings for the 20 minutes I played, especially with all of the bet camouflage (some of it very harmful in the long run) I threw in.

After I felt uncomfortable enough to leave, I told one of the starers, a black man who looked like a former football player, "Man, what luck I had! I almost never win playing blackjack and look how well I did!" The pit boss replied, "*Boy*, do you think it was luck or was it something else?" "I was just lucky," (which I was, considering all the bet camouflage). He answered, "By the way, do you know where the door is?"

I did and walked out it after I cashed out. Was this an official barring or just a hint? I'd find out later in the week. $\boxed{\text{Won: \$253}}$

Session Six. Horseshoe. 12:05-12:25AM. Swing shift. 1 deck.
In this session, the heat followed me. However, this time, it was given to me by a player, not the pit. As is usual in my play, I often went back and forth between one and two hands. There are two reasons that I do so. First, playing two hands somewhat disguises that I am increasing my bets (if I go from one hand of $25 to two hands of $50, I am increasing my wager four times, but it is much less obvious than going from $25 to $100 on one hand). Second,

playing two hands slightly reduces the financial fluctuations I'd go through than if I bet everything on one hand. Two hands of $50 will win or lose $100 less often than one hand of $100.

At times, some players get upset that I go back and forth between one and two hands. These players generally have the idiotic notion that my changing the number of hands I play will somehow change the order of the cards in a negative way (I sometimes use this stupidity as an excuse to switch the number of hands I play if I am in a losing streak—of course, the count is the really key factor). However, most of these players, if they do complain, do so quietly. But not tonight at the Horseshoe.

For a while, I played with an old, well-dressed, somewhat drunk player, who I recognized from last night. He is not a good player, and from his interaction with the dealers and the pit, I guessed that he was a Horseshoe "regular." The casino, I am sure, has made thousands, probably tens of thousands, of dollars from this player.

After we had played at the same table for about ten minutes, I was a little ahead. The drunk had often cursed his losses. He got up from his third base position. Now, I moved from my center seat to the seat to the right of third base. The drunk then yelled at me, "I can't play with someone as stupid as a fuckhead like you. I've never seen anyone who goes back and forth between one and two hands like you do. It totally fucks up my play. I'm not playing here again until you get the fuck out of here!"

I didn't say anything to the drunk, but I put on an act for the pit. To one female pit boss (women bosses can often be counted on to be sympathetic to plights like this), I acted very apologetic about upsetting this regular. The woman boss kept assuring me that I did nothing wrong and that I wasn't the problem.

After this, I played head-on for a few minutes, then left as the crowds came in.

> Won: $93

Session Seven. Four Queens. 12:40-12:50AM. Swing shift. 2 decks.

Usually this casino is just a dessert stop for me since I love their ice cream sundaes. But when I noticed some decent two-deck penetration I decided to play a little blackjack. I spread my bets wildly (one hand of $5 to two of $75) and then left when the table filled. I lost a little and skipped the sundae.

> Lost: $35

Session Eight. Fitzgeralds. 12:55-1:25AM. Swing shift. 2 decks.
I had glanced in here a few times, but the Fitzgerald's two-deck
$10 tables (their high tables) were always jammed. Tonight they
were not, so I decided to get in some brief play.

I spread my bets from one hand of $10 (in very negative decks off
of losses) to as high as two hands of $100 (often off wins in posi-
tive decks). This 1-20 ratio is enough to have a healthy positive expectation in almost any two-deck game.

I was given little heat by the pit. I fell behind early, but a run versus
Tran made this half-hour session a winning one. ⎿ Won: $212.50 ⏌

Session Nine. Horseshoe. 1:50-2:25AM. Swing shift. 1 deck.
The wild, angry drunk from my last Horseshoe session here of two
hours ago was nowhere to be seen. In addition, I had some head-
on play. And, when I played with others, no one openly complained about my one- and two-hand style.

However, there was another drunk at my table. He did something
I found amusing, though I don't know if the dealer (Kathy) did.
Whenever this drunk would double down, he would never look at
his double-down card, which is dealt face down in face down
games like the Horseshoe's. If Kathy made her hand (meaning that
she ended up with a 17-21), the drunk would let out a string of ob-
scenities, sometimes peppered with burps, even if Kathy had a 17
and he was doubling on a ten or an eleven (a situation in which he
was mostly a favorite to win). And, most of the time when Kathy
turned over the cursing drunk's double down card—even when she
pulled 18's and 19's—he would win. Still, the drunk cursed and/
or burped every time this double down scenario was played out.

I spread 1-8 (one hand of $25 to two of $100) and got so-so heat.
I usually bet bigger off the top if I did well at the end of the previous deck. Two good things occurred during this session. First, I
won despite some crazy swings. And, second, I got a comp, which
means that the pit probably accepts me and my play—for now!

When I stashed my winnings in various spots on me in the bathroom of the Horseshoe, I figured out that I was up over $7,200 on
the trip so far. I certainly didn't expect to win this much so soon.
Hopefully, my luck will continue. ⎿ Won: $793.50 ⏌

Session Ten. Lady Luck. 3:00-3:10AM. Graveyard shift. 2 decks.
It almost seemed as if Bev, my Lady Luck dealer, was in the
Horseshoe bathroom stall with me watching me secure my money.
She sure read me fast and spooked the crap out of me!

I won a little in the first deck I played (head-on). Early in the second deck, I had a blackjack and Bev had an ace showing. I did not
insure and Bev did indeed have a blackjack. I now pretended that
I made a mistake.

I moaned, "Boy, that was dumb. I just threw $50 (my winnings if
I had insured my blackjack) away."

Bev answered, "Taking even money on a blackjack is the one sure
bet in the game. However, professionals usually don't take it."

"I don't know why I forgot to."

"Really? You look like a professional gambler to me."

I laughed and said that my friends would find her comment funny.
Inside, I was shaking. After this exchange, Bev asked me on every
bet raise—even if the raise was a camouflage one—if I was counting the cards. I also started to lose nearly every hand after the un-
insured blackjack. After ten minutes of play and a $300 loss, I
decided to end the session and my work day and get some sleep.
This incident, the first drunk at the Horseshoe and the possible Plaza barring had worn me out.

Lost: $302

When I reached the sanctuary of my apartment, I half-yelled, "I
beat you bastards today, but you sure made me pay for it!"

March 8	Won: $765	Time: 6 hr
Week to date	Won: $2,926.50	Time: 13 hr, 55 min

March 9

Session One. Horseshoe. 3:00-3:40PM. Day shift. 1 deck
I continued to be careful in this casino. I used lots of camouflage
in masking my 1-8 spread ($25 on one hand-two hands of $100).
Still, the pit, especially one boss named Jeff, seemed to be looking
at me a lot. In addition, the cards ran lousy. When one loses, sometimes an act appears less believable.

Lost: $802

Session Two. Fremont. 4:05-5:05PM. Day shift. 2 decks.
I quickly fell behind by $800, and would have left if my losses had reached $1,000. Three straight $150 per round losses (two hands of $75) were the chief reasons for my slump.

Later, I managed to grind back some of the losses, but was still behind when the hour was up. After cashing out, I spoke a little with David, a pit boss from Spain. Surprisingly, he was very anti-Franco. I mentioned to David that I knew some people who had fought against Franco in the Spanish Civil War. This is not only true, but could help me to get more play in the Fremont! | Lost: $389.50 |

Session Three. Horseshoe. 5:45-5:55PM. Day shift. 1 deck.
One advantage to downtown Las Vegas blackjack play is the ease with which one can go from one casino to another. The walking distances are short. Sadly, the downtown casino in which I would really like to play, the Golden Nugget, I have to avoid for another two weeks. I don't want to wear out my welcome there, no matter what their alleged tolerance of counters is. Of course, non-counters (or amateur counters) don't have problems like these!

This Horseshoe visit was a pit stop. I played about four or five decks and then left when the casino got overcrowded. I was given less scrutiny on this visit than the previous one of just over two hours previous. | Won: $124 |

Session Four. Treasure Island. 6:35-7:35PM. Day shift. 2 decks.
The bad news was that I had my third losing session in four for the day. The good news was that I was very lucky to avoid losing $1,100. I would have probably stopped the session at that point. A fortunate dealer bust when I had three bets of $75 on the table kept me in the game. A split on one of my two hands accounted for the third bet, which resulted in three stiffs—(12's through 16's are considered stiff hands.) After this lucky $450 swing I battled back a little more but was still behind when my hour of play was up.

A loss of over $200 is not usually a happy occasion in my blackjack play, but when I realized how close I had come to losing $1,100 instead, my comped dinner at Treasure Island tasted just a little better. | Lost: $232.50 |

Session Five. Sands. 9:30-10:05PM. Swing shift. 6 decks.
After the hassle I received here yesterday, I decided to stick to just the shoes today. At least 4-1/2 decks, and usually closer to five, are dealt in them. Unlike yesterday, the bosses watched my six-deck play closely today. After a little over 30 minutes of undramatic play, I decided to leave with a small profit.   Won: $156.50

Session Six. Stardust. 10:40-11:45PM. Swing shift. 2 decks.
Before I began my 'Dust play, I spoke to Gorilla Lips, a sports bettor I know who often hangs out in the Stardust Sportsbook. He doesn't know of my new blackjack career. Gorilla Lips was speaking with a friend in the almost empty sportsbook as I sauntered in. We agreed to meet at the sportsbook at 11:45 and go to a nearby bar to talk. In a roundabout way, I then went from the sportsbook to the blackjack area.

In retrospect, I would have been happier and certainly wealthier if I had spent the rest of the evening with Gorilla Lips and his friend in the sportsbook. Not only did I have to put up with lousy players and their advice, but I had to endure another losing Stardust session as well. One of the lousy players criticized me whenever I hit a 15 or 16 and busted.

Some pit boss scrutiny and lousy penetration (less than 60 percent) didn't help my disposition either. A key double down loss on a $100 bet in which a dealer 21 beat my 20 clinched a losing session for me.   Lost: $358

After this loss, which put me over $1,500 down for the day, I got together with Gorilla Lips in the sportsbook. We went to a bar just across the street. For most of the time, he told me of his days as a high school and college basketball player. Now he bets mostly basketball. His opinion on sides (pointspreads) isn't great, but he does seem to have a decent feel for totals. Gorilla Lips and I enjoyed some interesting times at the Stardust, Riviera, and Mirage sportsbooks back in the 1991 NBA playoffs. I enjoy his down-to-earth approach to life; I felt that he would be a good tonic for this, my roughest blackjack day thus far on this trip.

Before I went to the bar with Gorilla Lips, I was considering playing some more blackjack. However, after we finished, I decided that some sleep would be a better idea. Hopefully, tomorrow would be a better day for me.

March 9	Lost: $1,501	Time: 4 hr, 30 min
Week to date	Won: $1,425.50	Time: 18 hr, 25 min

March 10

Session One. Stardust. 6:45-7:45AM. Graveyard shift. 2 decks.
I woke up feeling refreshed and ready to rebound from yesterday's losses. Of course, a player can still get slaughtered in blackjack even if he's totally refreshed and playing and counting in the best of games. Still, I felt optimistic when I woke up this morning.

Thus awake, I went into the Stardust, had some head-on play with up to 2/3 penetration and got beaten pretty badly. For a while, I played with one of the complainers from last night, the fellow who didn't like my hitting 15's and 16's. In this session, this player was too busy whining and complaining about all of his lost hands to think about or advise me. When this player left, after about a $3,000 loss, Diane, the dealer, said, "What a baby!"

Now I had my head-on play, but I couldn't win. I made one mistake when I doubled on an 11 versus Diane's eight when the true count was a little under -5 (my index for doubling). I lost the hand and an extra $25. I tried not to complain too much as my chips slowly dribbled away throughout the session. Diane, a 17-year veteran dealer, seemed sympathetic. | Lost: $743.50 |

Session Two. Sands. 8:10-8:40AM. Graveyard shift. 6 decks.
No two-deck games were open at this early hour. Since I had not yet played in this casino on graveyard, I decided not to give a name for rating.

I bought in for just $200 (usually at $25 tables I buy in for $500) and played. I quit play after 30 minutes because the construction work was creating dust in the casino, making it difficult for me to breathe. Though I won decent money for the session, this is fast becoming one of my least favorite casinos. | Won: $545 |

Session Three. Treasure Island. 9:05-10:05AM. Graveyard shift. 2 decks.
I spread from one hand of $10 to two hands of $100 in an uneventful session at the $10 minimum table. Penetration continues at a

consistent 2/3. The casino was very quiet and before I knew it my hour of play was up.   Won: $72.50

Session Four. "Cheat" Casino. 10:45-10:50AM. Graveyard shift. 2 decks.

I can't name the casino because an attorney tells me that doing so could bring a libel suit on me, as my allegations of what happened are, as yet, unproven. I cover the aftermath of what happened in my chapter "Dealer Cheating" beginning on page 71.

I sat down at a $25 two-deck table at first base. Three other players were present. I immediately noticed that the dealer's ID badge was on backwards, something I had never seen before. Since I often talk to dealers as I play, I look at their ID badge so I know what name to address them by. When I pointed this out to Juan, the name I saw when he briefly turned his ID around, he kept his badge on backwards. This rang a bell later.

I played the last two rounds of one-deck, using basic strategy, since I did not know the count. On the second hand that I played, I felt uncomfortable as I could not see the top card coming off the deck, something I always look for as a form of self-protection. I split these two rounds.

On the first hand of the new deck, I was almost sure that I noticed Juan holding back the top card with his thumb as he played out his hand. Luckily, I won that hand. On the second hand, I doubled down on an 11. On double downs in face-down games, the player turns his first two cards over and gets the double down card face down. Thus, Juan knew what cards would help me and which ones would not. As he dealt me the doubling card, I was now positive that I saw Juan holding back the top card. The card I got was a seven, which gave me an 18. The next card out was a ten, which broke the next player, but would have helped me a lot. Then I became even more sure that Juan was second dealing when he played out his hand—with thumb holding all the way! He ended up a three card 21 (a seven, eight and six combo). As I was leaving, one player said to me, "Maybe you are smart to leave; he's killing us."

I answered, "Maybe you don't know what's really going on in the game!" I left the casino very upset.   Lost: $25

What I must stress very strongly here is that I feel sure that cheating of players by dealers in Las Vegas blackjack is very, very rare.

If it was frequent, counters wouldn't win. No one else would win either! And if cheating were house policy (I've seen no evidence of that in Las Vegas), casinos would have no need to bar counters; they would just send in the mechanics to clean them out. What happened to me on March 10 was the only incident in my two months of playing in Vegas in which I was sure I was being cheated. And, while I am certain that cheating is not the house policy of this particular casino, I never played there again; this is the one casino barred by me. There were a few other incidents in my eight weeks of play in which I had suspicions about dealers. I would observe these dealers closely before playing at their table again.

Session Five. Lady Luck. 11:55AM-12:10PM. Day shift. 2 decks.
After recovering from the cheating incident, I went downtown and played first at the Lady Luck. Paul, my 3/4 penetration dealer of late last week was nowhere to be found. I played through just three decks and quit after the last two were shuffled at 40 and then 30 percent penetration. My win in this session was luck, plain and simple. $\boxed{\text{Won: \$138}}$

Session Six. Horseshoe. 12:25-12:50PM. Day shift. 1 deck.
I continued my camouflage here, but was watched very closely. I had a hot run early, then cooled down and then quit for the session and day to relax. I think that for the rest of my time in Vegas, I'll give myself a half day in the middle of the week. $\boxed{\text{Won: \$98}}$

The Nevada weather is starting to warm up and I feel more like driving into the mountains than playing blackjack. I had fun driving into the mountains off Charleston and later I stopped at the Big Dipper Ice Cream Shop to hear their inexpensive oldie jukebox and have their great ice cream.

March 10	Won: $85	Time: 3 hr, 15 min
Week to date	Won: $1,510.50	Time: 21 hr, 40 min

March 11

Session One. Horseshoe. 8:50-9:40AM. Graveyard shift. 1 deck.
This was a very uneventful session, considering the casino. I was able to play with just one or two other players. Early morning graveyard has the best conditions at the Horseshoe. I wasn't given any scrutiny. I quit at the end of a negative deck when the dealer let another player sit in my second hand spot. $\boxed{\text{Won: \$108.50}}$

Session Two. Treasure Island. 10:55-11:55AM. Graveyard shift. 2 and 6 decks.
I briefly played in the six-deck section and lost a small amount there. Then I moved over to the $10 two-deck games. I continued to lose in the two-deck blackjack and quickly fell $500 behind. It looked like a bad session was in the making.

Then Josephine, a dealer I've never seen here before, dealt 3/4 of the way and sometimes more into the deck. Lots of great count situations came up and I slowly battled my way back. I nearly pulled ahead and was very tempted to stay past my one-hour time limit, but I didn't want to overstay my welcome in a casino which has a good game and in which I have already been observed. I also didn't want to stay past the shift change at noon.

Two interesting players joined me in my two-deck play. One commented of how four aces came out on one round and two came out on the next. He stressed that he "wasn't a card counter or anyone like that." I much doubt that his overall play causes much concern to the pit at Treasure Island. Another player quit soon after Josephine came on because of "too many hands between shuffles!" Steve Wynn would probably pay a fortune to get a casino full of suckers like this one!   Lost: $11.50

Session Three. Treasure Island. 1:05-1:45PM. Day shift. 2 decks.
I ate lunch at the buffet between my sessions here. With a new shift on, I felt that I could come back; that's why I didn't stay past noon in my last session.

However, I was observed more on this shift than I was on graveyard. I cracked some jokes to the dealers and the pit bosses to make myself seem like an amateur player.   Won: $408

Session Four. Stardust. 2:30-3:25PM. Day Shift. 2 Decks.
This was another losing session at the 'Dust. Penetration never exceeded 60 percent, which makes this no DAS game tough. Once, I lost an insurance bet with a true count of +8 when I had two hands of $100 on the table. When the hand was played out, the dealer made a three card 21, which gave me a $300 loss. I guess it was fortunate I didn't have two hands of $200, on the table.

One dealer, Don, whom I also lost heavily to, looked exactly like a former uncle of mine: one who always felt I would never amount to anything. Figures!   Lost: $785

Session Five. Sands. 4:05-4:20PM. Day Shift. 6 decks.

I played just one shoe because the construction noise distracted me to the point that I screwed up my ace side count, which is more difficult to keep in shoes than in one and two-deck games. When I have count problems, I stop playing. So, I did. | Won: $85.50 |

Session Six. Plaza. 6:05-6:06PM. Swing shift. 1 deck.

I thought that I would avoid the crew that hassled me the other night (March 8) if I came in before eight. I was wrong. Swing starts early at The Plaza!

I sat down at the $25 one-deck game and was joined by two other players. Off the top, I played two hands of $50 and, luckily, won both. I then was slugged with a one-two punch. First, the dealer, with 75 percent of the deck left, reshuffled. Then, out of the corner of my eye, I saw the black pit boss of the other night who had asked if I "knew where the door was." I quickly colored up my chips and made up a story about forgetting about a dinner engagement. I went to the cashiers cage and cashed out. When I turned to leave, the black pit boss was standing right next to me. He seemed very ready to show me exactly where the door was! He said, "*Boy*, I guess we didn't make ourselves very clear to you the other night, did we? We don't want you in here to play anymore. Or for anything else!"

I answered, "What do you mean? I win one hand and you want me to leave?"

"Don't be a wise-ass with me. You are *not* going to be playing here anymore. I don't want to see you in here again. Get my meaning?"

I did and left. I now had been barred twice and could actually be arrested, and legally so, for trespassing if I so much as stepped into the Plaza again. | Won: $100 |

Session Seven. Horseshoe. 6:20-6:55PM. Swing shift. 1 deck.

I was given normal heat for this place. When the crowd and the heat picked up, I left. | Won: $157 |

Session Eight. Fitzgeralds. 7:10-8:00PM. Swing shift. 2 decks.

I continued the downtown circuit and found only one player at the $10 two-deck table, so I sat down to play. I fell behind by over $400 early and then came back late. I actually pulled ahead, but then lost a couple of $50 bets. Some pit boss scrutiny existed during my comeback.

Lost: $47

Session Nine. Horseshoe. 8:30-9:05PM. Swing shift. 1 Deck.
Since I knew that I wouldn't be back here for about a month, I decided to play once more in this wild casino. I bounced from $25 table to $25 table so I never played with more than two others. A few times I almost left, but I kept finding another table.

I fell almost $600 behind in just five minutes, but then ground my way back to a small win. After 35 minutes, and little heat, I decided this was a great time to say good-bye to the Horseshoe for about a month.

Won: $82.50

Before I drove up to do some blackjack playing on the Strip, I had a nice barbecue chicken dinner at Sassy Sally's. I was served by a cute waitress to whom I mentioned my blackjack playing. She mentioned having bad losses in the game at the Golden Gate (a small bettor place). It occurred to me that if I could get a playing partner like this woman, I could probably get away with a lot more in blackjack with less barring risk. Most casino personnel consider women, especially attractive women, too stupid to be intelligent blackjack players. However, after talking to this waitress some more, I decided that she would not be a good playing partner.

Session Ten. Treasure Island. 10:35-11:40PM. Swing shift. 2 decks.
In this session the cards just ran lousy. Gary, a pit boss who had witnessed my big winning session of March 7, could barely contain his glee as I lost hand after hand. Once he even said, "Different tonight, isn't it Stuart?"

Playing with two or three others gave me fewer hands and a worse expectation than normal, but tonight it probably cut down my losses and Gary's glee. I managed to keep my humor through it all. A couple of times when I won hands with Gary at the table, I asked him to stay next to me and bring me luck. A couple of times I called for him to come by from the other end of his pit and bring me luck on some big bets. Nothing really worked for me nor helped; though, seeming superstitious makes me appear to be—hopefully—a "normal" gambler.

Lost: $836.50

I decided after the loss at Treasure Island to end my play for the week. Though I usually want to get in 30 hours or more of play a week, I felt very tired. Blackjack can be a very exhausting game mentally. This isn't only because of the figuring and calculations that have to be made at casino speed, but also because of the acting job that any serious count player must do to survive for any length of time.

I just wanted to rest and not think much about blackjack for two days. I wanted to be rested for my third week of Vegas blackjack. I was happy to end up plus for the week, but wished that I had won more, especially considering the great first two days I had. Of course, I know that I'll almost assuredly have some losing black-jack weeks on this trip. Frank, has told me that losing months are not uncommon for him or other pros.

March 11	Lost: $738.50	Time: 6 hr, 46 min
Week 2 Total	Won: $772	Time: 28 hr, 26 min
Trip to date	Won: 4,860.50	Time: 58 hr, 31 min

Dealer Cheating

If one plays or even talks about blackjack for any length of time, the subject of dealer cheating is sure to come up. Nearly all of what I've heard and read on this subject can be classified as wild lies, paranoia and fables.

Even before I began to play blackjack for small stakes in the casinos, I was bombarded with falsehoods concerning dealer cheating. Two so-called counters in New York provided my introduction to fables of dealer cheating. One of these "counters," Al, estimated that over 40 percent of Las Vegas dealers and almost 20 percent of the dealers in Atlantic City (which has only shoe games—and therefore are much, much tougher to cheat in) cheat the players. Al's friend, Buddy, claimed that the main reason that the casinos in Las Vegas are well air conditioned is that the cool air makes it easier for dealers to perform seconds dealing!

Despite Al and Buddy's accusations of rampant dealer cheating of players, they both claimed to be huge long-term winners! After hearing these obviously ridiculous accusations, I "barred" Al and Buddy from my blackjack life (and all other parts of it, as well) even before I had played a single hand in a casino!

Other somewhat more realistic accusations, which I also believe to be largely false, were made by Lance Humble in his *World's Greatest Blackjack Book*, from which I picked up the Hi-Opt I count system. In his book, Humble, I believe, made the mistake of confusing short-term negative fluctuations, which can be violent in blackjack, with "evidence" of dealer cheating.

Before my blackjack trip to Las Vegas, I got to see, again, the tremendous negative fluctuations in my home practice sessions. While I won fairly significantly over the long haul (around 100,000 hands), I had a number of severe slumps that lasted many thousands of hands. In these practice sessions, I made fewer errors than I figured to make in the casino and I certainly wasn't cheating myself!

In his book, Humble lays down what he considers outward signs of dealer cheating. Some of these signs are: players whining over losses at a table, which one sees at just about every table; tough looking dealers; dealers wearing flashy jewelry; and so forth. Humble even printed the results of surveys that show that players are most likely to win against young female dealers and most like-

71

ly to lose against older male dealers. I don't know about Humble's respondents, but I can say that I have had many big losses against very attractive female dealers (as well as a number of big wins) and many big wins against tough looking male dealers (and a number of big losses). I would guess that for most male count players—and the majority of counters are men—it is more comforting to play and easier to concentrate against a young (and usually attractive) female dealer than against a tough-looking older man. (Interestingly enough, in Week Three, on March 15 at Harrahs, described on page 81, I was to have a play experience in which my reaction to the attractiveness of a female dealer probably cost me money!) Thus, the better results versus women. And though about ten hours of my play against each of two dealers hardly provide a real sample, I will say again that of the two dealers I know personally, I have done much better versus Mike, an older male dealer who wears jewelry, than against Mari, a very attractive lady in her mid-20's (though she does wear cute bracelets and rings; oh my God, that's why I lost to Mari!)

In terms of actually spotting dealer cheating via seconds, peeks, and false shuffles, Humble says that virtually no one, himself included, can do so. He urges readers not to waste their time even trying. (A point I strongly disagree with!)

If dealer cheating and casino tolerance of it were as pervasive as Humble implies and if no one, save for a few card sharps, could spot it, casinos would have no need to bar counters. Instead, the casinos would have the cheats (or mechanics or knockout dealers) destroy them. A few key false shuffles, peeks, and seconds at the right time would wipe out a counter's expected weekly winnings within an hour. If dealer cheating were rampant in blackjack, no counters—or anyone else excepting some confederates—would ever win a significant amount of money. However, some professional counters do win big bucks and casinos still do bar players that they consider a threat.

In addition, Nevada and Atlantic City—the two locations where a player is least likely to be cheated because of the expertise of Gaming Control Agents and most shift supervisors—are now in serious competition for consumer dollars from Indian and riverboat casinos. Any reported and proven incidents of dealer cheating would cause serious damage to the gaming in Nevada and Atlantic City. Because of the long-term damage that would result over just one proven cheating incident, I very much doubt that cheating is a house policy in any large Nevada or Atlantic City casino.

Does what I just wrote mean that dealer cheating is non-existent in Nevada blackjack, especially the hand-held games, in which dealer cheating via sleight of hand is much easier to perform? Of course not. But I do believe that it is very rare. Exactly how rare is hard to say.

By far, the most frequent scenario in which a dealer cheats a black-jack player is one in which the casino is totally ignorant of what's happening. It goes something like this. The cheat first helps a friend win at his table by seconds dealing, peeking, and false shuf-fles (putting player blackjacks on the top of the deck). The cheat dealer and his confederate have agreed to some split of this profit. The cheat then (the sequence can be reversed) cheats other players to make the table win level normal, which is done to prevent pit suspicion. In fact, a good cheat, I would imagine, would overcheat the other (ignorant) players so that his bosses would praise him for having such a "good" table!

However, this scam has at least two major risks. First, the dealer who cheats this way is forever under threat of blackmail by his confederate. In effect, the future of his gaming career is in his con-federate's hands. In other words, the dealer had better believe his confederate to be one of his best life-time friends! And the dealer's life-time friend had better be someone who can understand short term fluctuations. Even having a cheat help is no absolute guaran-tee the player can win in a 15 or 20 minute session, which these sessions would have to be held to because of potential pit suspi-cion over seeing losses with the same dealer-player combo.

The second major risk involves the heavy penalties. If the cheat and his confederate get caught they both will be arrested and faced with felony raps. In addition, the dealer can kiss his gaming career good-bye. In a sense the odds are against a cheat dealer because just one mistake or error on his part that can be picked up by a boss, the eye, or a local gaming agent, any of whom may be alerted by a smart player, ends the scam and brings out the handcuffs. These odds and penalties keep virtually all dealers in line.

Despite the rarity of cheating, a person playing for decent money in a hand-held game should always be on the lookout for it. He is most liable to be the player used by the cheat to make up for "losses" to his confederate. Because dealing blackjack is a fairly low-paying (especially considering the big money flying around), thankless job with little security, some dealer cheating will always probably exist. Though the odds are against its occurring, even one session with a cheating dealer can be very devastating, financially.

Steve Forte's *Gambler's Protection Video Series* has been a big aid for me (I've viewed it countless times) to learn about peeking, second dealing, bottom dealing and false shuffles. In their writings, Uston and Wong bring out good pointers on dealer cheating.

In my two months of blackjack playing in Las Vegas, there were instances in which dealers made me suspicious by certain motions and movements. On closer and later examination (when I observed from a table or so away) these were usually proven to be definite false alarms. There are a couple of dealers whom I do want to view again before playing again at their tables. I would guess that there is probably nothing wrong with these dealers, as well.

The one time on my Las Vegas blackjack trip in which I felt that I positively identified a cheat took place on March 10 in a casino that I have been legally advised not to name. What I will now write of is the aftermath of this incident—something that has troubled me more than the incident itself.

After my $25 loss in the four hands that I played, I cashed out and made a call to the Gaming Control Board from a nearby casino. The reasons that I did not complain to a supervisor or pit boss at the casino in which I believed I was cheated was that, I had no hard evidence of the seconds dealing (I would have needed a hidden camera working to get that) and, my complaint would have marked me as a knowledgeable player to the casino since the average player doesn't know how seconds (which must be combined with peeking) are dealt and why. Thus, I called the Gaming Control Board, whose job it is to investigate cheating allegations.

I related the details and time of the incident to an agent. Since I was positive that the unnamed casino tapes all of its $25 action, the agent just needed to view the tape to see the evidence. I was told that an agent would go to the casino before 12 noon. In case I ever wanted to play in this casino again, I thought that I should not be present during this agent's visit.

Early the following week (on March 14), I made a follow-up call to the Gaming Control Board. The agent I spoke to said that no dealer named Juan was in the casino I mentioned and that no $25 tables were open when the agent visited—just 30 minutes after the incident. I now asked to speak to this agent's supervisor.

In the conversation with a supervisor, I expressed my doubt that any agent had visited the casino for two reasons: 1) every time that I had been in this casino (even at times like 3:00AM) at least one $25 two-deck table was open. I much doubted that none would be open near noon time since the casino business picks up at that time. 2) Even if Juan had left the casino, some supervisor would surely know about him or whoever was working a $25 two-deck table by his description at 11:15AM.

This supervisor expressed doubt in my story. At first, he talked down to me as if I was some amateur who could never spot dealer cheating and would not know why a dealer would cheat in the first place. This supervisor was also amazed that anyone would complain of dealer cheating after just a $25 loss.

Patiently, I explained my knowledge and the whys of seconds dealing and peeking. I also stressed how rare it would be done in these times (as compared to 25-30 years ago). I also mentioned the bad ($743.50) loss that I had suffered earlier the same day at the Stardust in which the dealer definitely was not a cheat. Though I didn't explain this to the supervisor, I had lost at the Stardust—in mostly head-on play—only because the cards ran bad, which can often happen in the game of blackjack. I kept playing in that game up to my one-hour time limit because I was getting halfway decent deck penetration and was playing head-on; these factors created a positive expectation situation for me. That I lost was no fault of Diane, the dealer. However, at the unnamed casino, I was not going to stay and throw away money in a rigged game just because my losses totaled "only" $25 in the five minutes that it took me to figure out what was going on.

The supervisor finally took me seriously and said that an investigation would take place. He asked me to call him the next week.

I called back about ten days later. The supervisor now admitted that the casino mentioned had $25 tables and that a dealer named Juan did work there. However, no evidence of Juan's cheating was seen. Juan, he said, would continue to be watched.

I asked if agents viewed the tape of when I had played since cheats pick their moments and spots. The agent answered that this casino does not tape any of their games! I was very openly skeptical of this claim. Later, when I told Mike and Mari (the two dealers who know about me and my card counting), they were very skeptical of this as well. Mari almost wet her pants laughing and Mike nearly choked on the hamburger he was eating.

Thus, I was sure that someone was lying: either the Gaming Control Board supervisor to me or the casino to the Gaming Control Board agent. I figured that if the supervisor would lie to me he would probably say that the tape showed no cheating. Thus, I believed that the lie was probably told by the casino to the Gaming Control agent. Why he believed it is beyond me!

The casino's reasons for lying can't be good ones. My guess would be that they know or suspect that dealer cheating may be occurring in their blackjack games. They would probably prefer to find it themselves rather than be embarrassed by an outsider directing the Gaming Control Board to discover it.

With this in mind, I decided to bar this casino from any more of my play and have strongly advised other serious players to do the same.

Despite this incident and its unpleasant aftermath, I still think that blackjack dealer cheating is very rare in Las Vegas, the rest of Nevada, and in Atlantic City. Gaming agents and most supervisors have a decent amount of knowledge of what to watch for. If dealer cheating were frequent and/or house policy, I would have gone broke playing blackjack in Las Vegas. In addition, I would never have been barred or been flat bet: a fate that befell me on five sad occasions on this trip.

From what I know and have seen, dealer cheating appears to be much more of a possibility at Indian and riverboat casinos. Gaming and game protection supervisors in these locations often take their jobs with minimal, and sometimes no training, and nearly all have extremely limited knowledge of the hows and whys of cheating. In a sense, these locations are probably a lot like Nevada was in the 1950's and 1960's, times in which dealer cheating existed much more so than now. Thus, blackjack players should be very careful playing in Indian or riverboat casinos, particularly in any hand-held games.

Mirage, Harrah's, Imperial Palace, Las Vegas Hilton, Palace Station, San Remo

March 14

Session One. Mirage. 6:45-7:45AM. Graveyard shift. 2 decks.
I liked the Mirage blackjack conditions. I was able to play one-on-one most of the time and had no problem finding a $25 minimum two-deck game. The deck was dealt to a 2/3 plus depth. There was little heat, though I tried to minimize it even more by throwing in a couple of mistakes in which I didn't double on a couple of weak soft totals (a 13 versus a five and a 16 versus a four).

The only negative about this session was that I got clobbered for my worst loss yet in Las Vegas. I continued to play even after I fell over $1,000 behind, my usual cut off point. Why? Because of the superb conditions and rules (DAS and dealer stands on all 17's).

After my hour of play was over, I exchanged some jokes with the dealers, which I felt was good cover. How many serious, never-grinning counters would exchange jokes and laughter after losing over $1,000? Or any bettors for that matter? | Lost: $1,091.50 |

Session Two. Harrahs. 8:10-9:15AM. Graveyard shift. 2 and 6 decks.
I did something a little different in this casino. I often bet different amounts when I played two hands on a round. I usually bet more on the second hand since more information is available when playing it. This is especially true in face-down games since the player can't view his second hand until after he has finished playing his first hand (except when making the insurance decision). Sometimes when a pit boss watched, I bet more on the first hand in order to throw them off, especially if I had won on that spot and had lost the second spot on the previous round. This is something that I should have been doing from the very beginning of my Vegas play.

In another first, I had a dealer curse at me. Once in the face-up six-deck game I got a six when doubling a soft 15 versus a dealer six, which gave me 21. When I got the six, Tony, the dealer, said "Oh, shit!" He was probably pissed that I hadn't yet toked him though I was losing at the time. Usually I toke some, but not him after that!

I played mostly the six-deck game since there are no $25 two-deck games here. Penetration was great in both games: five decks plus in the six-deckers and 1-1/2 decks in the double-deckers. Despite that, I still lost again. | Lost: $184 |

Session Three. Imperial Palace. 9:35-10:35AM. Graveyard shift. 2 decks.

I spread wildly going from $10 on one hand to two hands of $150. By often parlaying hands in a seemingly haphazard manner, I seemed to avoid pit suspicion. Use of camouflage, such as betting big off-the-top at times, also helped.

As happened in my first two sessions of the day, I seemed to lose every insurance bet I made. When this happened, I often would lose three bets on such hands. Usually my insurance bets are made when I am playing two hands on a round. Let's say both hands are for $100. To insure both hands, I must bet another $100. If the dealer does not have a blackjack, I not only lose the insurance bet, but now must play my two hands versus a strong dealer up card: the ace. The insurance bet becomes a winning proposition if one wins it over a third of the time. Thus, the count player will lose it more often than not. In losing streaks, the "not" seems to disappear. A big comeback at the end fell short. As last week, I now have lost three straight sessions to start the week. Will I win the fourth session as last week? | Lost: $86 |

Session Four. Las Vegas Hilton. 12:15-1:15PM. Day shift. 2 decks.

Before this session, I made a downtown stop at Leroy's to see my sports betting friends. I also got a San Francisco Examiner next door. This bulldog edition of the Examiner is the only paper in Vegas from which I can get the Saturday NBA box scores. Though I am not betting the NBA, I still paste every box score in a notebook, and I still record each game and pointspread. I do this in case I decide to end my sports betting retirement.

My session at the Hilton put my sports betting retirement end on hold. I not only had a big win, but I used a unique occurrence to my advantage.

On one play, I hit a 12 and received a nine. I don't know why, but I felt that I had busted on this play. When I threw my cards in, casino procedure after a bust in a face down game, Michelle, my dealer, informed me that I had a 21 and gave me back my cards. (I have often caught dealer mistakes, but this was the first one I made that I was aware of.) After Michelle performed her honest deed, I loudly praised her and tipped her fairly well. In return, Michelle started going much further into the deck than is Hilton policy (2/3 plus versus 50-55 percent), and I profited. After the session, I praised Michelle to the pit bosses and even the executive casino manager as someone who "didn't take advantage of me." How many counters or even non-counters do that? | Won: $1,084.50 |

Session Five. Palace Station. 2:00-2:45PM. Day shift. 4 decks.
The Palace Station deck penetration was excellent. They dealt out over three decks out of four. Some of the other conditions and rules, such as the dealer hitting soft 17 and cards dealt face down, are not.

I used a popular, and probably Palace Station regular, high roller as cover. He was betting $500 per round. In his shadow, I was easily able to progress from one hand of $25 to two hands of $175.

An early high-count shoe created a winning session for me. A comp given me for the Iron Horse Cafe at the end of my play provided me not only a decent meal, but also a signal that my play, for now, is welcomed here. | Won: $695 |

Session Six. San Remo. 7:55-8:40PM. Swing shift. 2 decks.
Only $5 minimum tables were available in the double-deckers, so I bought in for $200 and spread in crazy patterns from one hand of $5 to two hands of $100. What I first did at the Golden Nugget on March 2 continues to pay dividends. I won and was given no real scrutiny. | Won: $575.50 |

Session Seven. Harrahs. 9:35-10:35PM. Swing shift. 2 and 6 decks.
I mostly played the two-deck game with $5 and $10 minimums. I used my "crazy" bet patterns again. For a while, I forgot that surrender was offered in this game. Dumb! A pro must always be totally aware of the rules and the effects they have on the game he is playing. A bad drunk player chased me from the six-deck game. I later returned to it when he, and the other players, had left. Despite continuing great penetration, I lost here again. I was able to joke with Debbie, the dealer I had most of my losses to. | Lost: $528 |

Session Eight. Imperial Palace. 11:00-11:55PM. Swing shift. 2 decks.

I played at a $25 table and received more scrutiny than I did earlier today. Was it because of the large spread I used on graveyard? I don't know. I fell behind by over $600 in the first five minutes and spent the rest of the session battling back.

I was watched mostly by Don, a look-alike of one of the young Nazi killers in the movie, *The Boys From Brazil*. Ironic, considering the reputation of the owner. When I finally left the table a small winner, Don said to me, "I'm happy that you came back. You don't know how happy I am that you came back." What was it that Hitler once said about big lies?

> Won: $58.50

Session Nine. Mirage. 1:05-2:05AM. Swing shift. 2 decks.

I might have gone back to my apartment and called it a day, but with the Mirage right across from the Imperial Palace and Harrahs and with my car parked in the Mirage garage, I decided to play one more session there.

I made a lot of dealer bets in this session—probably too many. I felt a little tired near the end of my play and perhaps should have quit sooner, but the great conditions (very little heat, good penetration and rules) kept me at the table. However, it would have been even nicer if I had won. Though I am now 0-2 in my Mirage sessions, I am positive that I'll win there at least once before the week is up. They will get more of my play than any other casino this week.

> Lost: $191.50

| March 14 | Won: $332.50 | Time: 8 hr, 30 min |

This was my longest playing day in Las Vegas thus far. Except for a brief rest stop at my apartment between sessions five and six (Palace Station and San Remo), I was on the run all day. After getting down about $1,400 early in the day, it was nice to end up slightly ahead. However, I want my long-term hourly win rate to be somewhat more than the $39 per hour that I won today.

March 15

Session One. San Remo. 1:20-2:10PM. Day Shift. 2 Decks.

I played and acted like a wild man at a $5 two-deck table. I acted superstitious about what spot I'd put my money in. My head-on play gave me lots of choices in terms of seating and where I'd put my bet down. I also acted impulsively when chasing losses, especially when the count was high.

Financially, I fell behind by $200 early, then got about $400 ahead. I was hitting another slump when a pit boss came to watch. At this point, I left.

Won: $140

Session Two. Mirage. 2:40-3:40PM. Day shift. 2 decks.
My session record at the Mirage fell to an imperfect 0-3. I spread from $25 on one hand to two hands of $200 (the optimum bet spread for me), and this time was given some heat. Jim, a pit boss, engaged me in conversation and was obviously looking to see if I was looking at him or the cards. Looking at the cards in our talk would tell him that I'm a counter. I'm scared that I may not have totally passed this test.

I had some wild money swings. First, I fell $1,000 behind. Then I won some big bets in a few high-count decks and got $400 ahead. A losing streak in the very last deck I played, one with a high count, sealed another lost session.

The Mirage may not be as heat free as the Nugget, despite what I was told by Frank and others. I wonder what will happen if I win here at some point!

Lost: $114

Session Three. Imperial Palace. 3:55-4:40PM. Day shift. 2 decks.
I fell $500 behind in the early going in a head-on game with a male Asian dealer. This dealer then started giving me the preferential shuffle treatment, dealing deep in negative decks and shuffling early in positive decks. I tried tipping once, but this didn't help. Playing against preferential shuffling is hopeless. I switched to a more crowded table, which had consistent and decent penetration, and I ended up a small winner.

Won: $118

Session Four. Harrahs. 5:00-5:45PM. Day shift. 2 decks.
Again, I briefly forgot the surrender rule at Harrahs (I am really angry about that) early, and I know that this cost me a partial bet or two. Why did I forget? Who knows?

I received another lesson as well. Don't play when tired! At the end of the session, I was playing against Anne, a very attractive dealer. Anne has cute, curly, light brown hair and has the thin body type that I like. She also has sparkling brown eyes. I lost a couple of hands very late in the session and suddenly noticed that my play decisions were taking me longer and longer. I was dead tired. Anne's attractiveness had made me unaware of how exhausted I was. The second I realized this, I quit the game and got comped to dinner. When tired, don't play no matter who is dealing (though I doubt very much that Anne realized or tried to contribute to my problem). | Lost: $20.50 |

After my dinner at Harrahs, I slept for about three hours at my apartment. This sleep refreshed me.

Session Five. Las Vegas Hilton. 9:50-10:45PM. Swing shift. 2 and 6 decks

I played the two-deck game first and lost almost $1,000. The loss would have been worse, but a couple of correct insurance bets (I'm finally winning some of those) prevented even worse carnage. Correct insurance play is critical to winning blackjack. Because of its frequency in one-deck games, it is the most important strategy variation in that game; it is also important in two-deck games.

I then gave the six-deck game a try and used some correct surrender plays (I didn't forget that rule in this casino) to help fuel a small comeback. | Lost: $708 |

Session Six. Palace Station. 11:20PM-12:15AM. Swing shift. 4 decks.

I played with mostly two or three other players at the table. All were lousy players (all never hit with over 13 versus any dealer up card). Sometimes players like this get me angry, making it a good time to leave. It didn't here because I remembered many times when a stupid play by someone causes the whole table to win.

In this session, the last shoe I played was the killer. Or, more accurately, the last two hands. On the first, I lost $600. I originally had two hands of $200 on the table. The count was, of course, sky-high. Versus a dealer six, I stood on one stiff (a 13) and doubled on ace-three (soft 14) on which I received a ten. The dealer then proceeded to get a four card 18. He could have busted on either of his last two cards. I then lost $400 on the next and final round of the shoe. This was my worst session to date. | Lost: $1,191.50 |

I decided to give the good game at the Mirage another try. Being down close to $1,800 on the day has shown a little of the real world negative fluctuations of blackjack. The almost $1,900 I've lost in my last two sessions shows that these losses can occur quickly.

Session Seven. Mirage. 12:50-1:50AM. Swing shift. 2 decks.
I finally got a win at the Mirage! It came at a needed time. However, my win also had its dark lining. One dealer, Rayshell, shuffled far earlier then any other dealer I've seen here, at just 50 percent. Have the pit bosses put out the word on me?

I quickly left her table and played with another dealer, Samantha, who went 1-1/2 decks in. I did very well at her table. On one hand, with no floor people watching, I doubled on a soft 20 versus her six and won a big bet for me, as well as a bet for Samantha; I doubled her bet as I did mine. Samantha seemed not in the least surprised that I made this play; I suspect she knows that I am a counter. It was nice to win at the Mirage, though my win there did not put me in the black for the day or the week. | Won: $865 |

March 15	Lost: $911	Time: 6 hr, 10 min
Week to date	Lost: $578.50	Time: 14 hr, 40 min

At home, during my practice blackjack sessions, I came to see how bad some negative blackjack fluctuations could be. I'm now getting a little taste of these negative runs in the real world. I'll see what tomorrow and the rest of the week brings. I just remind myself that the long-term odds are in my favor even if I should lose thousands in the short haul.

March 16

Las Vegas had beautiful weather today, 60 degrees, blue skies, and a swift breeze. I looked forward to enjoying it after playing for about three hours. Today was to be my mid-week half-day.

Session One. Palace Station. 9:05-9:50AM Graveyard shift. 4 decks.
I started out with one great shoe and one fairly good one. These shoes got me about $800 ahead. In the last three shoes I played I lost back about $300 of the profits; I also was getting some pit scrutiny. One of the bosses, Ross, said that I played like a professional player. I guess that I need to avoid his pit for the rest of this week. | Won: $505.50 |

Session Two. Las Vegas Hilton. 10:35-11:35AM. Graveyard shift. 2 and 6 decks.
I won in the one shoe I played doing fairly well when the count increased. I also got some pit scrutiny and was getting tired of it.

Thus, at the end of the shoe, I complained loudly of an upset stomach and went to the gift shop for some Peptol Bismol (I like its bubble gum taste!). When I came back, showing the Peptol Bismol to the pit, I played in the two-deck games instead. The deck penetration was fair (60 percent), but I lost more than I had won playing six-deck. Thus the session had a red bottom line, in more ways than one!

Lost: $61.50 plus a bottle of Peptol Bismol

Session Three. Mirage. 12:30-1:30PM. Day shift. 2 decks.
For the first half hour of my play, I had one of my hottest blackjack runs ever; financially, it was my hottest run ever. In several high-count decks, I reached my high bets (two hands of $200) and was winning the majority of them. Since I was running so hot, I often was starting out new decks with bets as high as two hands of $100. After a half hour, I was ahead close to $2,500. With my loss limit rules, I was going to make a minimum of $1,250 for the session.

When a card counter is the beneficiary of a run like this, he considers the blackjack count books to be bibles. On my big bets I got several blackjacks, just as the books say I should. On my big bets, the dealers were busting most of their stiff hands, just as the books say they should. I received several tens on my ten and 11 double downs (once, when the ace side count was high, I received an ace on my ten double down), just as the books say should happen.

But, as the blackjack count books say, big winners—especially those suspected of being counters—get heat. And that also happened! At the height of my session, Ralph, the shift supervisor, started prowling around the table and glared at me like an angry shark. I joked with the dealer that she might lose her job since I was doing so well. The dealer replied that I "misunderstood" Ralph who she called "a sweetheart." Probably to Ralph's delight, my hot streak cooled down after he came out of his lair to observe me.

It is now obvious that the Mirage is not nearly as heat-free as the Nugget. I best be careful the rest of this week if I want to continue to have access to these good games. Good penetration continued today, despite the biggest win I've earned in Las Vegas or anyplace else, thus far.

Won: $1,925

Session Four. Harrahs. 1:45-2:00PM. Day shift. 2 decks.
I bet wildly in the $5 minimum two-deck game in this short session. I often started out with two hands of $50. I would go as high

as two hands of $100 if the count got high or gradually cut back to one hand of $5 or $10 if the count got lousy. I parlayed my bets like a "normal" gambler and acted like I was playing high because I felt "lucky." After 15 minutes, I decided to enjoy the rest of the nice day outside the casinos. In retrospect, I probably should have stayed since the game was good and I was getting little heat; also, generally, I am much more likely to quit off a big losing streak than a big winning streak. But I was impatient to enjoy a splendid outdoor day.

		Won: $481.50
March 16	Won: $2,850.50	Time: 3 hr
Week to date	Won: $2,272	Time: 17 hr, 40 min

As I crossed Las Vegas Boulevard to pick up my car at the Mirage, I realized that I was now close to passing my high money point of the trip. I was ahead around $7,100; my high trip point had been about $7,200, reached before my last session of last Tuesday (March 8). Would I pass this point tomorrow? Was my losing streak of late last week and early this week now a distant memory? Tomorrow, I would start receiving answers to these questions.

Today, I enjoyed the nice weather with a slow walk in the downtown part of town. I recalled that when I used to bet sports in Las Vegas, I was always running someplace. Running to catch the start of a game; running to a sportsbook to catch a price before some other bettor or betting group took it away; running to be first in line in the morning at the Las Vegas Hilton. I remember doing some of this frantic running downtown. Today, I ran no place.

Later, I had dinner at a small Chinese and Thai restaurant, downtown. During my meal, I spoke to a friendly, elderly couple from Minnesota, who are visiting Las Vegas for a vacation. This couple comes here once or twice a year to play for small stakes and have fun doing so. Though for them it is entertainment, I can't imagine wagering anything more than a dollar or two total at a time (and this I do very seldomly) "for the fun of it" on games in which the house has an unassailable house edge such as slots (the only bets I make "for fun" are on these), keno, or roulette. I can't imagine losing $100 or $200 in one session "for the fun of it." However, if all bettors were like me, Las Vegas could not exist.

March 17

Session One. San Remo. 7:15-7:45AM. Graveyard shift. 2 decks.
For some reason, I had a nervous feeling as I drove up I-15 on my way to the San Remo. I was excited because I was on the verge of breaking into high ground for the trip. However, I was also fully aware from my home sessions that, in my first 13 days of play, I had not yet encountered any of the real bad runs that are part of the blackjack experience.

I opened the day with a disastrous session. I played at the $5 minimum table and only once did I even bet as much as two hands of $100. I lost every single double down bet I made and also got beaten by about six dealer blackjacks in my mostly head-on play. I wasn't happy about my losses, and I put on an angry impulse act (especially when I progressed to two hands of $50) that showed more anger than I really had. Lost: $727

Session Two. Mirage. 8:10-9:10AM. Graveyard shift. 2 decks.
My losing streak continued for the first 40 minutes of this session. Playing mostly one-on-one, I received zero blackjacks in this time period. I also lost most of my double down bets.

I also blew one double down when, on a very close play decision, I did not double down on a ten versus a dealer ten (my true count index for this play is +5 and the true count at this time was about +5-1/4). I guess with this very small difference and my double down losing streak, I was playing a little scared. I got angry at myself; one has to play like an unemotional machine and always make the right plays if one is to win at blackjack. On the play, I got a ten and beat the dealer's 18.

By this point, I was down about $1,000, but I kept playing because play conditions were very good and there was no heat. The better the game, the more deeply I am willing to play into a loss.

In the final 20 minutes, right after my double down error, the cards turned. Two very hot decks pulled me back to even. And some pit boss scrutiny followed. To this boss, I gave a rap on how to make time seem to go by twice as fast as it really does! (I said he could use this if he couldn't wait to go home from a dull day's work.) This little talk must have made a good impression because the pit boss now looked in less and he also gave me a buffet comp even after I had ended the session a winner! Won: $365

Session Three. Imperial Palace. 9:45-10:40AM. Graveyard shift. 2 decks.

In this session, I used a technique that Frank, the professional counter I've spoken to, taught me. I played at a table with two young female Chinese players who each were betting much more than I. Twice, I even switched tables to follow them, saying that they brought me good luck. The pit crew watched the $500 bets of these ladies much more than they watched my "puny" bets of two hands of $150. Good penetration, sometimes exceeding 3/4, continued.

$\boxed{\text{Won: \$156}}$

Session Four. Harrahs. 11:05AM-12:05PM. Graveyard and day shifts. 2 decks.

After my bad start at San Remo and the first 40 minutes at the Mirage, I was within $200 of pulling ahead for the day and within about $300 of breaking new financial ground for the trip. However, I received another tumble down the mountain in this session.

I had some suspicions of Marty, who hesitated a lot before playing out his hand. However, I could not see the top card being held back, so I stayed at his table for a while and dropped about $200 there. Though there is probably nothing to my suspicions, I would want to observe him more closely before playing at his table again.

At two other tables with dealers I wasn't at all suspicious about, I lost another $367. One of these dealers, whose name now escapes me but who reminded me in looks of Ken Stabler, the former pro football quarterback, would yell out to the pit in a weird bartender-like voice, "Another hundred dollar bill," each time I bought in for another $100. (Dealers must announce and have approved by the pit virtually all large buy-ins.) Though I was losing at Bartender Voice's table, I almost broke out laughing over the way he announced my buy-ins. I probably should have; this would have been a great act!

$\boxed{\text{Lost: \$567}}$

Session Five. Palace Station. 1:45-2:25PM. Day shift. 4 decks.

I definitely was not laughing during this session! As seems to happen in all blackjack losing streaks, I lost consistently on my high-count bets. The really big loss came in the last shoe in which I suffered my biggest losses in the highest count shoe of the session. I also received some pit glares at the end. Since I was getting serious scrutiny at the end and since I felt that cutting down from two hands of $200 to one hand of $25 between shoes would appear very counter-like, I decided to cut this session, my worst thus far in Vegas, a little short. $\boxed{\text{Lost: \$1,295.50}}$

Session Six. Las Vegas Hilton. 3:00-3:55PM. Day shift. 2 decks.
For the second straight session, I set a new record for my worst session for the trip. What are the odds of that, with this being my 14th day of play?

Once again, I won very few of the high-count bets. A $150 double down loss was the real killer. A win on that bet almost seemed as if it would shift the momentum of the session. In the last deck I played, I lost over $400 in a very high-count deck. This high count was the reason I continued my play after I reached $1,000 in losses. After this deck, I decided that I had lost enough. Penetration and crowd conditions were not the best. $\boxed{\text{Lost: \$1,304.50}}$

In the last 2 hours, 35 minutes of play I had managed to lose close to $3,200. I decided to go back to my apartment and get some rest. My mind felt kind of numb after the consecutive big losses at the Palace Station and the Las Vegas Hilton. I was now starting to experience in real life just how much of a grind blackjack can be.

Session Seven. Mirage. 7:50-8:50PM. Swing shift. 2 decks.
Ahead in this session on my very first hand, I was ahead until the next to last hand. On the very last round I lost two hands of $50 to make the session a loser.

Despite few early high-counts, I won. Late, in high-count decks, I lost as I had continual stiffs versus dealer tens. After sessions like these, the blackjack books, instead of being they bibles they seem like during the good sessions, seem as if they were written by the pit bosses! One plus was that I got absolutely no heat because of the semi-crowded conditions. $\boxed{\text{Lost: \$82}}$

Session Eight. Mirage. 9:50-10:55PM. Swing shift. 2 decks.
After a nice dinner at the Mirage buffet, I decided to continue my play in this casino because of the total lack of heat in the previous session. At dinner, I met an interesting young woman who mentioned that her mother is a professional poker player. Hopefully, her mom is having a better day than I am.

My play slump continued. Few high-count situations presented themselves. In this session, I did not do as well on the negative counts as I had in the last session. I moved from table to table to avoid crowded conditions. Nothing helped, though the heat stayed away from me once again.

	Lost: $416.50

This was, by far, my worst day in Vegas. Hopefully, tomorrow will be better.

March 17	Lost: $3,871.50	Time: 7 hr, 5 min
Week to date	Lost: $1,599.50	Time: 24 hr, 45 min

March 18

Session One. Mirage. 9:55-11:00AM. Graveyard shift. 2 and 6 decks.

I gave myself a long pep talk this morning. In it, I reminded myself that disastrous days and losing streaks are to be expected in blackjack. However, I do figure to win over the long haul. I reminded myself that I expected to have one losing streak here which would stretch between eight and thirteen thousand dollars. I felt better after eating two turkey sandwiches and drinking some fruit juice for breakfast before going out to play.

Thus inspired, I lost again at the Mirage! It was the same old story. It seemed as if my high-count winning percentage was about 20 percent. I seemed to have hand after hand where I had a 15 or 16 versus a ten; in high-counts I'd stand and the dealer would have another ten as the hole card. In high-count decks, as I wrote in the chapter on card counting myths, a player is more likely to get stiffs like 15's and 16's versus dealer tens. In the six-deck games, I could, at least, employ an important cost-cut measure and surrender many of those hands (many in high-counts). On the more unlikely side, I lost nearly every insurance bet (well over 2/3). I also lost the majority of my double down bets. Fewer than normal high-counts prevented a total slaughter.

	Lost: $704

Session Two. Harrahs. 11:20AM-12:20PM. Graveyard and day shifts. 2 decks.

Early on, I did fairly well in the non-smoking area (I love this feature of Harrahs). However, several high-count losses prevented me from getting significantly ahead. When this pit filled up, I moved.

Then I played at Anne's (the attractive dealer I met on March 15) table. I planned to spread my bets in my wild $5-two hands of $100 fashion, except that I never went past two hands of $55 in the half hour I played at her table. The count just never got very high.

Anne is very pleasant, and more importantly, she deals far into the deck, I tip dealers like her pretty well. Or, usually I would, I should say. In this session I never did tip her (by placing a bet for her on a hand when the count is good at a critical deck penetration time). At the end of this losing session, I said to Anne, "You know I feel bad because I didn't play any hands for you. I just never had a 'good' feeling about my bets. I'm in a real losing streak."

Anne answered me, "That's OK."

"No, it really isn't. I've screwed up and I'm hurting you as well."

Smiling—and Anne's smile is a very radiant one—Anne then winked at me and said in a low voice. "Don't worry about it. I understand. I also know exactly what's going on." I guess Anne has figured me out as a counter even though I bet in crazy patterns in this $5 minimum game (weeks later, my hunch was to be confirmed). I did tip Anne $2 when I left; I really didn't want her to give a bad report about me to her bosses. Her wonderful smile said that she wouldn't. I hope my hunch on that is correct as I plan to play in Harrahs good games again in a few weeks. | Lost: $146 |

Session Three. Imperial Palace. 12:45-1:55PM. Day shift. 2 decks
At first, I played in the $5 minimum game using my crazy betting patterns and quickly fell behind by $1,000. Hasn't this happened recently? Because the game was very good, I bought in for another $500 and played on. I finally started to win some key bets. I recouped about $600 of losses at the $5 table. Then I saw a $25 two-deck game open up.

As soon as I entered this game, a much higher-betting player bought in, as well. This player bet in a wild way, such as betting $300 on one hand off the top and then reducing to one hand of $100 even if the count went up. However, every time the deck went negative, this player asked to sit out some hands. He was leaving the negative decks for me!

The third time this player jumped out of a negative (the true count was always less than minus one) deck, I was certain that he was counting. I decided to let him know that I was angry without it being obvious to anyone else. I said, "What's wrong, my friend? Do you have some negative vibes concerning these hands?"

The now exposed counter (he knew now that I knew what his game was even if he didn't make it obvious to the pit or the dealer) said,

"I think that I want to take a little stroll right now." Now I had a head-on game. In it, I actually overcame my earlier session deficit. Suddenly, I looked at my watch and saw that I had gone past my hour session limit! Time for lunch.   Won: $9

I asked for and received a restaurant comp for lunch. I wondered if my tiny win meant that my violent slump was coming to an end.

Session Four. Mirage. 3:00-3:55PM. Day shift. 2 and 6 decks.
Mirage conditions were fairly crowded as I bounced between the two and six-deck pits. I made sure to play the two-deck games in a different pit from my big win of two days ago.

I fell back again into my losing ways. Few high-counts appeared. I had very few wins when they did. After 55 minutes of play, I decided to stop for the day and the week. I didn't want to think at all about blackjack until Sunday night when I would plan my Week Four activities.   Lost: $1,202

March 18	Lost: $2,043	Time: 4 hr, 10 min
Week 3 Total	Lost: $3,642.50	Time: 28 hr, 55 min
Trip to date	Won: 1,218	Time: 87 hr, 26 min

I now further understand, in the real world of the casinos, the meanings of negative fluctuations in blackjack play. In two days and 11:15 hours of playing time, I have lost $5,914.50—over $500 an hour! One can go to a doctor or lawyer for less. I have also lost $5,708.50 in my last 8:50 hours of playing—well over $600 an hour. It's possible to lose a lot very quickly in blackjack. Or as Stanford Wong wrote in his *Blackjack Secrets*, "If you bet big, you'll often lose big. Expect it."

On Saturday night I had dinner at a Red Lobster with Paul, the sports betting money mover I spent time with at the Stardust sportsbook on February 28, and his wife, Joan. Paul reminded me to keep an eye on the long haul. Of course, he's right. I watched some basketball games, went to some movies, and in general took two days away from blackjack.

I still thought that the games at the Mirage, Harrahs, and Imperial Palace were among the best in Vegas, and I wanted to return to them, as well as the Palace Station. The Las Vegas Hilton with its poor penetration and the San Remo, I would play more sparingly.

Golden Nugget, Excalibur, Luxor, Aladdin, Circus Circus, Maxim, Desert Inn

March 21st

Session One. Golden Nugget. 5:30-6:30AM. Graveyard shift. 1 deck.

I fell asleep at 8:30 last night and had eight sound hours of sleep. Being rested is critical for good card counting, even more so during a losing streak! Hopefully, I can garner a winning week in Week Four. At least, I know the odds favor me.

This morning I played only the $25 one-deck game. This is the casino and game in which I feel most comfortable.

I received much more scrutiny here than I ever have before. (If only these bosses knew about my disaster of last week!) The scrutiny caused me to use much more camouflage than I have ever used before at the Nugget. I often played two hands of $50 or $75 off the top.

This session ended on two good notes. First, I won! My minor $280 win represents my best session of the last eleven. I also received a comp for the buffet, a sign that my play is still welcomed here; Frank has told me that a refusal of a comp is a warning sign that a barring is imminent.

Won: $280

Session Two. Excalibur. 7:15-8:20AM. Graveyard shift. 6 decks.

This was my first session in this casino on this trip. I played just the six-deck game since the one- and two-deck games are all $5 minimum, and were all very crowded even at this early hour. The deck penetration was not great in any of the three, six-deck games I played in. Four weeks ago, the penetration seemed better.

The session got off to a rocky beginning as I fell behind $500 to Jane, an unfriendly dealer who seemed upset that I didn't tip her; she did not take any of my broad hints that I wanted better deck penetration.

Much later, I won some high-count bets in a game dealt by Franco, who gave me the deepest cuts I received this morning. Him, I tipped, and we won a few bets together. In the last shoe that I played at Franco's table, I noticed that I was being observed from behind. I quit this session with the shoe having a true count of -5 (running count -10 with two-decks left) and being short three aces (only five left). My win here was my biggest since my monster triumph at the Mirage on March 16: 15 lifetimes—oops, I mean sessions—ago.

Won: $877

Session Three. Luxor. 8:50-9:50AM. Graveyard shift. 6 decks.
I made the walk between the Excalibur and the Luxor for the first time. Just as noted in my scout trip of four weeks ago, the Luxor has uneventful six-deck games that are marginally playable; unfortunately, I can't camp out at the Nugget or few other casinos that have the great games.

I got ahead by $175 early, and then behind about $400. I worked my way back to about even and then, lost several bets in a negative shoe. I definitely quit the session most of one shoe too late. Live and learn! The casino clothing was very drab. Hopefully, ancient Egypt was more exciting than this joint.

Lost: $206

Session Four. Aladdin. 10:30-11:20AM. Graveyard. 2 decks.
I thought that my act was now good enough to play in the Aladdin, the casino with supposedly the sharpest pit crew for spotting counters. Last year, I played here once for about 45 minutes and won $115 spreading from $5-$80 playing one hand. Later, I found out that the Aladdin almost never bars counters who don't wager over $100 on a round.

I decided to play at the $10 two-deck table rather than the $25 one and use camouflage similar to what I started using at the Nugget almost three weeks ago (March 2). I was able to get away with a $10-$200 ($100 on two hands) spread without any apparent heat.

The deck penetration was great: over 1-1/2 decks dealt out of two. However, the cards ran lousy and I lost. Has my slump now returned? A sympathetic pit boss told me that my luck might change if I switched tables. Instead, since my hour was almost up, I asked for and received a coffee shop comp. The prime rib was good, but the service was slow.

Lost: $874

Session Five. Circus Circus. 1:25-2:25PM. Day shift. 2 decks.
The cloudy day on the Strip matched my mood as I drove from the Aladdin to Circus. I had been warned by Mari, the dealer I know at Treasure Island, that some dealers at Circus are alleged to be great seconds dealers. I will keep my eye on the deck, as I always

try to, though I believe Mari's tale, though well-intentioned, is probably just dealer gossip. I saw absolutely no evidence of any funny business by any Circus dealer. Dealing blackjack can be, at times, an extremely boring job (as both Mike and Mari have told me). To alleviate their boredom, dealers probably create bullshit stories. Some probably sound convincing.

I played at the $25 two-deck game in the main casino. Almost from the start, a pit boss was practically sitting in my lap. I was very careful in changing my bet sizes, especially increasing. I was slightly ahead for most of the session. When I left, so did my lap-sitter. This can be an emotionally draining business! | Won: $75 |

After this small win I drove down to Leroy's to talk to some sports bettors about the stretch drive for the NBA playoffs. This conversation took my mind off the blackjack grind for a couple of hours. Then I rested a little at my apartment.

Session Six. Maxim. 7:10-7:50PM. Swing shift. 2 and 6 decks.
I played the six-deck game briefly. Nothing much happened in this 3/4-dealt game.

When the two-deck game became less crowded, I moved my chips over there. I went on yet another high-count losing streak. CJ, an older woman dealer, seemed to be hesitating in the play of her hands, but I always saw the top card coming off the deck and the thumb moving in the correct way. This was just another lousy session, the type I've had much too often of late. | Lost: $854 |

Session Seven. Desert Inn. 8:15-9:10PM. Swing shift. 6 decks.
The Desert Inn was even better than when I scouted it four weeks ago. Usually I was getting five decks out of six dealt to me. The surrender rules and the resplit of aces make this a great shoe game.

I had some wins in high-count bets for a change. Late in the session, I won some $300 bets (two hands of $150), which helped me overcome a slow start. Some late session pit boss scrutiny and a delicious hot chocolate (brought by the cocktail waitress) were other low and highlights of the session. | Won: $122 |

Session Eight. Golden Nugget. 10:20-11:25PM. Swing shift. 2 decks.
I rushed downtown and made it just in time to use my buffet comp (given to me when I played graveyard) for the dinner buffet, which

closes at 10. The food was excellent and even healthy. Who says that everything that tastes good is unhealthy?

Unfortunately my after dinner activities were less pleasurable. I played in, and, as usual, lost in, the baccarat pit area two-deck games. My loss almost made me throw up my dinner.

I've done so badly, last year and this, in the Nugget's baccarat area games that I almost wonder if some group like Gambler's Anonymous films these games to warn recovering, sick gamblers what will happen to them if they return to gambling!

I left after going through almost two $500 buy-ins. I am depressed because my continuing slump unchecked from last week, has now actually put me behind on my trip. | Lost: $927 |

After my Nugget loss, I walked across the street to the Pioneer Club and got a snack in their Carl's Jr. restaurant. I thought back to the fall of 1985 when this restaurant was a buffet in which I had many of my dinners. I recalled the ups and downs of the NFL betting that I did in those long-ago days and I remembered rehashing many of my wins and losses, as well as my handicapping thoughts, in this location. I also remembered that over the years I ended up well ahead in football and sports betting despite many rocky days and periods. Hopefully, this history will repeat for me in blackjack. I decided to go back—for a while, anyway—to the Nugget.

Session Nine. Golden Nugget. 11:50PM-12:15AM. Swing shift. 1 and 6 decks.

I performed my wild betting act in the $5 minimum one-deck games and then quit when the tables filled. I played two shoes in a six-deck game and quit this, the session and the day when the second shoe quickly got very negative; my experience at the Luxor (when I didn't quit soon enough in a negative shoe) taught me something. At least, this session was a winner. | Won: $195.50 |

| March 21 | Lost: $1,311.50 | Time: 8 hr |

This was my third straight day of losing over $1,000. However, my win in the last session, though a small win, made it easier to accept the day, even its putting me behind on the trip, mentally.

March 22

Session One. Circus Circus. 10:00-11:05AM. Graveyard shift. 2 decks.

Today, I was given much less heat in this casino than I was yesterday. At the $25 table, penetration was great, sometimes up to 75 percent. That was the good news.

The bad news was that I continued to lose almost all of my high-count plays. Once, I had two hands of $125 on the table. I received a 20 and a blackjack on my two hands versus a dealer picture card (ten value). Naturally, the dealer had an ace in the hole for a blackjack: this one round represented a $437.50 minus swing (assuming I had won the 20 versus the 10 up, a hand that I am favored to win).

Right after this round, a happy pit boss asked me if I wanted him to set me up in one of Circus' eateries. Maybe it was a mistake, but I answered that right then I felt more like throwing up than eating! I'm now starting to wonder if I'll ever have a good day playing blackjack again. | Lost: $862.50 |

Session Two. Desert Inn. 11:35AM-12:30PM. Graveyard and day shifts. 6 decks.

Sessions like this one probably go far in convincing players—especially those in the midst of a violent losing streak like mine—to quit counting and try silly systems like the New Blackjack (mentioned very briefly in Appendix D beginning on page 200) or the Core System. This streak I've had is maddening, but it hasn't, and hopefully won't, make me insane!

I won hand after hand in negative counts and in very negative shoes as tens helped me even though the odds were against their appearing. In one stretch, I won 14 of 15 hands, all at negative or neutral counts and virtually all of them $25 minimum bets. (Occasionally, I'll parlay winnings in neutral or slightly negative shoes to appear to be a "normal" gambler.) These winnings and some in some slightly positive shoes, in which I never got beyond two hands of $50, got me ahead almost $1,000.

Then I encountered a shoe in which the count got very high, never came down (usually a disaster for a counter since his bets and play strategies in high counts are predicated on the expected tens coming out), and got clobbered. I was roundly criticized by all for increasing my bets to as high as two hands of $125 (not going higher only because I couldn't parlay winnings—there were so few) and for making plays like doubling on a ten versus a ten and losing.

On another hand, I didn't split two tens versus a five when it was correct to do so because a pit boss was watching; I won the hand, but would have won two hands had I split (but might have been really hassled or even been on the road to barring). This seems to be another unwritten rule of losing streaks in blackjack; unconventional plays that are made, lose; those that are passed because of fear of pit reaction would have won. I quit a small winner and left dodging eggs and boos by all for my "stupid" money management. No, I still wasn't ready for New Blackjack, yet! | Won: $103.50 |

Session Three. Excalibur. 1:00-1:50PM. Day shift. 1 and 6 decks.
This was my best session in six days. I played for 15 minutes in a one-deck game and left when it got crowded. In my six-deck action, I received better deck penetration than yesterday; over 4-1/2 decks out of six were dealt. And, for a change, I won several high-count bets. My "money management" may be getting better! I not only won, but did so without heat and got a comp for lunch. The food tasted good coming off a big win. | Won: $978 |

Session Four. Luxor. 3:10-4:10PM. Day shift. 6 decks.
I did well despite both a grouchy dealer named Sary, who seemed to want a tip after every bet I won but wouldn't deal far into the shoe, and, crummy penetration that seldom exceeded 4-1/4 decks.

Outside of winning some money in a casino that I doubt I'll play in much more, my main enjoyment was sharing some laughs with a cute woman at the cashier's window who looked like the witch in Hansel and Gretel—a young version of the witch that is! If I play here much more, the lousy deck penetration will cook me for sure! | Won: $633.50 |

Session Five. Maxim. 5:00-6:00PM. Day shift. 2 decks.
I ran hot even with the pit bosses watching. My streak gave me a natural reason to parlay my bets. One play that helped was my yelling, "Even money!" on a blackjack insurance bet when actually insurance was not the right play (the true count was +2-1/2 and I need a true count of over +3 for insurance to be the right play). It turned out even better when the dealer did have a blackjack and I explained to the pit boss that I insured my blackjack because "the dealer wanted to punish me for my hot streak." This little show got

the pit boss to leave since he, like almost all pit bosses, knows that insuring blackjacks is a sucker bet.

Jackie, the dealer I had my best run against, gave me 2/3 penetration plus. I tipped her at the appropriate times. Maybe my slump is finally ending!

> Won: $1,148.50

Session Six. Golden Nugget. 6:50-7:40PM. Day shift. 1 and 6 decks.

I played the six-deck shoes nearly the whole session because the one-deck games were mostly jammed. Sammy, the main dealer I played, was full of jokes and talked a mile a minute. He also dealt very rapidly—so rapidly that between his dealing and jokes I sometimes had problems keeping the count and ace side count. Once, I actually lost track and left the table (the count was negative and I had lost the last hand, so this maneuver was not suspicious). Losing the count virtually never happens to me these days.

After a few minutes of one-deck play, I returned to Sammy's table as he was reshuffling. I did well despite almost never having a high enough count to bet more than two hands of $50. Whenever I won Sammy yelled out, "Easy money, easy money!" I quit after 50 minutes of play because Sammy was starting to drain me and I was hungry for the Nugget buffet.

> Won: $742

Session Seven. Golden Nugget. 9:05-9:45PM. Swing shift. 2 decks

I must be getting hot! I actually won money in the baccarat pit area two-deck game. It was a minuscule win in an uneventful session. I joked with Pam, a pit boss in the area. I had come to feel that even if I were guaranteed a 20 on every hand, I couldn't win playing blackjack in this pit!

> Won: $7.50

After my very small Nugget win, I checked out some basketball scores across the street at the Las Vegas Club. While there, I ran into Matthew, a retired sports bettor I know. Our conversation was far more interesting than the Vegas Club's blackjack games that I never play: three decks dealt out of six; this takes away from all of the good rules of the "world's most liberal blackjack."

Session Eight. Aladdin. 10:25-11:00PM. Swing shift. 2 and 6 decks.

I continued to steer clear of the $25 tables and played at the $5 and $10 tables, which allow me more camouflage, less heat, and a bigger bet spread. I quit the session and for the day when all the tables filled up. This place is in its own world in terms of deck penetration.

		Won: $103
March 22	Won: $2,854	Time: 6 hr, 55 min
Week to date	Won: $1,542.50	Time: 14 hr, 55 min

This day provided a very welcome relief from my recent brief, but violent slump. In this slump, I had lost over $8,000 in just over three days of playing time. Right now, I am on a $3,700 or so up-hill streak (which started with my Desert Inn session). I am now on a six-session winning streak. However, this won't really become a winning streak until my losses of the bad streak are wiped out. Hopefully, I am now once again on the up cycle of the blackjack roller coaster.

March 23

Today would be my mid-week half day. I'd like to keep yesterday's winning streak going. Unfortunately, mathematically one day of blackjack play is totally unrelated to the next.

Session One. Maxim. 8:00-8:55AM. Graveyard shift. 2 and 6 decks

I was a little suspicious of Earl, who seemed to hesitate a lot when playing his hands. It also seemed like the more he hesitated the less likely he was to bust. Though I could see no direct evidence of any peeking or seconds dealing, I left the table after he made two 21's in a row versus my 20's when I had big bets on the table. I then went to the shoe game.

Though I made a comeback in the shoes, I noticed the cuts getting worse and worse. When the dealer cut off 2-1/2 decks out of six, despite some subtle hints I gave about wanting deeper cuts, I left. Hopefully, this doesn't represent a new trend.

Lost: $182.50

Session Two. Circus Circus. 9:25-10:25AM. Graveyard shift. 4 decks.

The $25 two-deck game was crowded so I played in two different four-deck games. Losing two rounds of $100 (two hands of $50) cost me a winning session. At one table, the dealer admonished me for hitting a 12 versus a three (a correct basic strategy play) and later a 12 versus a five (not a basic strategy play, but one I made because the true count was less than -1). I just shrugged off both criticisms and said that I play hunches. The dealer replied that hunches cost money as I busted both hands.I received no heat during this session.

Won: $15.50

Session Three. Desert Inn. 10:55-11:55AM. Graveyard shift. 6 decks.
This was an uneventful session. A minor hot streak made it a winner. I quit when the shoe got very negative after a couple of $25 losses.

Won: $195

After this session, I thought about quitting for the day. Unfortunately, I decided to play at the Nugget instead. It's very easy to second guess yourself after the fact in this game!

Session Four. Golden Nugget. 12:55-1:35PM. Day shift. 1 deck.
An early cold streak on high-counts destroyed this session. Of course, one can often do badly even in good games such as those at the Nugget.

Lost: $892.50

After the 40 minute Nugget disaster, I did quit for the day. I believed that any further losses would ruin the half-day I wanted to take off. Mathematically, there was no justification for stopping the Nugget session after 40 minutes. But, psychologically, I felt there was. Everyone has to do what makes him comfortable in this regard. The only rule I try to keep for myself is that I never want to allow myself to lose more than what I will allow myself to win. Actually, I put virtually no limits on my wins, but do always set up limits on losing streaks.

March 23	Lost: $895.50	Time: 3 hr, 35 min
Week to date	Won: $647	Time: 18 hr, 30 min

March 24

I ended up taking 1-1/2 days away from the game. I did not get to sleep until four in the morning, and I slept through until four this afternoon. I must have needed the rest.

Session One. Aladdin. 6:50-7:50PM. Swing shift. 2 and 6 decks.
My clear and rested mind helped me to make an unusual decision that may have thrown off the alert Aladdin pit crew and the eye. Once, in the two-deck game, I had a very close insurance call. I had two bets of $100 on the table for which I received a blackjack and a hard seven (a four and a three) versus a dealer ace. The run-

ning count was +3 with .4 decks remaining, but four aces—even taking into account the two aces on the table—still remained in the deck. Aces count as small cards for insurance purposes, so the true count was +2-1/2 or not quite high enough for insurance to be the right play. What I did was to insure the blackjack (of course, yelling, "Even money!") and not insure the other hand. The dealer did not have a blackjack and eventually I won the second hand. This one play may get me lots more time at the Aladdin.

Financially, I fell behind by $500 at first, then got $650 ahead before a late cold streak made me a small loser. | Lost: $90 |

Session Two. Excalibur. 8:55-10:05PM. Swing shift. 6 decks.
I was incredibly lucky to garner a big win in this session in that I progressed to two hands of $100 just once (and won $300 on that round because one of the hands was a double down winner). Most of the shoes stayed in the neutral range. I had other players at my table. They made many mistakes, but most often their mistakes helped me. This is something many players forget; they always remember the stupid plays that hurt them (like me at the Flamingo Hilton on March 2). Tonight, I praised all the stupid plays that helped me. +$1,044 | Won: $1,044 |

Session Three. Luxor. 10:25-11:10PM. Swing shift. 6 decks.
Penetration continues to be lousy here with 4-1/4 decks the best I could find. I really don't think that this place is worth playing anymore. Despite the lousy penetration, the count in one shoe went high, but I got murdered in it. The dealers were friendly and seemingly sympathetic as I lost, however when my losses reached $1,000, I left. | Lost: $1,016 |

Session Four. Golden Nugget. 1:00-2:20AM. Swing shift. 1 and 6 decks.
I played the one-deck game at some $5 tables for almost an hour-much of it heads-up. I spread from $5 to two hands of $100 and got nearly 2/3 penetration and still lost. I lost about $150 in this great game and began—despite my weird betting patterns—to get some glares and scrutiny: very rare at the Nugget. I cooled it by slipping away to a six-deck game where, the opposite of the Luxor, I got good penetration (five out of six-decks dealt), but virtually no high-counts. I lost in this game as well. I may be slipping back again. | Lost: $368.50 |

Session Five. Circus Circus. 3:00-3:50AM. Swing shift. 2 and 4 decks.

Tonight I got heat from the dealers. First, Nancy shuffled up on me in the two-deck game when I raised my bet with 1.1 decks left. In the two four-deck games I played, one dealer suggested I get rid of my cough by swallowing some lighter fluid followed by a match, and then another answered my dislike of cigarette smoke by shuffling at 60 percent penetration. These dealers are probably all vying for pit boss jobs!

Lost: $63

Session Six. Desert Inn. 4:15-5:25AM. Graveyard shift. 6 decks.

This session made me feel better about the blackjack world. I was behind from the very start of the session until the last shoe. I had played for 55 minutes and could have ended the session, but I decided to play one last shoe. And what a shoe it was!

Before this shoe, I hinted to Dave, the dealer, about how I wanted a deeper cut. His cuts had been 4-3/4 decks, good but not great. Dave now cut 5-1/4 decks into play. I tipped him on the first hand—a good way to say thanks.

In the shoe, the count slowly went up, as did my bets. I was slowly falling further behind (which, as I've said, tends to happen as the count rises). With 1-1/2 decks left (3/4 left to deal) the true count had reached +6 (the running count was at +9). Two extra aces—a total of eight—were still also in the deck; this pushed my true betting count to about +7-1/2. I now had two hands of $200 on the table. Despite the high-count and big bets, I knew—as I wrote in "Card Counting Myths" beginning on page 10—that I might be a favorite to win money but that I also was a favorite to lose any individual hand before the cards were dealt.

However, I overcame the odds by being virtually unbeaten for the rest of the shoe as I got 19's, 20's, and blackjacks on nearly every hand. Dave (very luckily for me) was getting sixes and sevens as up cards. In six rounds, I won about $2,000. The tens and aces were there and I got them! But without a good final cut, this session would have been a losing one for me. Dave's reading of my hint paid off!

Won: $1,432

Session Seven. Aladdin. 6:00-6:55AM. Graveyard shift. 6 decks.

Penetration continues to be super here. Over 5-1/2 decks out of the six-deck shoes were dealt. Again, I played at the $5 table so that I could vary my bets more with less heat.

I had a feeling that the dealer who looked like Bum Phillips, the former Houston Oilers coach of the late 1970s knew that I was counting despite my camouflages. He described himself to me and the other players as someone "who knew too much about the game." Perhaps he has been barred as a counter in spots.

Austin, the Bum Phillips look alike, was extremely personable and friendly. Circus could probably use dealers like him. Or maybe they can't! I always thought that if I could have played in the NFL, I would have wanted to have played for a real human coach like Bum Phillips. Austin strikes me as the same kind of guy. I'd bet that he takes in more than twice as much in tips as a normal dealer at an equivalent table.

Though my winnings were small, I greatly enjoyed this session. For one of the very few times on this trip, I truly enjoyed blackjack as just a social event. However, even with a genuinely nice guy like Austin, I have to remember why I am here! | Won: $51.50 |

Session Eight. Golden Nugget. 7:45-8:20AM. Graveyard shift. 2 and 6 decks.

For the second straight day, I played one too many sessions. And for the second straight day, I ended my day getting creamed at the Nugget.

First, I went back to my losing ways in the baccarat pit area. I lost about $450 there in about ten minutes. Then I got slaughtered in the six-deck game losing another $600 plus there. After 35 minutes, I just wanted to go to sleep. Almost forgotten was the peaceful session I had enjoyed at the Aladdin not much more than an hour ago. | Lost: $1,066.50 |

March 24	Lost: $76.50	Time: 7 hr, 45 min
Week to date	Won: $571.50	Time: 26 hr, 15 min

The loss of over $1,000 at the Nugget in just 35 minutes was frustrating and very mentally draining. Crazy and fast fluctuations such as happened today show why blackjack is a long-range betting proposition. Anyone who says otherwise is a fraud or a fool who is looking for fools to believe him.

March 25

Session One. Golden Nugget. 4:45-5:45PM. Day shift. 1 and 6 decks.

At the end of today's blackjack play, I would be at the halfway point of my trip: four weeks of eight. I realized that it was possible—though not probable—that I could be behind at that point.

The day began well with my best Nugget session since Week One. I enjoyed most of my success in the one-deck game where I joked a lot with Leonard, the dealer. I had had a huge session with him back on March 3. No heat was given me in this session, during which I tipped very liberally (about $15). I tip best when I win and get good deck penetration, which is what occurred today at the Nugget.

Won: $1,055

Session Two. Aladdin. 6:45-7:40PM. Day shift. 6 decks.

I played again in the $5 six-deck game. I did well in the last shoe as the count, and my bets, soared. I was given intense pit scrutiny, which made me lose the count for just the second time on this trip (my session with Sammy at the Nugget on March 22 was the first), right at the end of the shoe. I may have blown a surrender play on a 13 versus a 10 because of this on the last hand of the shoe. I quit at the end of this shoe, angry that I let something like this happen.

I like the Aladdin games but their pit reputation probably makes me more paranoid than I am anyplace else. I will be returning in four weeks and will definitely use a different name as far as rating is concerned.

Won: $82

Session Three. Maxim. 8:10-8:55PM. Swing shift. 2 decks.

I garnered my second $1,000 win in three sessions. I had a hot early high-count streak, which created this win. Of course, some pit boss scrutiny followed. I followed this with some lewd jokes, which made the pit bosses and Joy, my dealer, laugh. Deck depth varied.

Won: $1,094

After my profitable session, I met Gregory, a friend of mine employed at Circus Circus, who took me to their steakhouse for dinner. I had won the dinner in a bet on a Chiefs, 23-16, Monday night win over the Packers—my friend's favorite team. Though I did not get involved seriously with the NFL last season, I did keep records. On this game, as I try to do in blackjack, I got the best of the bet by giving my friend 2-1/2 instead of three—the predominant line—on the Chiefs. I had fun collecting the dinner. During dinner, Gregory mentioned his search for employment in the non-wagering arena. I told him of my blackjack successes and failures.

Session Four. Circus Circus. 11:00-11:25PM. Swing shift.
After chowing down on prime rib and drinking about a half gallon of soda, I was ready to go back to work. I had a short hundred-yard walk to reach the Circus blackjack tables.

As has been usual for me today, I had an early hot run and got over $1,000 ahead. Then the dealer started doing the early shuffle in one deck, and then in the next, she shuffled whenever I varied my bet. It was time to leave. I was relieved that my week of play at the Circus was over. | Won: $920.50 |

Session Five. Desert Inn. 12:00-12:20AM. Swing shift. 6 decks.
For different reasons than at Circus, I had a brief session here as well. I kept my session brief because I won big on some high-counts in the second shoe I played. Cutting back from two hands of $200 to $25 or $50 bets would have made my counting obvious. Though much less important, I've won every time I've played here this week. Since I want to return to this casino in a few weeks, I don't want to appear too piggish to the pit. | Won: $941.50 |

It has been amazing how well my day has gone so far. In just over three hours of play I have won over $4,000. I remind myself that hot streaks can end at any time in blackjack, and I am still well over $1,000 away from passing my top money peak of the trip.

Session Six. Excalibur. 1:00-1:55AM. Swing shift. 6 decks.
My five-session winning streak came to a halt. I quickly fell behind by almost $1,000 then almost came all the way back, but a key $300 loss (two hands of $150) doomed the comeback. I was engaged in some conversation by the bosses. I'm sure that I'll be back here in a few weeks; I suspect I'll try the two-deck games more often since it is hard to find Excalibur six-deckers that exceed 3/4 deck penetration. | Lost: $488 |

Session Seven. Golden Nugget. 2:55-3:50AM. Swing shift 1 and 6 decks.
I considered going to the Luxor after my session at the Excalibur, but decided to make that Egyptian joint history. Lousy penetration

in six-deck games is not worth my time. The Nugget, of course, is at the other end of my blackjack spectrum.

I did fairly well in the one-deck game, getting ahead as much as $500. When the game got crowded, I shifted to the six-deck shoes. For most of the time, I held my own. Then I went on a ten hand losing streak to Yon. Though I only bet $25 on each hand, I still lost $300 in this streak (two hands were losing double downs).

After my tenth straight losing hand, I decided to stop the session, the day, the week, and the first half of my trip. After I cashed my chips, I had a nice talk with Christy, an idle, one-deck dealer. Christy is a very friendly gal from Colorado Springs, whom I have played a couple of times. Though part of me wishes that I could talk to her honestly about what I am doing, she and just about everyone else associated with the casino in blackjack games can not be trusted in this way, especially since I am now playing for decent stakes. That's a very sad fact of life in this tough business.

Last year when I got to know Mike (the Riviera dealer) and Mari (now a Treasure Island dealer), I was playing for much smaller stakes and was willing to open up a bit—hopefully not a mistake—with these dealers. Since Mike also watches sports, we ran into each other several times at the sportsbooks (I was betting the NBA playoffs last year when taking time off from my blackjack play).

March 25	Won: $196.50	
	Won: $3,801.50	Time: 5 hr, 15 min
Week 4 Total	Won: $4,372	Time: 31 hr, 30 min
Trip to date	Won: 5,590	Time: 118 hr, 56 min

Though this was a great week, I am slightly disappointed in my overall hourly win: under $50/hour. However, this is close to my financial expectations for the trip. Maybe, after the great ending of the first half of my blackjack trip, I am getting greedy and piggish!

I decided that after my play of next week, I would take a weekend trip away from Las Vegas. I wasn't yet sure where I would go though San Diego and Sea World seemed to be the favorite.

Treasure Island, Riviera, Rio, Flamingo Hilton, MGM, Stardust

March 28

This was the start of the second half of my Las Vegas blackjack trip. I hope it will be better than the first half. However, I fully realize that a good player can easily lose over a four-week period. And, if the cards ran very badly, I could still be a loser in blackjack for the trip. But, hopefully, my violently bad streak at the end of Week Three and the beginning of Week Four was the worst period of the trip.

Session One. Treasure Island. 6:50-7:50AM. Graveyard shift. 2 and 6 decks.

I lost some in the two-deck game and broke even in the six-deck game. The $10 minimum two-deck game never had more than 2/3 deck penetration and often had worse. They dealt up to five decks in the six-deck game. With its surrender rule, this probably made that game more profitable than the two-deck one. I was watched little by the pit during this session.   Lost: $94.50

Session Two. Riviera. 8:20-9:15AM. Graveyard shift. 2 decks.

The penetration averaged just under 60 percent for most of the session. I surged ahead by about $400 early and used lots of bet camouflage, often betting big off the top. Near the end, Gil came on and dealt less than 50 percent, so I quit.   Won: $114

Session Three. Rio. 11:00AM-12:00PM. Graveyard and day shifts. 1 Deck.

Despite the Rio's reputation of being tough on counters, I continued to avoid heat. Frank told me that if I won at the Rio with any consistency, I wouldn't be tolerated for long.

During this session, I made jokes and bet very carefully, often using a parlay system (with penalties since I was not always consistent with the count) in my play. I was rewarded with up to 2/3 penetration and a decent financial windfall.   Won: $415

Session Four. Flamingo Hilton. 12:35-1:15PM. Day shift. 2 decks.

I played my 40 minutes at the $10 table. Crowded conditions and lousy penetration (sometimes under 50 percent) were constant.

Why do I play in this casino at all? As matters turned out, I never did again! When a blackjack player wins any money in atrocious conditions like this, he is lucky. I was lucky. | Won: $83.50 |

Session Five. MGM. 1:45-2:25PM. Day shift. 6 decks.
In the last two shoes, the count got high. Lost late bets in both shoes prevented a huge session. In the second high-count shoe, I was up to two hands of $200 at the end. This was a good time to leave. The penetration was seventy-five percent or better on all shoes. | Won: $196.50 |

With the MGM win tucked away, I drove downtown to Leroy's to talk about the NBA. Tonight, in my now layman's NBA opinion, I'd favor the home Sonics (at -11-1/2) over the Nuggets. The Sonics lost to the Nuggets in their last meeting, and they seem to have won a lot of home blowouts this year.

At Leroy's I was informed that Chuck Sharpe, a very respected player with a big following, bet the Nuggets and that he and his followers knocked the price on the Sonics from 13 to 11-1/2. I well remember that when I bet the NBA, Sharpe's bets were very important, not for me to follow, but as a way of knowing which way the line would move and thus knowing when was the best time to bet. Tonight, if Sharpe is still a huge NBA betting factor in the lines of games, the best time to bet the Sonics would be five minutes or less before tip-off!

Session Six. Treasure Island. 7:15-8:15PM. Day and night shifts. 2 decks.
I was ahead until the very end when I lost a series of high-count bets and about $600. A mistake I made in this session was that I tipped far too much: $10. I didn't even get good penetration for my tips! I did get a dinner comp, a plus for my act. | Lost: $194 |

I saw in the sports book that the Sonics won and covered, 111-97. They pulled away from the Nuggets very late in the contest in what had been a close game throughout, which made a winning bet on them lucky. I also saw that the line on the Sonics went back up to 13 right before tip-off. The next day I was informed that a computer group (called The Computer) bet the Sonics and thus against Chuck Sharpe's group. I would guess it is probably easier these days to remember all of the blackjack play indexes than it is to keep track of who each big betting group figures to bet in the NBA.

Session Seven. Stardust. 10:00-10:30PM. Swing shift. 2 decks.
Penetration was decent at the Stardust for a change. Some dealers were going in 2/3. Unfortunately, conditions were mostly crowded. It was difficult to get a table in which I could use two spots, a mandatory requirement for me to play. When a woman behind me whined that she wanted to play and that I wasn't always using two spots, I left.

Won: $73

Session Eight. Riviera. 10:40-11:40PM. Swing shift. 2 decks.
In Lawrence Revere's book, *Playing Blackjack as a Business*, it is pointed out that a player will lose about 2/3 of the hands in which he gets a total between 12 and 17. Though Revere wrote of single-deck games, I am positive that this percentage would be about the same in multiple-deck games. An intelligent player, aware of these odds, realizes that the goddess of wagering is smiling on him when he often turns his stiffs (12's-16's) into made (17-21) hands or has the dealer bust a lot when he (the player) stands on his stiffs. This happened to me frequently during this one-hour period.

Denny, a pit boss, was extremely friendly towards me even as I won. He probably thought I was just a typical sucker, who was on a lucky streak (particularly as I parlayed), the type of gambler who will pay with heavy interest later.

Won: $769

Session Nine. Stardust. 12:00-12:35AM. Swing shift. 2 decks.
I went back to play at the 'Dust again even though I had been here just two hours ago. I figured that if I kept my total time in the two sessions to around an hour total, I'd be OK. Penetration continued to be decent, but conditions were still crowded. Dwight, a pit boss who comped me to dinner on March 7th, remembered me and seemed glad to see me.

After a little over a half hour of play, I was getting tired and decided to end the session and the day's play.

Won: $98

| March 28 | Won: $1,460.50 | Time: 7 hr, 20 min |

This was an incredible day in one respect. In my nine playing sessions, I never had to go into my pocket after my first buy-in (usually $500). Once again, I've crept within about $300 of my trip's high point. Maybe this time I'll pass it.

March 29th

Session One. Treasure Island. 12:40-1:40PM. Day shift. 2 decks.
I fell far behind in the early going, but then I won some high-count bets to get ahead. Then I lost most of the profit in a slump near the end. I'm sure that I passed my high point of the trip in this session, only to slip a little. Frieda was my friendliest dealer in this session. She was full of smiles and talk. | Won: $77 |

Session Two. Stardust. 2:35-3:35PM. Day shift. 2 decks.
Penetration is back to normal at the Stardust: lousy! I probably should play only head-on in Stardust blackjack. The brief time that I enjoyed head-on play was the only time that I won money in this session. Several high-count bet losers doomed me. I received a comp to Ralph's, a 50s style restaurant, located in the Stardust's arcade. I'll eat lunch there after playing at the Riviera, which is right across the street. | Lost: $322 |

Session Three. Riviera. 3:55-4:55PM. Day shift. 2 decks.
A slump may be in progress. I played at the $10 table, allowing me a bigger, but much less obvious, bet spread in this, once again, poor-penetration game. I never was ahead the whole session, and could never get any run going. No heat. | Lost: $414.50 |

Session Four. Rio. 6:35-7:35PM. Day and swing Shifts. 1 deck.
The dinner at Ralph's was good, but didn't change my luck. For the second straight session, I was behind from start to finish. In fact, I lost every single hand in the first deck in which I played. I played head-on and two hands on a few rounds in this deck. The only plus, but potentially a big one, was that Evelyn, a dealer I played in the second half of the session often dealt down to about the last ten cards (80 percent plus penetration!) of the deck.

Financially, this session was a disaster, especially considering that I never went past two hands of $75 and reached that level on just two or three occasions. | Lost: $1,144.50 |

Session Five. MGM. 8:15-9:20PM. Swing shift. 6 decks.
Though this was my fourth straight losing session, at least I was ahead at the beginning of it. My profits were wiped out by a few $150 losses (two hands of $75 each). Shannon was a very friendly dealer, though I probably would have liked her even more if I had won! Penetration continues at 75% plus. | Lost: $306 |

Session Six. Riviera. 10:45-11:35PM. Swing shift. 2 decks.

Though I won money in this session, I was forced to pay a price. A drunk jerk (the only other player at the table) slowed down the game and slurred insults at Peggy, our dealer. I wished that the pit bosses would have gotten rid of him and later Peggy told me (the pit concurred) that they would have if I had complained. It offends me that the dealers—the ones who really get abused—have no say. And, they are the ones who keep the games running. Whenever the drunk lost a hand, he complained that Peggy hated him because he was a "New York Jew." Anti-Semitic nutcases would get plenty of ammunition from a jerk like this!

Won: $722

Session Seven. Treasure Island. 12:10-1:15AM. Swing shift. 2 decks.

Wouldn't you know it, I ran into two more abusive drunks here. There must be a full moon out or something! When I complained about the first drunk, the pit boss said that he could do nothing because the drunk "was a guest of the hotel." I was so disgusted that I moved to another table—leaving on a decent (+1-1/2) true count.

At my next table, another drunk joined us and loudly told the dealer, me, and the pit boss that he had just lost more money at the Mirage next door than the pit boss "would make in the next six months." This drunk made several sexually suggestive remarks to the dealer (Michelle) and cursed at the pit bosses with defiance any time he got winning hands.

Of course, the pit bosses let this man play on (though cutting off his alcohol) since he was a high roller. I muttered to the dealer that if I ran Treasure Island, I'd throw this drunk out no matter how much he was losing. The drunk then told me that he could "buy and sell" someone like me. At this point, I almost decked him. If he hadn't left soon after, I would have. I absolutely detest people with money (assuming this guy was really rich), who think their wealth gives them the right to treat people like garbage. There is one well-known very wealthy sports service operator like that in Vegas. Once, when he put out his hand for me to shake, I spat at it.

I don't know how dealers put up with the crap such as what I saw at the Riv and especially at Treasure Island. I couldn't. I may see the dealers and everyone else employed by the casino who is involved in blackjack as enemies, but I still think that they should be treated like human beings.

In the play session itself, I fell way behind early and won some key bets at the end after the drunks had left. As I spoke to Michelle about her work hassles (she told me that she ignores and really "doesn't hear" any derogatory comments made at her), I compared myself to Houdini over the financial escape I performed during the session. Still, even this escape could not come even close to creating a winning day for me.

		Won: $275
March 29	Lost: $1,113	Time: 7 hr
Week to date	Won: $347	Time: 14 hr, 20 min

March 30

I decided that I would visit the new MGM theme park after my play today: my mid-week half-day.

Session One. MGM. 9:10-10:20AM. Graveyard shift. 6 decks.
Today's blackjack conditions were the worst that I have faced in the MGM. I never had a table of less than three other players, the dealers were slow, and the counts never got high. My biggest bets came on the two occasions that I progressed to two hands of $50.

With some negative counts, I sometimes varied from basic strategy. Once, I hit a 12 versus a five and busted with a ten. The dealer and the other players at the table criticized this play and used it as an example as why I was losing this session. I said that I hit on a hunch. Should I have said, instead, that the true count was -3 and called for a hit, a variation from basic strategy?   Lost: $138.50

Session Two. Treasure Island. 11:00-11:50AM. Graveyard shift. 2 decks.
I traveled through one of my wilder sessions. After falling behind by $500, I hit a hot streak, and got up almost $900. Very late, I lost some $200 (two hands of $100) rounds to Bruce. I also was the object of some pit boss scrutiny by Patti, a dead ringer for Devine, the late transvestite movie star. It was probably wise that I did not tell Patti of this resemblance!   Won: $323.50

Session Three. Riviera. 12:40-1:40PM. Day shift. 2 decks.
This was another wild session. I lost almost $1,000 in the first 20 minutes, and would have quit had I reached that point. I came back and actually got $100 ahead before losing a few $100 rounds to finish in the red.

One occurrence at the Riv that made me angry was that Mike, the dealer I had gotten to know last year, seems to have soured towards me. He ignored any conversation I directed to him when I passed his $100 minimum table. I believe he was recently admonished by a pit boss, who probably suspects that I'm a counter. Sadly, this proves, through no fault of Mike, that I have no friends in the casino. This is a hard, but accurate, truth.　　| Lost: $405.50 |

Session Four. Stardust. 2:10-2:15PM. Day shift. 2 decks.
This being Wednesday, my half-day, I almost decided to take the rest of the day off. I was impatient to go to the MGM theme park, and I was also bothered by Mike's cool reception, or rather, the probable reasons for it.

I probably would have quit for the day if the Stardust, in whose parking lot my car was parked, was not right across the street from the Riviera. I decided to play at the 'Dust when I found an empty $25 table. I played just one deck (55 percent penetration), but didn't continue. I just didn't feel like playing anymore today.

I really wish that I didn't feel that way because head-on is the only way to play the usual poor penetration games at the Stardust. However, forcing myself to play isn't right, either. Doing that could well lead to mistakes and angry second-guessing of myself for playing when I didn't feel like it.　　| Won: $74 |

March 30	Lost: $146.50	Time: 3 hr, 5 min
Week to date	Won: $201	Time: 17 hr, 25 min

The MGM theme park was OK even if overpriced at $15. The park got my mind off blackjack for a few hours.

March 31

Session One. Stardust. 10:50-11:50AM. Graveyard shift. 2 decks.
I started a little late today. When my alarm rang at 5:30, I fell back asleep. I woke at ten, feeling much more refreshed. It can cost plenty to be a tired card counter.

In this session, very few positive counts occurred and thus I made few big bets. Very little fluctuation took place.

Susan, my dealer for most of the session, complained about players who jump in and out of the game. Susan complained and shuffled up when one player jumped in at a true count of minus nine!

(Probably, good ideas will pop into some readers minds for team play!) I openly questioned Susan if jumping in mid-deck gives a player an edge. Two-decks later, I quit the game with a very negative count in mid-deck to "prove" my point. | Lost: $54.50 |

Session Two. Riviera. 12:15-1:20PM. Day shift. 2 decks.
Usually a bad record on double downs equals blackjack financial disaster. Today at the Riv, it did not. I did well enough on my big bets to make up for my double down losses; of course, if I had a normal winning record in double downs (the player should win close to 60 percent of them), I would have enjoyed a huge win.

With no pit observance, I once split tens and won both hands; this is a play which, on this trip, I have passed on over half the time because it sends up such a strong red flag to the pit. I did not talk to or even look at Mike. | Won: $59.50 |

Session Three. Rio. 3:10-4:10PM. Day shift. 1 deck.
Evelyn, the 80 percent penetration dealer of March 29, was dealing the shoes today. I don't play these at the Rio because of the bad rules.The player has over a 3/4 percent disadvantage off the top in this game. However, another lady, Dawn, was dealing over 2/3 on single-deck. Nonetheless, I lost at the Rio again. And, as two days ago, I never progressed past two hands of $75. A couple of players whined about how I "changed the order of the cards" by frequently going back and forth between one and two hands. I wish that some of these players would quit their present jobs and become shift supervisors in the Las Vegas casinos! | Lost: $221.50 |

Session Four. MGM. 4:50-6:00PM. Day shift. 6 decks.
Two high-count shoes near the end of the session doomed me. Once, a dealer forgot to deal me a second hand when I spread to a second hand. I lost a stiff on the one hand I played. I lost several 20's to three-card or more 21's; in fact, that has happened to me a lot today. Penetration continues at 3/4 plus. | Lost: $669.50 |

Session Five. Treasure Island. 6:45-7:50PM. Day shift. 2 and 6 decks.
Penetration at TI is definitely going downhill. It is difficult to find 2/3 penetration in the two-deck games. I played in one six-deck shoe, and I fell behind by over $500, then got $200 ahead and ended up by losing that plus a tiny bit more in the last deck.

After dinner at the buffet, I watched the Lakers, led by their new coach, Magic Johnson, give the West-leading Sonics a very tough game before losing by three. | Lost: $12.50 |

Session Six. Treasure Island. 9:00-10:05PM. Swing shift. 2 and 6 decks.

Though I love watching the NBA, I do remember that I am on this trip to make money in blackjack. Thus, I tore myself away from the Laker struggle to make the playoffs and learned of their three-point loss later. It's doubtful that the Lakers will make the playoffs. They trail the Nuggets for the last playoff spot by 4-1/2 games with time running out. I'm sure, however, that the media would be delighted if the Lakers did crash the post-season party.

I seem to be on a new losing streak as I lost at Treasure Island again. First I lost over $500 in the baccarat area six-deck game (shades of the Golden Nugget where I almost never win in that pit), and then I tried to make a comeback in the two-deck games.

I fell further behind and my comeback efforts were thwarted by several more 20 losses to three-card 21's. I must have had over 20 such losses today through this session; this is another way in which blackjack's negative fluctuations strike. | Lost: $522.50 |

Session Seven. Riviera. 10:50-11:50PM. Swing shift. 2 decks.

The penetration varied between over 2/3 to under 50 percent. One can guess which dealers I patronized and followed around! Once again, as happens in all blackjack losing streaks for counters, I did poorly in high-counts. Plus, I lost about four more 20's to three-card plus 21's. This just hasn't been my day! Strangely, some lucky dealer busts on negative counts prevented a very bad session. | Lost: $370.50 |

March 31	Lost: $1,791.50	Time: 7 hr, 25 min
Week to date	Lost: $1,590.50	Time: 24 hr, 50 min

I have decided to drive to San Diego and visit Sea World and other sites there after my play tomorrow. I've heard many positive reports about San Diego. I look forward to this short and much-needed break from Las Vegas.

April 1

Session One. Riviera. 8:20-9:20AM. Graveyard shift. 2 decks.
I played at the $10 table to get a bigger bet spread and because the
$25 tables had at least three players; since Week Three I have sel-
dom played with more than two others in any face down game.

This was my best session of the last 13 (another Riviera session,
ironically) though I never went past two hands of $75 on any
round and, experienced lousy penetration. In the very last deck,
Brenda, the dealer, dealt only 2/3 of a deck: 1/3 penetration! A pit
boss once went through the discards, not realizing that it was extra
aces left in the deck that made me increase my bets. (The tens and
low cards were about even.)

This is the last time that I'll play at the Riviera on this trip. Last
year, I made a good deal of money here. This year I was luckier to
do so because of much poorer deck depth. | Won: $640 |

*Session Two. Treasure Island. 10:15-11:20AM. Graveyard shift. 2
and 6 decks.*
The $25 two-deck games are not open on graveyard and the $25
six-deck games were all crowded. I played in the $10 minimum
games. I took a beating at the two-deck tables and broke about
even in the shoes, which I played about 2/3 of the time. I received
no heat. | Lost: $444 |

Session Three. MGM. 12:30-1:45PM. Day shift. 6 decks.
This was my best session of the week. I won because of one successful high-count shoe in which I won a few $400 (two hands of
$200) rounds. I played one shoe after this, starting with a medium
bet since I realized this was my last session here for this venture.
It helped me greatly that my table was blessed with a great dealer.

Summer dealt 5-1/4 decks out of six. Her relief, Stan dealt under
the 4-1/2 decks that I need for six-deck play, but I stayed at the table and played, awaiting Summer's return. Her first shoe after her
break was the one I won big in. I tipped her on the first hand of the
last shoe, as well as at the end of the session. | Won: $903.50 |

After the win at the MGM, I slept for a few hours, so I would be
fresh for the drive to San Diego later. I made up some sandwiches
for the trip, but would eat my dinner at Treasure Island since I had
received a comp for that earlier.

Session Four. Continental. 7:35-8:30PM. Swing shift. 2 decks.
I have not played at the Continental because low maximum bet limits ($200) kept this casino off my original list. However, I have kept hearing about their excellent deck penetration, so I decided to try some play there. I decided that I would never bet over two hands of $100 in this visit. Since their highest minimum table was a $5 one, I planned to use my "crazy" betting patterns that I first performed at the Nugget on March 2.

During the session, I bounced from table to table according to crowd conditions. Penetration was close to 3/4 with all dealers. With little floor scrutiny, I did my "wild" betting. I first fell $500 behind, then got up by $300 and finally left a small winner. I think this is a place in which I can do some playing.

I saw one weird thing after the session in the parking lot—a security guard and a cocktail waitress handcuffed together. He wasn't arresting her; they were just headed for some fun sex! Or so I guessed since they were holding hands in a very affectionate way. Maybe it's time for me to leave town! | Won: $37 |

Session Five. Treasure Island. 9:20-10:25PM. Swing shift. 2 decks.
As I just mentioned, maybe it was time for me to leave town. But, I did play one more session after I used my dinner comp. I was aware that a good session could make me a winner for the week. That would have been a solid accomplishment considering some of the tough times I endured. I also knew that this accomplishment would make the drive out to San Diego much cheerier. I realize, of course, that this is psychology, not mathematics.

But, the above scenario didn't happen. Instead, I did poorly in high-count situations. Two straight rounds of $150 losses (two hands of $75) were critical. More important, just before I left a floor supervisor stood behind me and observed my play. I had been considering playing either here or at the Mirage or Nugget for a third week. After this supervisor observation, I've ruled out Treasure Island for any more play on this trip. | Lost: $470.50 |

April 1	Won: $666	Time: 5 hr, 20 min
Week 5 Total	Lost: $924.50	Time: 30 hr, 10 min
Trip to date	Won: $4,665.50	Time: 149 hr, 6 min

Though I am ahead on this trip, my win rate is significantly below what I expected. I am not really sure if this is due to negative fluctuations, play conditions, or mistakes on my part (both in my play and game selection). Probably all three are playing a role.

I wish I could have someone like Frank, a real pro, evaluate my play (and act). However, while he is a competent player, he is also an unreliable recluse whom I probably won't see on this trip. As it was with my sports betting, I'll have to discover nearly all of the in-battle answers by myself. I don't think I can ask the pit bosses for answers!

I enjoyed San Diego. Sea World was the highlight, though I did wonder if the intelligent animals aren't wasting their talents by just being used to entertain people.

What I could not have realized during my San Diego and Sea World visit was that my most violent negative fluctuation in the game of blackjack was just ahead. This fluctuation was so violent that I was to consider quitting the trip and the game. In retrospect, I would have been better off staying in San Diego even if it meant going swimming at Sea World and getting bounced around by Shamu, the killer whale. This activity would have been much less painful than what awaited me in Las Vegas on my return.

Mirage, Harrahs, Imperial Palace, Sands, Desert Inn

April 4

Session One. Mirage. 3:50-4:55PM. Day shift. 2 decks.
Before I started play, I dropped by the Gambler's Book Club and spoke to a couple of blackjack players, as well as Paul Keen, the resident blackjack expert, who works there. I hope no pit bosses were listening to our conversation.

At the Mirage, I fell behind by about $700 early but kept battling. The deck penetration, unlike Treasure Island's next door, is still pretty good: about 2/3. In some head-on play, I made my move and actually got $600 ahead before some late lost big bets turned the session into a small loser.

Lost: $114

Session Two. Harrahs. 5:15-6:15PM. Day shift. 2 decks.
Despite the great penetration and a $5-$200 (two hands of $100) wild spread, I lost. It seemed that whenever the ace side count was high, the dealer got a blackjack or was able to use an ace for a three-card 20 or 21. This loss made it easy to forget the extra 50 percent that a blackjack is worth to a player versus the dealer. The loss also made it easy to forget how extra aces in the deck make double downs on nine and ten more profitable: double downs, of course, are options not available to the dealer.

Lost: $611.50

Session Three. Imperial Palace. 6:35-7:45PM. Swing shift. 2 decks.
The penetration was good here as well (2/3 plus), but once again I lost. Well, if one has to lose, it is easier to take in good games. There is less second guessing that way.

In this session, the dealers never seemed to bust on my large bets. I realize that even when the dealer has a five or a six up, they are still better than even money to make a particular hand (get a 17-21) unless the true count is very high. However for them to practically never bust was frustrating.

During my losing session, I shared a table with probably one of the most blatant counters in recent casino history. This counter would start every deck with one hand of $5, the table minimum. He would have one red chip on the table. If the count became positive, he would go immediately to two hands of $25—one green chip in

119

each bet spot—and then to two hands of $100—one black chip in each spot—if the count stayed strong. This fellow was watched much more than I was. I wonder how often he has been barred? This was a bad session even for him though he wasn't asked to leave. | Lost: $856 |

Session Four. Harrahs. 8:55-9:20PM. Swing shift. 2 decks.
I bounced around and bet wildly in several two-deck games. However, I quit after 25 minutes for three reasons. First, I noticed that I was being closely watched and followed around by some fellows in suits. Second, the penetration got bad for me in the last game when the dealer suddenly dealt just one-deck rather than the usual Harrahs' deck-and-a-half out of two. And, third, though probably least important, I wanted to enjoy winning at least one session on the day: a poor mathematical reason to stop. | Won: $367 |

Session Five. Sands. 9:40-10:30PM. Swing shift. 2 and 6 decks.
I played the six-deckers almost exclusively. I remembered from four weeks ago that the Sands' two-deck games were watched much more closely than the six-deck games. I had one very bad high-count shoe and I ended the session after this shoe. Going from two hands of $150 to one of $25 would not be a wise move for me in this casino. | Lost: $645 |

Session Six. Mirage. 10:50-11:50PM. Swing shift. 2 decks.
Some of the games were occupied by drunken Arkansas rooters, who were celebrating their team's NCAA title. I don't drink alcohol, don't follow college basketball, and felt even less like celebrating.

The very last hand of this session was the killer. I had two hands of $175 on the table and just as the dealer was about to send out the cards, another (non-counting) player sat next to me at third base and threw some money on the table. I had a double down on one hand and the dealer ended up making a three-card 21 right after the new player at third base took two high cards that would have busted the dealer. This hand alone was a $1,050 negative swing against me. When it rains, it pours! | Lost: $741 |

Session Seven. Desert Inn. 12:25-1:40AM. Swing shift. 6 decks.
My lifetime Desert Inn session record became 6-0. Strangely, I did better in neutral and negative counts than in positive ones. At

times, I raised my bets somewhat in the neutral and slightly negative decks; this camouflage, which costs in the long run, won this short-term session for me.

However, Art, a pit boss didn't seem fooled by my betting camouflage. He actually asked me to admit that I was a counter ("C'mon, admit that you're counting; you can tell me"!). I admitted that I could count to 21 and could keep track of soft totals. The penetration was decent (about 4-3/4 decks, the standard Desert Inn cut), but not great. ⎿ Won: $93 ⏌

Session Eight. Rio. 2:00-2:50AM. Swing shift. 1 deck.
I was willing to come back to the Rio this week because I played there just three hours last week. Decent penetration in a one-deck game can be very profitable even with the .433 percent disadvantage against the player off the top that is created by their Reno rules (double down only on first two card 10 or 11 and dealer hits soft 17). Tonight, I often was able to get 2/3 penetration.

I got ahead by over $750 early and then the penetration went down and the heat went up, so I left. ⎿ Won: $252.50 ⏌

Session Nine. Mirage. 4:00-5:10AM. Graveyard shift. 6 decks.
Even though I came into this session down over $2,200 on the day, I felt confident that good conditions here would lead to a good session. This would end my day well and give me some momentum, a meaningless term in blackjack, for the rest of the week. (In sports betting, especially a day-to-day sport like basketball, winners to tend to beget winners.) All my premonitions were incorrect.

First off, all of the $25 two-deck games had three or more players, making them too crowded for me. I thought that almost everyone would be asleep.

I played a six-deck game and got murdered in the last shoe. I lost a series of $300 (two hands of $150) bets at the end. I felt angry, frustrated, and a little tired. ⎿ Lost: $922.50 ⏌

April 4 | Lost: $3,177.50 | Time: 8 hr, 45 min

Thus ended my second worst day of the trip. In the last five days of play, I have lost about $5,000. I sure hope I can start to turn the tide tomorrow.

April 5

Session One. Desert Inn. 3:55-5:10PM. Day shift. 6 decks.
Maybe I should play only in this casino! I ran my undefeated Desert Inn session string to seven despite very few high-counts. This represented my best session in two weeks and my first $1,000 plus session since the last day of Week Four, 11 days ago. I had almost forgotten what it felt like to win big!   Won: $1,108.50

Session Two. Mirage. 5:40-6:40PM. Day shift. 2 decks.
It's totally frustrating to play in a game as good as the one at the Mirage and lose. But, it happens and will happen to all counters a lot. And, as I've written, it is easier to take losing in good conditions because I don't have to second guess myself. I got ahead by over $400 and then went into a late, high-count slump. My key loss was a $400 one in which I doubled down both of my $100 hands and lost to a three-card dealer 21.

I played briefly with Teresa, a dealer who also works with AIDS patients. It would have been interesting to talk to her about this, but I wasn't at her table long since she did not deal much past one deck out of two. Is the Mirage following in Treasure Island's footsteps? Teresa, for now, seems an isolated case.   Lost: $557.50

Session Three. Harrahs. 7:05-7:45PM. Swing shift. 2 and 6 decks.
I did well in the two-deck game. When someone started watching me (don't these assholes realize that I've been getting slaughtered lately?), I moved to the $25 six-deck game in which the cut card was placed at the 5-1/2 deck dealt mark. Three bad events then transpired. First, in the second (and last) shoe I played, I lost a series of high-count bets to make the session a losing one. Second, I noticed what I knew was a casino employee watching me (he tried to appear nonchalant by leaning against the slot machines, but he was watching every hand). And, third, the dealer in the second shoe, abruptly reshuffled with 1-1/2 decks left: one-deck before the cut card (and this was the high-count shoe that I was losing in). As soon as I left the table, the slot machine leaner ran to a casino phone. I assume that he called the eye-in-the-sky to compare notes on my play. The heat is on at Harrahs!   Lost: $237.50

Session Four. Imperial Palace. 8:00-8:55PM. Swing shift. 2 decks
This was yet another frustrating, losing session. Typical of the week!

I fell $400-plus behind early, and battled back to get $100 ahead fairly late in the session. I then lost two key high-count bets (two hands of $100) when the dealer twice made hands off of 16's with the true count above +6 in both instances. These two non-busts caused an $800 negative swing for me.

I also ran into some preferential shuffling. Chang, an Asian dealer, shuffled up on me early in plus decks. I have been told by some players (and Ken Uston wrote in one of his books) that Asian dealers are more likely to try to protect the house by preferential shuffling. They shuffle early on plus-counts and deal deep on minus-counts. I didn't stay at Chang's table for long! | Lost: $236.50 |

Session Five. Mirage. 10:05-11:05PM. Swing shift. 2 decks.
After a nice dinner at the Mirage buffet—to which I had been comped earlier—I resumed the wars. I enjoyed my first win in four sessions and just my fifth winning session (out of 14) for the week.

I not only had another counter at the table, but we also helped each other out by flashing our cards to each other. Once, on a close insurance call, our shared information saved me $150 when the dealer had a blackjack.

I noticed that this player basically spread his bets (with much less camouflage than me) according to the count, but used basic strategy for nearly all his playing decisions even when the count called for variation. Once, on a 12 versus a four, he stood in a very negative deck (on any minus count, my count system—and virtually all others—say to hit). The exception was the above-mentioned insurance bet (basic strategy says never bet insurance).

The worst penetration in the two-deck games came in the machine-shuffled two-deckers—50 percent seems the rule in those games. In most of the dealer-shuffled two-deck games 2/3 penetration is often available. | Won: $396 |

Session Six. Rio. 11:55PM-12:25AM. Swing shift. 1 deck.
I did well early versus Debbie, then quit after losing six straight hands to Mike and feeling intense pit scrutiny. I probably have to cool it in this casino for the time being. | Won: $132.50 |

April 5	Won: $605.50	Time: 5 hr, 15 min
Week to date	Lost: $2,572	Time: 14 hr

After the Rio session, I felt a little tired. I decided to rest, get up early tomorrow, and play graveyard. Usually, I take time off on Wednesday, but I may not this week because I started late on Monday and also because I want to give myself time to improve my financial position for the trip, which has just over two weeks left.

April 6

Session One. Desert Inn. 7:00-8:00AM. Graveyard shift. 6 decks. What better place to start a momentum-turning day than the casino in which I am undefeated? For most of the session, an 8-0 session record at the Desert Inn seemed probable. Conditions were superb. I was winning, I was getting dealt five decks out of six in head-on play, and I was barely being observed. Lastly, the hot chocolate I was sipping for most of the session was delicious.

Then came the last shoe. The count was going up steadily and I was losing most of the hands and not getting the key bonuses that enable one to win at blackjack despite losing the majority of hands (especially player blackjacks). With one round to be dealt I was $370.50 behind. I wagered two hands of $150 on this final round; the true count was over +5 with just under 1-1/4 decks left in the shoe. Two extra aces (seven were still left in the shoe) pushed the revised true count to over +7. I was dealt an eight on one hand and a nine on the other (the cards that created these hands pushed up the true count even more) versus a dealer four. Because of the high-count (plus the extra aces), I doubled down on both hands. I now had a total of $600 on the table. If I won both hands, my Desert Inn record would remain perfect since this was the last shoe I planned to play. And the cut card had come out, which meant that this was my last hand.

My double down cards were an eight on the eight and a nine on the nine; I would live or die with totals of 16 and 18. I needed a dealer bust to win both hands. As the dealer began to turn over his hole card, a pit boss, seeing the large amount at stake, rushed over to the table to see the result unfold.

The dealer turned over a ten on his hole card and now had a total of 14. If he pulled an eight or more I would win both hands; if he pulled an ace or a two from the shoe, the suspense would last for another card. A dealer pull of a five, six or seven would spell disaster for me. The pit boss yelled, "C'mon, bust, bust, pull a picture (a ten value card). Make this man a winner!"

The dealer turned over a five, the player's worst enemy (partially because it turns all dealer stiffs into made hands) giving him a 19 total and me a $600 loss on the round. I pulled up the very few remaining chips I had ($29.50 worth) and said, "Well, you folks beat me today," and cashed out. Such are the big, scary, and wild swings of blackjack on even one round. | Lost: $970.50 |

Session Two. Mirage. 8:20-8:55AM. Graveyard shift. 2 decks.
My slump continued and got even more violent. I managed to lose over a $1,000 in just over 35 minutes. One hand was key.

I had two hands of $200 invested on the round. With a sky-high-count, I had gotten my bets this high by doing a little parlaying. The dealer had a ten showing, and I had a ten on one hand and a 20 on the other. Because the count was so high, plus the fact that three extra aces were left in the pack, I doubled on my ten (a true count of plus five or better is needed for this play). On my peek of the double down card, I happily saw that one of the extra aces was my draw giving me a 21 total. But before I could celebrate, the dealer turned over another of the extra aces as her hole card (in the Mirage, as in most Vegas casinos, dealers do not check under tens until the dealer starts play on his hand) for a blackjack. The dealer sympathetically said, "Well, at least, you lost only one bet on your double down." Really made my day. | Lost: $1,044.50 |

After my last loss, I realized that I am barely ahead for the trip. I have lost about $7,000 in about six days of play. Instead of needing to find places to stash extra cash as in my winning streaks, I needed to make another trip to my box to fortify my carrying bankroll. I also went to my apartment to rest a little and relax.

Session Three. Desert Inn. 2:15-3:20PM. Day shift. 6 decks.
Even the Desert Inn couldn't stop my losing streak. I managed to get $500 ahead in the early shoes, but then I got clobbered by an attractive female Asian dealer who had lots of blackjacks and 20's on my key bets. | Lost: $420 |

Session Four. Mirage. 3:40-4:20PM. Day shift. 2 decks.
The first ten to fifteen minutes was probably the hottest run I ever have had in blackjack. It looked as if the session would not only provide a big win—which it did—but also wipe out most of the misery of the last six days. (Realistically, I knew that wouldn't happen, but huge plus and minus runs in blackjack make one be-

lieve that anything is possible.) This streak made the early part of my huge Mirage win of March 16 look almost like a cold streak; I got over $2,500 ahead in less than 15 minutes, not the half hour it took me to do so then.

In this streak, I seemed to be getting blackjacks on almost every key bet. The double downs all won. The dealers busted every stiff and even many non-stiff starting hands. I once stood on a 14 versus a ten (on an over +8 true count) and the dealer turned over a five then busted with a ten. My green ($25) chips were changing into a small army of blacks ($100 chips). I even had some of the blacks changed into purples ($500 chips).

At the height of my streak, I gave myself slightly over a $1,000 loss limit. This quickly occurred as the cards got ice cold. Still, I had a very good session, which may mean that my slump is ending. | Won: $1,591.50 |

Session Five. Harrahs. 4:45-5:50PM. Day shift. 2 decks.
The heat on me at Harrahs has spread to days. All eyes appeared on me in every pit I played. No camouflage helped. Penetration was OK (though 2/3 rather than the usual 75 percent), but I lost. A bad record on double downs spelled my doom. | Lost: $610 |

Session Six. Imperial Palace. 6:05-6:45PM. Day shift. 2 decks.
Despite losing a large majority of my high-count bets, I won a little. Sometimes, when I lose consistently on high-count bets (especially when I go on double down losing streaks), I almost wonder if my count is off. All counters probably have such self-doubts. My count was probably accurate in this session because it seemed that other players at my table (and/or the dealer) would get blackjacks when the count went up. In one 20-hand stretch, an old lady (one of two others at my table then) got seven blackjacks, while I was dealt none.

When the pit boss scrutiny picked up, I decided to leave and end my day. I should have taken the whole day off on this my usual half day! | Won: $34 |

April 6	Lost: $1,419.50	Time: 5 hr, 5 min
Week to date	Lost: $3,991.50	Time: 19 hr, 5 min

I stopped off at Circus Circus to watch some NBA games and forget about my blackjack problems. I saw the very end of the Hornets—who are finally healthy—rout of the Pacers. They are 5-1/2 games out of the last East playoff spot with just ten games left. It is probably too late for them to make the playoffs. I saw the beginning of the Lakers overtime five-point non-covering win over Sacramento. This win got them within 2-1/2 games of the Nuggets for the eighth and last West playoff spot. Their playoff run may not be too late. Is it now too late for me to make this a good blackjack trip?

April 7

Session One. Mirage. 7:20-8:20AM. Graveyard shift. 2 decks.
After making $400 early in the session, disaster struck. I not only went on a high-count losing streak, but I lost every single insurance bet I made. One such loss was typical of the session. I had two hands of $200 on the table and drew a soft 19 and a hard 12 versus a dealer ace. The running count was +9 with .7 decks left, making the true count about +13. In addition, the aces on the round (in my soft 19 and the dealers up card) were the last two aces of the two-deck pack. This made insurance (aces count as low cards for the insurance decision) an even better bet since the true count with regard to this decision was about +17! I put another $200 on the table for my insurance bet, covering both hands. The dealer did not have blackjack so I lost the insurance bets. I then hit my 12 and, naturally, busted with a ten. I stood on my soft 19. The dealer then turned over a nine in the hole giving her soft 20. Another $600 was lost. On every close call when I did not bet insurance (like on true counts-including ace adjustments-of +2 or +2-1/2), the dealer would have blackjack.

Because of the head-on play, the good penetration and lack of heat, I played far into this loss, my biggest yet.   Lost: $1,613

Session Two. Harrahs. 8:40-9:50AM. Graveyard shift. 2 and 6 decks.
I got ahead early in the two-deck action and then in a deeply penetrated shoe, I got killed on the high counts. Once again, I was winless on insurance bets and on one key hand (two hands of $200), the dealer had a three-card 21 to beat my 19 and 20. One plus was that I got no heat on this shift.   Lost: $493.50

Session Three. Sands. 10:00-10:45AM. Graveyard shift. 6 decks.
I reached new lows in this session. It ended in yet another disastrous high-count shoe. For most of the shoe, I was playing heads-up. Then an old lady (not a Wonging counter) joined me as the true count reached the roof. I had my high bets of two hands of $200 out. On the first two rounds after this lady joined me, she received a blackjack and a 20, while I lost everything, including one double down. By now, I was taking money out of my shoes. The betting money that had been in my wallet and money belt had already been lost. On the next hand, the lady stood on a stiff, while I drew a 19 and a 20 versus a dealer two. Maybe, my luck was turning. Not! The dealer turned over an ace in the hole and drew an eight for 21. I had thus lost $1,400 on the last three rounds and left the table seriously thinking blackjack retirement. | Lost $1,922 |

I was in a daze when I reached the warm weather outside. I had lost over $4,000 in just under three hours this morning and was now behind over $8,000 for the week. I was also down over $3,400 for the trip and was on close to an $11,000 losing streak. I realized that it was now very possible that I would lose money for the entire trip.

I felt very worn out and numb. I decided to return to my apartment to rest and think. I asked myself if playing blackjack was really worth the aggravation. I was being scorched with heat, though I hadn't been barred since Week Two, and wasn't even making money for the hassle. Would I eventually go broke and get barred everyplace at the same time?

I decided that I had trained too hard to give up. I had put the best part of a year and 250,000 practice rounds or more into the game. I owed it to myself to play out the eight weeks. Maybe that amount of time was not even close to a true test in terms of statistical significance but I would play it out. I'd do my best and the cards would fall where they would. My home play and my play out here (and in Michigan) last year told me that the odds were in my favor. And that is all anyone can ask in terms of a business proposition, which is how I see the game of blackjack.

Before, I had overcome adversity and early losses to win in sports betting. The long-term odds in my favor had prevailed there. Blackjack, even though a different sort of proposition, would be the same. I was ready to go back to war against the casinos and their agents.

Session Four. Desert Inn. 2:15-3:20PM. Day shift. 6 decks.
After falling behind by $500 early, which extended my losing
streak to over $11,000, I made a comeback. My apartment talk
session with myself helped make me very detached during my early losses. The high-count bets ran well, for a welcome change.
One correct play that I did not make was a double on a soft 19 versus a four. The true count was +3-1/2 (the index for doubling this
hand is plus three), but a scrutinizing pit boss made me decide to
stand on the play. (I won the hand, though I would have also won
on the double-down.)   Won: $1,070.50

Session Five. Mirage. 3:55-4:10PM. Day shift. 2 decks.
This session played itself out in a rush. I actually got $1,000 ahead
in the first deck! I then set a $500 loss limit to assure myself of at
least a $500 profit. I made less than that because on my final hand
I lost $400. I started with two hands of $100. As continues to happen every time I bet insurance, I lost $100 on the bet. In addition,
I lost both hands, including one in which I lost a double down on
an 11 versus an ace. Thus, my loss for the round was double my
original investment.   Won: $333.50

*Session Six. Imperial Palace. 4:35-5:20PM. Day shift. 2 and 6
decks.*
I played the six-deckers more than the two-deckers, which were
crowded. The session went back and forth. In my last shoe, I went
as high as two hands of $150 and then quit. I received very little
heat. Maybe the casinos all know how badly I am doing! There
was good penetration in all pits and games.   Lost: $92.50

Session Seven. Harrahs. 5:40-6:40PM. Day shift. 2 decks.
Today, I was given little heat. I guess with all of my bad sessions
at Harrahs, the bosses are thinking, "How can this loser be a
threat?" This session probably reinforced that thinking.

On one hand, not being able to see the cards of another player (one
needs to be careful looking at the cards of other players in face
down games, since that is a symptom of card counting) cost me
$400 as I stood on a 12 versus a dealer three, a standing play for
me when the true count is over +1. The nine that the dealer drew
to make his hand would have given me a 21. If I had seen the four
tens of the other two players, I would have hit, since this lowered
the true count enough. As one can see, blackjack can be a good

game for second-guessers! A key loss of two hands of $150 was also a killer in this good-penetration game. ☐ Lost: $371 ☐

Session Eight. Sands. 7:00-8:00PM. Day shift. 6 decks.
My most boring session ever. Despite the over 3/4 penetration, the true count never became very positive. Only once during the whole hour did I progress to a $50 bet: a loser. I varied between $200 behind and $200 ahead. Borrrrrring! ☐ Lost: $16.50 ☐

Session Nine. Mirage. 9:50-10:55PM. Swing shift. 2 decks.
Before my play, I ate in the Mirage steakhouse. A pit boss insisted on comping me to that earlier today; he must know how badly I've done this week!

Once again, I had a huge early Mirage run. At my peak, I was ahead over $2,000. The swings that I've had in the Mirage have been the biggest I've ever had in any casino. The good rules and deck penetration create a situation in which I can not only easily raise my bet (even on a true count of one, I can safely raise my bet), but also, because of the penetration, I have more opportunities to do so. Plus, I sometimes throw in large camouflage bets (especially going big off the top).

I quit a couple of tables because the dealers started shuffling early, and left another when a third other player joined. The shuffling may be a sign of Mirage heat; I'll see. ☐ Won: $1,662 ☐

April 7	Lost: $1,442.50	Time: 8 hr, 5 min
Week to date	Lost: $5,434	Time: 27 hr, 10 min

Though the day was a bad one, I did make a $2,600 comeback after my morning disasters ended at the Sands. I continue to try to swim through the turbulent waters of the fluctuations of blackjack.

April 8

Session One. Desert Inn. 10:00-11:00AM. Graveyard shift. 6 decks.
I lost badly early. I made a little comeback at the end, but still had my third losing session in my last four Desert Inn appearances.

Near the end of the session, I made an unusual play. With a true count of -8, I did not split aces versus a nine. I drew two tens and busted to the shock of the players and dealer (and to myself, though, for a different reason). I was unsure if I had made the right play since, with rare exceptions, I've studied mostly just indexes of plus through minus six. Later, I called Paul Keen, the blackjack expert of the Gambler's Book Club. Paul said that the play was a very close one, but that I was right in not splitting. In the long haul that is more important to me than the $75 negative swing I had on that hand.   Lost: $564.50

Session Two. Mirage. 11:40AM-12:50PM. Graveyard and Day shifts. 2 decks.
I bounced from table to table as they filled up. I fell $200 behind early, but one good run won the session. I never progressed past two hands of $100.   Won: $479.50

Session Three. Harrahs. 1:00-2:00PM. Day shift. 2 decks.
Though I did not play at her table today or this week, I have seen Anne (the attractive dealer I played a couple of times in Week Three) a few times at Harrahs. Today, I mentioned my recent bad run to her. Anne then cutely winked at me and said, "I think you'll still come out ahead, Stuart. I'd *count* on it!" Can't fool her!

For a change, I came out ahead in this casino. I managed to win despite a huge betting mistake. On one hand, I bet two hands of $50, thinking that the dealer would shuffle, instead of the two hands of $150 that I would have bet (progressing from a win at two hands of $75) had I known that more cards (going past 3/4 dealt) would be dealt. I won both hands, but blew $200 in the process. I wonder if Anne still would respect my blackjack abilities if she had seen this whopper of a mistake?   Won: $385

Session Four. Imperial Palace. 2:25-3:00PM. Day shift. 2 decks.
I did very well versus Joanne, a friendly middle-aged dealer from Massachusetts. When her table filled, I bounced to Wilson's table. It soon was evident that he was a preferential shuffler, so I quit to go eat lunch.   Won: $431

Session Five. Sands. 4:10-5:10PM. Day shift. 2 decks.
Near the end of the session, I again ran into preferential shuffling. I sometimes put out big bets early in the deck, but the nonsense continued. This was my last Sands session. I can't say that I'll miss this casino. Between the construction and pit heat in Week Two and my 0-4 session record this week (including the loss yesterday

that had me contemplating retirement from blackjack), I don't
have very fond thoughts of this joint. | Lost: $55 |

Session Six. Mirage. 5:50-6:05PM. Day shift. 2 decks.
I sure played at the Mirage a lot this week! This is the last week I
will play at the Mirage on this trip, so I want to make it worth my
while. Next week, I'll give the Nugget a third week since I've gotten almost no heat there.

This session was very brief because the tables quickly filled up. I
won because of one hot run. On the next deck, the table filled when
the count got negative, so this was a great time to leave: a reverse
form of Wonging. | Won: $684.50 |

Since yesterday's disaster at the Sands, I have won almost $4,000
and have again pulled ahead for the trip. I know that it is now very
unlikely that I will win enough money the next two weeks to average the $40-$50 an hour in winnings that I figured would be the
minimum acceptable win rate.

When I began this venture, I thought that I would have routine
$5,000 up- and down-swings (more up than down) and would en-
counter one very bad swing that would cost me between $9,000
and $13,000. I've endured two such swings: one that ended this
week that cost me about $11,000 and one that bridged the third
and fourth weeks that cost me about $8,000. Other factors may
have played a role in my perceived underachievement on this
trip—factors I'll try to examine in my days off and perhaps after
the trip. (These factors are discussed in "Conclusion" beginning
on page 170.)

I decided to play once more on graveyard at The Mirage in what
would be my final session there.

Before getting a little rest, I watched the Lakers get shocked by the
Nuggets at home. This key loss puts the Lakers four games behind
the Nuggets, and they have a schedule disadvantage the rest of the
way, which includes a game next week in Denver. It appears that
the momentum that Magic Johnson brought the Lakers is fading.

*Session Seven. Mirage. 3:10-4:45AM. Swing and graveyard
shifts. 2 and 6 decks.*
I got less sleep than planned, but was eager to end this terrible
week on an upswing. Didn't happen.

I first got a little ahead in the two-deck game then switched to the shoes when the two-deckers got too crowded. On a Friday night, this is not unexpected.

I lost in the six-deck game when confronted with both a bad player and bad luck. Once the bad player hit on a hard 17 versus a ten (no, the shoe was not astronomically negative!) and got an ace which would have gone very well with my nine. Instead, I busted. Of course, I again realize that an idiot like this will help me just as often as not in the long run. Later, a much worse disaster hit when I had two hands of $100 on the table. The first card on each of my hands was an ace (which, according to blackjack expert, Peter Griffin, gives the player an expected win rate of 52 percent) and the dealer's up card was a five (which, I'm sure, further increased my edge, as did the high count). But instead of receiving a ten on my second card, I received fours on both hands. I doubled both hands and *then* got two tens for two stiffs. The dealer then efficiently turned over a six in the hole and pulled a ten from the ten-rich shoe for 21. This round cost me $400.

After this tough luck in the last round of the shoe, I went back to the two-deck games and came back about $200 before finally calling it a week and saying good-bye to the Mirage. | Lost: $583 |

April 8	Won: $777.50	Time: 6 hr, 35 min
Week 6 Total	Lost: $4,656.50	Time: 33 hr, 45 min
Trip to date	Won: $9	Time: 182 hr, 51 min

The day after my terrible week ended, I purchased Arnold Snyder's book, *Blackjack for Profit* at the Gambler's Book Club. In this book, Snyder has an excellent index showing the profitability of virtually any blackjack game based on its deck penetration, rules, and number of players at the table, as well as the bet spread a player uses. I've instinctively tried to play in the types of games that the system gives high ratings to and stay away from those that rate poorly. However, the numerical ratings that can be attached to games and their various conditions will be helpful to me in the future.

Though I have tried to concentrate on playing good-expectation blackjack games, Snyder's book did point out to me that there were some games I've played that I should have avoided. For instance, I should have avoided the Stardust and Flamingo Hilton games altogether unless I was able to play with no one else at the table (and those games would barely be worth playing even then).

In my visit to the Gambler's Book Club, I also spoke to Paul Keen. I told Paul of my just concluded blackjack disaster. Paul mentioned that he once had 17 straight losing sessions in blackjack! That is a fate I have thus far avoided in my play. However, I suppose that if I play as much blackjack as Paul has—about 20 years—I will at some point hit such a negative fluctuation.

Later in the weekend, my rereading of some of Ken Uston's books was also helpful. He (along with Arnold Snyder and Stanford Wong) is one of the few blackjack authors who mention the negative swings that will occur in the game. Best yet, Uston mentions personal and team examples of these nightmarish swings. Mirroring my just ended week, Uston says that virtually every serious player he knows has considered retirement from blackjack because of rough losing streaks or negative fluctuations.

Reading Snyder's and Uston's books reminded me once again that blackjack will always be a learning experience. Those blackjack players who say that they know it all know very little about the game.

**Las Vegas Hilton, Horseshoe, Golden Nugget,
Palace Station, Maxim**

April 11

Session One. Las Vegas Hilton. 2:25-3:20PM. Day shift. 2 decks.
Except for Sheila, who would deal 1-1/4 decks, I could not get much over 50 percent penetration. I played head-on as much as possible at all tables.

I used a lot of camouflage, which enabled me to get a 1-16 ($25-two hands of $200) spread with little heat. I often bet $100-plus off the top. Sometimes, I would progress after a win even if this was in violation of the count.

The camouflage came easy since I was winning. Strangely, I did well despite only a so-so double-down record. I quit very soon after a two-hand loss of $150 (two hands of $75) in which I lost a 19 and a 20 to a multiple-card dealer 21. The tables got crowded right after this.

Won: $891

After my Hilton win, I drove downtown to play at the Nugget and the Horseshoe: the two casinos on my list for Week Seven. Before I commenced my play, I stopped to see some sports bettors at the Las Vegas Club. In my visit I spoke with Richie, a supervisor of this book. Richie, a Las Vegas Club sportsbook employee for about ten years, is one of the few really nice sportsbook workers. In my sports betting days, Richie often told me at which sportsbooks the best prices on games were and were not located; this was something which he had no obligation to do.

However, I spent most of my Las Vegas Club pit stop talking with Sam, a sports bettor I've known for about ten years. I have yet to hear him mention any losing streaks he has had in these ten years. Sam, as he did today, always tells me of his latest wins against the "weak" lines of the sportsbooks. I have long realized that Sam has either been: a) incredibly lucky (about a .1 percent probability) or b) lying (about a 99.9 percent probability) concerning his record.

I believe that I'm probably underestimating the chance of (b) because Sam has been working at the same civil service job for about nine years. More important, Sam once answered my proof that he took bad odds on a bet he (allegedly) won by saying, "Hey, I got to the cashier's window. That's all that matters." Those are the catch words of a sucker who will always have a long-range negative bottom line. I got my day's amusement hearing his latest fables, though. Much later, I was to need this humor.

Session Two. Horseshoe. 4:45-5:45PM. Day shift. 1 deck.
Surprisingly, I was given so little heat at the Horseshoe today that I dropped my usual heavy camouflage for the last three decks I played. The bad news was that I lost badly, anyway. I also bounced around a lot so that there were never more than two other players at my table.

Lost: $730

Session Three. Golden Nugget. 6:00-7:00PM. Day shift. 1 and 6 decks.
This is the one casino in which I will play for a third time. I'll play extensively at the Nugget this week because of the lack of heat given me and their good games.

I fell far behind early versus Glenn, a professed "hot" dealer. I saw no evidence of any nonsense (cheating) on Glenn's part, so I kept playing. And losing! I was easily able to use Glenn's "hot streak" as a good excuse to leave when the table got crowded.

I drifted to the six-deck tables and did very well at Sammy's table. Sammy is the very talkative Hawaiian I played three weeks ago. He gives decent (4-3/4 to 5 deck) penetration, but it is a struggle to keep count as he rambles on and deals very quickly. Sammy is the only dealer I still have this problem with.

After my big win ("easy money, easy money," Sammy always would say as he paid my wins) at Sammy's table, I played the one-deck game again and broke even in it. I then ate a healthy dinner at the Golden Nugget buffet.

Won: $561

Session Four. Golden Nugget. 8:30-9:30PM. Swing shift. 6 decks.
The one and two-deck games were very crowded so I played the shoes once again. This time I got killed.

I made $400 in the first 40 minutes of the session and then got slaughtered in two high-count shoes in the final 20 minutes. The biggest loss came on one round in which I lost $800. I had two hands of $200 on the table and not only lost the $400 to a dealer four-card 21, but lost an insurance bet and a double down as well. In this six-deck shoe I had absolutely no problems counting, just winning!

Lost: $1,308

Session Five. Golden Nugget. 9:40-9:55PM. Swing shift. 1 deck.
After a quick trip to the restroom, I played at the Nugget some more—after I first flushed some money into my wallet! I found an empty one-deck table and sat down to play. I lost a couple of high-count rounds and left when the table filled up. Lost: $176

Session Six. Horseshoe. 10:00-10:05PM. Swing shift. 1 deck.
I found a table with one other player and played two-decks. Then, the mobs moved in and I left. Lost: $50

Session Seven. Palace Station. 10:30-10:50PM. Swing shift. 2 decks.
I played in the $5 minimum two-deck game which was 2/3 dealt. I had two break even, one good, and one bad deck. The good deck was better than the bad. Despite some wild bet patterns, I was given some heat and stopped the session. Won: $197

Session Eight. Palace Station. 11:00-11:45PM. Swing shift. 4 Decks.
After a quick break, I decided to try the four-deck $25 game. The heat did not follow. I did well early, but got beaten in the last shoe when I had six stiff (12's-16's) hands on the last three rounds and lost them all. Lost: $229

Session Nine. Maxim. 12:10-1:00AM. Swing shift. 2 decks.
Because of reports of occasional good penetration here, I put the Maxim casino on my Week Seven list. I found such with Cindy, the first dealer I played, she dealt inside 2/3 of a deck.

I fell behind by over $1,000 early, but played on because of the good conditions. I came all the way back in one hot and high-count deck. Shortly after this, Monica relieved Cindy and the great penetration vanished; no hints of possible tips would bring it back.

I was also getting some mean looks from the pit. I left two-decks after Monica came on to deal. Won: $731.50

Session Ten. Rio. 1:45-2:10AM. Swing shift. 1 and 2 decks.
Since I did not play on the night shift at the Rio two weeks ago, I returned for a brief session tonight.

I did well in the one-deck game, but quit it when I started to lose to Nick, who made some suspicious hand motions as he dealt. I could find nothing definitely wrong, but I won't play Nick again until I observe him closely when not playing.

Then I played for a while in the two-deck game, but was bummed by the poor penetration. When another player returned from a brief bathroom visit, I lost three straight hands. This gave me a good "superstitious" reason to leave since I had done well when he was gone!

> Won: $123

Session Eleven. Horseshoe. 2:50-3:35AM. Swing shift. 1 deck.
As soon as I sat down, I knew that there was a large potential for trouble. Two bosses, one of them the shift supervisor, were obviously talking about me. They repeatedly pointed at me. The pit boss looked familiar, but I couldn't yet place him.

Despite my very heavy bet camouflage, the pit boss seemed to be trying to convince his supervisor that I was counting. I did some depth charging (betting more when deeper in the deck no matter what the count was; this is a somewhat viable single-deck strategy assuming that a player can see every card and always makes good play decisions, often going contrary to basic strategy). In some very negative decks, I saw the supervisor laughing at the pit boss. It was if he was saying, "How can that moron be a counter? He has $100 (or more) on the table and look how many pictures (how negative the deck is) have come out."

After about 35 minutes of observation, the supervisor seemed to have won the argument and he and his pit boss went their separate ways. Or so I believed! I was a little ahead in the session and happy that I had seemed to have survived this major test.

Since I knew that I would be leaving in about ten minutes, I decided to play it straight (no camouflage) the rest of the way. I just had a desire to show these stuffed suits how stupid they were, I guess. Two decks after I reached this decision, I started the deck with one hand of $25. I won, the count went up, and I increased to two hands of $50. I won both hands, and the count was good enough to increase to two hands of $100. I won both hands on this round, as well. This deck was a big winner for me.

About two minutes after this lucky deck, I got a tap on the shoulder from the pit boss, who had been suspicious of me. He wished to talk to me, and asked me to step away from the table for this conversation. The pit boss then told me that if I were to play anymore at the Horseshoe I would be flat bet, meaning that I had to bet the same on every hand of a deck. I asked why, and this boss said that I had just gone $25-$200 which was an "intolerable" 1-8 spread. I questioned this (since I had played two hands of $100, not one of $200) and the boss answered that two hands of $100 was the same as one of $200. When I still protested, he referred me to his boss, the shift supervisor, the man I thought was my ally.

The shift supervisor mentioned the same $25-$200 progression, and I said that I often parlayed winnings. He answered, "Well, you never did that in negative decks."

I answered, "What do you mean by 'negative' decks?"

"If you don't know what I mean by positive and negative decks, I won't tell you."

Of course I wanted to say, "Why don't we view the goddamn tapes made from the 'eye' and I'll show you how I parlayed in negative decks." Of course, I couldn't say that!

I continued to act puzzled by this flat-bet ruling and even said that I bet sports and that no one had ever restricted my bet range (though I didn't mention that several outlaw bookies had thrown me out) except within house limits that apply to all. The supervisor then answered that, "Blackjack ain't sports." No, I guess, it ain't!

Despite my protests, the flat bet ruling stood and my days at the Horseshoe are over (for now). I had been warned by Frank and Mari (the Treasure Island dealer; she had once dealt at the Horseshoe) about the Horseshoe flat betting of counters. | Won: $296 |

Later, I was able to place the face of the suspicious pit boss. He was one of the four bosses who had stared at me intently on March 8 at the Plaza—a casino that later barred me. This fellow had evidently quit the Plaza and had moved down the street. Damn!

Though I had won a little on the day, I was depressed that my dropping of my act at the Horseshoe had gotten me flat bet (and thus barred, since flat betting is a slight losing strategy in their game). Unlike my barrings at the Gold Coast and the Plaza, I could have avoided that fate at the Horseshoe if I hadn't tried to flaunt things. I'd have to be more careful for the rest of my trip in any place that I was getting heat.

April 11 | Won: $306.50 | Time: 7 hr, 20 min

April 12

Session One. Golden Nugget. 3:00-4:30PM. Day shift. 1 and 2 decks
For memory's sake, I lost $100 in a $10 two-deck baccarat pit area game. If I even see the baccarat pit of the Golden Nugget two life-times from now, that will be too soon!

However, today the baccarat pit was paradise compared to my one-deck play on the main floor. The penetration was decent, but the cards were a disaster. Lots of stiffs. Very few blackjacks. A los-ing record on double downs. I have now fallen behind on my trip once again. | Lost: $1,176 |

Session Two. Golden Nugget. 5:00-6:50PM. Day shift. 1 deck.
Obviously, this must be my favorite place to play! Penetration sometimes reached 2/3 plus. But the cards continue to run lousy. I joked to cover up my hurt. I used some bet camouflage and re-ceived no heat. | Lost: $449.50 |

Session Three. Maxim. 7:40-8:40PM. Day and swing shift. 2 decks
This was another typical losing session. I got up $500 early by winning mostly little bets. Penetration was again surprisingly good, so I waited for some high counts to materialize.

In the last half hour, they mostly did. And, I got routed. I fell $900 behind before a very late comeback, mostly on low-counts, almost got me even. When some dealers started to shuffle up early, I de-cided it was time to leave. | Lost: $157.50 |

Session Four. Golden Nugget. 10:00-10:55PM. Swing shift. 1 and 6 Decks.
I did very well in the single-deck games, but gave most of the win-nings away in the six-deck (you guessed it) baccarat pit area game (my two-deck jinx carried over!). My loss in this game was high-lighted by a $150 loss (two hands of $75) when I did not take in-surance with a 20 and a blackjack on a very close insurance decision (the true count including the ace adjustment was +2.6 and I need over a +3 true count to bet insurance). Several onlookers and Pam, the pit boss, said that I had played it dumb when the dealer turned over a blackjack. ("You should insure blackjack and those good hands like 20's".) I left in disgust even though I had garnered my first winning session of the day. | Won: $181.50 |

Session Five. Las Vegas Hilton. 11:40PM-12:30AM. Swing shift. 2 decks.

Though my win was not huge, I made all the right moves. In other words, I played like a professional!

Early on, I did well versus Jimmy in a head-on $25 game. When he suddenly started shuffling at less than 50 percent, I switched tables after a losing hand.

At my next table, the woman at first base seemed to get angry whenever I switched between one and two hands. I took advantage of this to get the table to myself by switching back and forth like crazy. (I was helped by the Hilton's rule in which a player playing two hands at a $25 table can bet the table minimum on both.) My "erratic" play made this woman leave in disgust, which gave me some more head-on play.

Won: $193.50

Session Six. Palace Station. 1:00-1:30AM. Swing shift. 2 and 4 decks.

I bounced back and forth between the two and four-deck games. I quit whenever a third other player joined the game (my usual rule in all face down games). I received some pit boss scrutiny, but made no really big bets, never going past two hands of $75, to bring down the real heat.

Won: $50

Session Seven. Golden Nugget. 2:00-3:30AM. Swing shift. 1 and 6 decks.

This may have been my most frustrating session ever. Play conditions were superb with sometimes up to 3/4 depth on the one-deck games, but I couldn't win.

I got $600 ahead early in the single-deck, and then a total imbecile joined the table. Once, in a very negative deck, he resplit tens to make four separate hands to destroy the deck. After this move, everything went downhill for me. I got practically nothing but stiffs for the rest of the session. While the imbecile got blackjack after blackjack, I received none. I also lost every single insurance bet I made. I think I won one of those about a month or so ago!

There is a mathematically illogical occurrence I've noticed about my blackjack experience. Whenever there is a player who upsets me, I always lose money once I decide that I am upset. Logically, this should not happen, but it does. Perhaps, I get upset enough that I start to miscalculate.

I very seldom *do* get upset at other players. It usually takes much more than mere stupid play to upset me. And, face it, if there were no bad players, counters couldn't play, and beatable blackjack would probably cease to exist. But the fellow in this game had a crummy and haughty personality, which pissed me off. My recent struggles didn't help my mood either.

I may have to set a rule for myself to quit games the minute another player upsets me. As I just wrote, this seldom happens, but when it does, I never have won. My session record is exactly 0 percent in these rare situations.

		Lost: $773
April 12	Lost: $2,131	Time: 8 hr, 5 min
Week to date	Lost: $1,824.50	Time:15 hr, 25 min

Thus far this week, I have an even 9-9 session record, yet have managed to lose over $1,800. I win small and lose big. Hopefully, this disturbing trend won't last much longer.

April 13

Session One. Golden Nugget. 8:50-10:05AM. Graveyard shift. 1 deck.

Though I got just four hours of sleep, I woke up refreshed and— who knows why after my recent blackjack play—optimistic. I've decided to play my normal Wednesday half-day, today. I well remember the bad Wednesday I had last week when I did not take a half-day off.

My positive premonitions came true in my first session for the day. I played most of it against Christy, the friendly gal from Colorado Springs whom I have played a few times and have talked to on a few occasions.

I sensed early on that a turning point of sorts had been reached when I finally won a couple of insurance bets (making correct insurance plays is the single most important variation from basic strategy in single-deck play). I won steadily in the hour I played at Christy's table, most of the time, head-on. I also enjoyed our conversation. My winning, I admit, made this more likely.

When Christy took her break, I played for a little while against Audray, her relief. When I hit a $200 losing streak, I saw that I had played for over an hour. I decided then to leave and savor my best session of the week. I also got a comp for lunch from the pit bosses, who had made a show of "rooting" me on. Perhaps, my recent hard times at the Nugget have them actually feeling sympathetic towards me!

Won: $911

After my win, I had some breakfast and then stopped in at Leroy's. I was tempted to bet the Bulls at plus three over the Heat tonight.

The Bulls are one of the most amazing stories in sports this year. After losing the best basketball player (and maybe athlete) ever, in Michael Jordan, and also being hit with many injuries this season, the Bulls are just 1/2 game off the best record in the East with a 52-23 record. I would have bet serious money that the Bulls would not have won over 45 games this season.

Tonight, in a revenge situation, even in a back-to-back spot, the Bulls should win in Miami. Getting an underdog that figures to win straight up is the best type of bet in sports. However, I have not really kept abreast of the NBA this season, so my betting in this spot would be bad short-term value.

Session Two. Golden Nugget. 1:25-2:35PM. Day shift. 1 and 2 decks.

In this session, I had several good and bad runs. I fell $300 behind early, then got $600 ahead. Then I hit a slump, which left me just a small winner. I did most of my playing against a dealer named Lynn.

Won: $73.50

Session Three. Palace Station. 3:35-3:55PM. Day shift. 4 decks.

I may or may not have run into a house shill in this session. For the most part, two other players were at the table with me (my limit for face down games, as this one is). At the end of my first shoe, in which I entered late and played basic strategy, a fourth player started to enter. When I started to leave, so did he. He then left the pit. I stayed and continued to play.

In the next shoe, this player came out of nowhere and tried to enter on the very last hand (the shoe was neutral). Again, as I started to pack up my chips, this player declined to enter and disappeared again. At the end of the next shoe, with the deck slightly positive, this player again tried to pop in. At this point, I cashed out.

Since the shoe often reaches its best value at the end (since a counter is dividing by the smallest number to get his true count and because of the additional value of deck penetration) I wondered if the Palace Station was sending this player in to dilute the last and potentially most profitable hand? Were they testing me to see if I would be willing to stay in the last (positive) shoe and thus identify me as a definite counter? I'll probably never know for sure.   Won: $35.50

April 13	Won: $1,020	Time: 2 hr, 45 min
Week to date	Lost: $804.50	Time:18 hr, 10 min

April 14

Session One. Palace Station. 7:05-8:05AM. Graveyard shift. 2 decks.
I got the least heat I've gotten in this casino on this trip. I played at the $5 minimum table and was able to vary from one hand of $5 (in very minus counts off losses) to two hands of $75. I probably could have gone up to two hands of $100 with no hassle.

Mostly, I played with just one other player whose cards were easy for me to see. Since I ran fairly well, I told this player (whose errors often helped me) what a great player he was. Not! (Once he doubled on a ten versus a ten on a -7 true count).

The dealers consistently went 2/3 into the deck and sometimes even up to 3/4. If only I could always get such a hassle-free, deeply-dealt game!   Won: $376.50

Session Two. Golden Nugget. 8:50-10:10AM. Graveyard shift. 1 deck.
Penetration was very good on this shift—as much as 2/3. However, I was behind the whole way and was probably lucky to garner even a small win. A $250 one-round win (an extremely rare one-deck bet of two hands of $125, which I would only progress to in an almost heat-free place like this) was the turning point.

I played a part of my session with Bill, an almost perfect single-deck basic strategy player. He is a non-counter, though he has noticed and even openly stated (causing me to cringe) that good things, like blackjacks, tend to occur more often than usual on his hands when I have big bets out. I have shared tables with him a lot this week. He has been fairly pleasant to play with, but today he did make one huge error in judgment.

Bill quickly left the table when Jeff, a Korean dealer, came on. As he left, Bill whispered to me, "Be careful." I guess that Bill was trying to tell me that he thought that Jeff was a cheat.

However, I had played Jeff on several occasions and was positive that he was not (and, I'm always on the lookout in hand-held games). Nothing Jeff did in this session made me change my mind. The fact that I won a little in the 30 minutes that Jeff dealt to me in a head-on situation was further proof (though I realize that cheats usually pick their times and spots). If Jeff was pulling she-nanigans, my winning for over 30 minutes in a head-on game would have been near impossible.

As I left the casino, I explained to Bill that Jeff's "fluid motions" (what Bill found suspicious) in no way made him a cheat. I tried to teach Bill what to look for (peeking and pull-back thumb motions when the thumb should be going forward among other things).

Though I had one definite incident of cheating five weeks ago (which I mentioned to Bill), I'll stress again that I am sure that dealer cheating is very rare in Vegas these days. Bill and others should study cheating tapes and demonstrations so that they know what to look for rather than guess and employ generalities. Generalities such as "the guy is too fluid with the cards," do a horrible disservice to the vast majority of honest dealers and casinos that try their hardest to deal and employ a clean game. | Won: $60 |

Session Three. Maxim. 11:15AM-12:15PM. Day shift. 2 decks.
Somehow, I continue to find dealers who deal deep in this casino. Lenore went almost 3/4 in!

For a change, the high-count bets ran well. I got about $1,300 ahead and seemed headed for my first $1,000 plus winning session in a week. However, I had a high-count losing streak and left just as the hour ended, locking up half the profit. | Won: $648.50 |

Session Four. Las Vegas Hilton. 2:05-2:15PM. Day shift. 2 decks.
This was a quick wipeout, pure and simple! I played head-on for three decks, two of which were very plus despite the lousy (50 percent or so) penetration. I got slaughtered and was unwilling to lose more money in this lousy penetration game. | Lost: $904.50 |

Session Five. Golden Nugget. 2:50-4:20PM. Day shift. 1 and 2 decks.
Though I played for 1-1/2 hours and made a few dollars, the session was very uneventful. I bounced from table to table, leaving as tables filled. Despite my very heavy Nugget play this week, heat on me continues to be minimal. However, I won't play in the Nugget next week, my last in Vegas for this trip. ┌──────────────┐ Won: $352.50 └──────────────┘

Session Six. Four Queens. 9:00-9:10PM. Swing shift. 1 deck.
Though the Four Queens is not on my usual play list, I decided that conditions (head-on) were such that I could play for a few minutes. I started with one very hot deck. This was highlighted by a $200 (two hands of $100) win, which made this quick stop a winner. Right after this, I noticed that Pai, the dealer, went deep into a negative deck and then shuffled early in a positive deck. I quickly left the casino rather than face this preferential shuffling.

Pai should perhaps go find work across the street at the Horseshoe! He'll take care of those sneaky depth chargers (whose strategy will obviously not work against preferential shuffling)! No need for the bosses to flat bet counters at his table! ┌──────────────┐ Won: $189.50 └──────────────┘

Session Seven. Golden Nugget. 10:25-10:35PM. Swing shift. 6 decks.
After dinner, I decided to try to play here again. The casino was now very crowded. I was able to find one uncrowded six-deck game. However, when the table got crowded, just as the shoe got negative, I decided this was a perfect time to leave. ┌──────────┐ Won: $49 └──────────┘

Session Eight. Maxim. 11:10PM-12:05AM. Swing shift. 2 decks.
This session had a terrible beginning and a shocking end. I'll have trouble sleeping tonight because of the ending.

On the first 23 hands I played, the dealer did not bust once! Even considering that I played most of these hands heads-up (and thus the dealer could not bust if I had busted first, as sometimes happened), the odds against this are astronomical even though the dealer has just a 28 percent chance of busting when his hand is played out. In this bad-luck period, I fell over $1,000 behind. However, since the deck penetration was good, I continued to play.

After about 20 minutes of play, the cards started to turn, and I mounted a comeback. I varied my bets, with camouflage, from one hand of $25 to two of $200. There seemed less heat on me in this casino than ever before.

After another 25 minutes of play, I had come all the way back. Two other players were in the game and I was joking around as I played. I figured that I would play about two or three more decks and then call it a session and day. I still had time to pop a big win.

After two more break-even decks, it happened. I got a tap on the shoulder from the night shift supervisor, who wished to speak to me away from the table. He introduced himself and told me that I was "too tough for the Maxim."

I answered, "What do you mean? I got lucky tonight. You had me buried and I was lucky to come back."

Impatiently, the supervisor answered, "Look, you don't have to play games with me. We know what you are doing and we feel that we have no edge dealing to you. You've been under observation all week. We'd prefer that you not play any more blackjack here. You are welcome to play any other game at the Maxim and be any place else in the casino, but no more blackjack."

The conversation and "friendly" barring ended shortly after this, and I cashed out and left. I have been told that barrings are a fact of life in this business for counters; in fact, if a player is not barred, he is probably betting peanuts and/or not playing a winning game (true of most counters). Still, this barring came as a shock.

What really terrified me is that the Maxim was and still may be the headquarters for the Griffin Detective Agency, an agency used by some casinos to check up on and bar and/or harass card counters. Would this agency now have my picture and description and show it all over town? These were questions that I certainly could not ask the shift supervisor as he barred me.

What is also frustrating is that this is my fourth barring (including the Horseshoe flat-bet decree) and I haven't even really started to win yet. I'm now down a microscopic $2 in my play for the trip. Maybe it's good that I'm leaving Las Vegas in a little over a week. The town may be getting too hot for me.

Won: $22

April 14	Won: $793.50	Time: 6hr, 15 min
Week to date	Lost: $11	Time:24 hr, 25 min

April 15

It was difficult for me to get out of bed this morning. The Maxim barring of last night and its possible consequences made me almost want to leave town right now. But, I won't. I came here planning to play for eight weeks and I will.

Session One. Golden Nugget. 8:45-10:05AM. Graveyard shift. 1 deck.

Though I have been given little heat at the Nugget, I decided to use more camouflage than usual. I almost always opened the deck with decent-sized bets (though keeping my total bet variation from one hand of $25 to two of $100). I was given no heat.

However, the cards were bad. I lost to every dealer I faced. I don't believe that I was distracted because of what happened at the Maxim yesterday, but I guess I'll never know for sure. Perhaps I should have asked the eye or the pit if I was making the correct count plays!

Lost: $953

Session Two. Palace Station. 10:40-11:20AM. Graveyard shift. 2 decks.

I played at the $25 and then the $5 two-deck games. Surprisingly, the $5 tables had fewer players (though only one $25 two-deck game was open).

With not much heat, I did well. I liked Eddie, a very friendly black dealer from Louisiana. I have doubts that I would be very friendly as a dealer. Hearing losing bettors whine all day (and many blaming me), getting asked the same dumb questions hundreds of times a day, and dealing with casino political bullshit would wear on me quickly. Dealing seems like a thankless job.

A key $200 loss on two hands of $100 kept me from having a big session. However, it was nice to bounce back a little from the Nugget disaster.

Won: $413

Session Three. Las Vegas Hilton. 12:00-12:45PM. Day shift. 6 decks.

With the lousy two-deck penetration, I decided to play the shoes. I played at the $5 six-deck game which allowed me great variance as I started with what would seem medium-sized bets and could easily go up or down.

The bad news was that in the 45 minutes in which I played, there was only one high-count shoe, in which I broke even. I quit the session in a negative shoe as the table and the casino became crowded.

| Won: $25 |

Session Four. Golden Nugget. 1:25-2:35PM. Day shift. 1 and 2 decks.

This session ended up being a decent, but not great, one. Near its end, I suddenly felt very tired and worn out. I bid good-bye to the Nugget at the session's conclusion.

| Won: $321 |

This was an extremely frustrating and draining week for me. I was barred twice, and have now fallen behind for the trip. I had a great 22-11 session record for the week and yet managed to lose money! This week my average winning session netted me about $304, while my average losing session made me $625 poorer. I endured three losing sessions of over $900 this week, and just once won over that amount. Doesn't make sense!

April 15	Lost: $194	Time: 3 hr, 55 min
Week 7 Total	Lost: $205	Time: 28 hr, 20 min
Trip to date	Lost: $196	Time: 211 hr, 11 min

The next week will be my last week of this venture. I'll give it my best shot and draw conclusions later.

Player Barrings

At first glance, barring blackjack players looks like a very simple issue in which the casinos have taken an untenable position. The casinos are offering a game, blackjack, in which the player has options on his betting and playing strategy and is trying to win money from the casino. The same type of player options, in play and bet variation, exist in all other casino games—craps, roulette, keno, etc. (Maybe slot machines don't have player options in strategy, though I suppose one can use different types of pulls on the handle!) However, since the player has the potential to have a long-term edge in blackjack, casino bosses in all jurisdictions, except Atlantic City, reserve the right to ask blackjack players whom they consider skilled to leave the casino or at least not play blackjack in their casino anymore.

Allowing casinos to bar skilled blackjack players seems like a position that only a greedy person or a fool could agree with. If a casino offers blackjack to its patrons, anyone, save disorderly patrons, should be allowed to play at the tables. If a casino thinks that the game of blackjack really *can* be beaten, it has the option of not offering it to its patrons anymore. It seems ridiculous for a game to be offered to players who are in effect, being told, "You can play this game, but only if you are a sucker. If you are not a sucker, we don't want your action." Again, only a greedy person or a fool could agree with such a business position.

However, we live in the real world, not in a world in which problems and solutions are simple and can all be solved by perfect logic and debating school points. The barring of blackjack players by casinos is a very complicated problem.

The complexity of the blackjack barring problem has been shown very clearly in Atlantic City. Since September 15 1982, because of a lawsuit won by Ken Uston, Atlantic City casinos have been forbidden to bar blackjack players for being skilled (card counters). The casinos in Atlantic City responded by setting up their blackjack games in such a way that even the most skilled counter has a minuscule edge, if that.

Virtually all of the Atlantic City blackjack games are eight-deck games in which usually two-decks are cut off from play. These games, it has been shown in Arnold Snyder's *Beat the Eight Deck Game*, are virtually unbeatable for someone who plays every hand. This is because there are too many negative or neutral count situations to overcome with any but monstrous bet spreads, which will result in gigantic fluctuations. The house has about a .43 percent edge in these games. For Wongers who table hop, any small profits will probably be eaten up in the cost of the aspirins needed to relieve aching feet, which will be caused by the endless walking around looking for the few positive situations.

Even with these virtually counter-proof conditions, the Atlantic City casinos are allowed still more options that can make life for counters even more miserable. These options are the following:

1) The dealer can be told to reshuffle the cards at any time. Thus, if the counter has finally gotten a good count situation, the pit boss can have it taken away. Though this horrible form of preferential shuffling seldom happens in Atlantic City—and usually just to big-money counters—it, or even worse penetration, can be imposed at any time.

2) Virtually all of the few six-deck games in Atlantic City, as well as the one four-deck game (a $100-minimum table at the Claridge) prohibit mid-shoe entry. This rule was imposed specifically to stop Wongers. If a player plays in a six-deck game, he must play from the beginning or he can't play at all. Even if a player like an 85 year old grandmother, who can barely see the cards much less count, leaves a game to go to the bathroom, she can't re-enter the game until the cards are reshuffled. With 2/3 penetration standard in Atlantic City six-deck games, playing every hand of such a game is really a waste of time. Even a huge bet spread would probably gain not much more than a 1/2 percent edge: an edge that would need close to 200,000 hands of absolutely perfect play and absolutely perfect bet spreading with no camouflage and experiencing no casino countermeasures for a counter to have a significant edge—one in which he would be ahead even if two standard deviations south of expectations.

3) Though the Atlantic City casinos are not allowed to bar obvious counters who use big bet spreads, they can still stop the use of these spreads by changing table limits. A $25-$1,000 table can be changed, for example, to a $50-$100 table in which the same number of spots must be played on each round of a shoe. In other words, in this example, a 1-2 spread would be imposed on the counter, thus making the game unbeatable.

A few years ago a four-deck game with 50 percent penetration was used in Atlantic City. The table limits were $25-$100. I believe (but am not positive) that mid-shoe entry was prohibited. I wouldn't play in such a game with your monopoly money! And neither should you!

Because of these allowances by the New Jersey Casino Control Commission and the bad games, the casinos of Atlantic City attract virtually no professional card counters. Thus Atlantic City has found the way around the no barring law. They make the games unplayable for card counters.

What has happened in Atlantic City would very possibly happen in Nevada and all other areas that offer blackjack if a no-barring rule took place. There could be even tougher variations such as the dealer shuffling after every round in any hand-held game with any suspected counter at the table, or very widespread preferential shuffling.

Thus stopping the casinos from barring skilled players probably would make the game much tougher to beat than it is even now. So what is the solution?

I believe the only casino person who has tackled the barring problem at all rationally is Bill Zender of the Aladdin Casino of Las Vegas. Zender knows all about card counting (and hole carding and shuffle tracking) and he also fully knows how a casino can create basically unbeatable blackjack games.

However, Zender, being light years of intelligence ahead of most casino executives and supervisors in Las Vegas, also realizes a few other facts. These are:

1) Most card counters won't win because they make too many play and bet mistakes. Frank, the long-time counter I know in Vegas, often told me that if a casino opened and permitted no one but self-professed counters to play it would make more money than any casino in history. I am not sure if I agree with Frank's strong statement. However, I will say that most counters I have witnessed do not play a winning game and should not be considered a threat by intelligent casino personnel.

Zender knows that the few counters who will win probably won't win that much money because of limited bankrolls and/or marginal play. Thus, very few counters are real threats to the casino.

2) The more hands that a casino deals in the shortest possible time, the more potential profits it can make. The casino makes no money while the dealer is shuffling the cards. Thus, the more deeply the games are dealt, the more money the casino potentially makes.

3) The more options allowed the player, such as DAS and surrender, the more mistakes a player will make. This creates a better casino bottom line. DAS and surrender are good options for a good player, however, the number of players who make mistakes with DAS and surrender outweigh the number of players who use them correctly. This translates to a better profit for the house.

On points two and three, Zender realizes that the few competent counters who can take advantage of these conditions will be far outweighed by the masses of players who will lose far more money by their existence.

Supposedly, Zender protects the Aladdin blackjack games against the few real threats by taping from the eye and with an alert, competent pit crew. From my understanding these "threats" are defined as a "competent counter who sometimes bets over $100 a round."

For small-stakes, competent counters, the Aladdin is perhaps the best place in the world to play blackjack. (Only the Golden Nugget is close to the Aladdin's equal in this regard.) They can play in great games and have virtually no fear of being kicked out if they play well and win. And the games at the Aladdin provide excellent win potential because of the superb penetration and rules (except for the soft 17 dealer hit).

For Zender and the Aladdin, the few long-term, small-stakes winning counters provide great advertising. Wannabe counters, see these winning players not harassed and think blackjack can be beaten, and feel comfortable that the Aladdin won't hassle them if they do win. Of course, as Zender knows, probably less than one wannabe counter in a hundred will actually win money in the long run; thus these few winning players probably profit the Aladdin Casino far more than themselves.

I would guess that, on average, maybe one blackjack player in every 1,000 constitutes a financial threat to a casino's bankroll. A financial threat means not only that the player is an excellent blackjack player, but also that he is betting enough to take away a significant portion of the casino's expected profit in the time that he plays in it. Obviously, the definition of "a financial threat" is different to different casinos. And "significant portion of expected profits" is open to wide interpretation. Only the casino bookkeepers know these definitions for sure!

Zender has set up the Aladdin blackjack games in such a way so that the 999 players can play there comfortably. How well he has kept out (protected the Aladdin) from the 1,000th player—the real threat—is something that probably can't be answered objectively at this point since Zender has been running the Aladdin blackjack games for only about three years.

Most other casinos are so counter paranoid that they set up inconveniences for the other 999 players because of the 1,000th player. The casino's fear of this player also costs it money. Decks are shuffled early. Dealers preferentially shuffle. Shoes are broken in half. All these actions mean fewer rounds dealt, less total money wagered in a given time, and less profits for the casino. Most casinos sweat winners and glare at them. They often bar skilled, and even sometimes unskilled, players in an obnoxious way, which is not only stupid, but alienates the other customers (like my barring at the Gold Coast on February 28). In Atlantic City, and I would guess in some Nevada casinos, table limits are jacked around. Ironically, most of these paranoid casinos I would guess are more injured by the 1,000th player (the real threat) than the Aladdin is!

So, the question isn't whether casinos are right or wrong in barring skilled blackjack players. If casinos are not permitted to bar skilled players, they could always set up games that would be unbeatable by counters or anyone else (such as, say, a game in which there is continuous shuffling by a machine, as the Nugget and Mirage once had at a few tables). Atlantic City now comes close to this type of nightmare as do a few Vegas casinos (such as Bally's and Caesars Palace).

The reality is that blackjack and card counters—a few of whom are very competent—both will continue to exist in casinos. And, casino owners will continue to want to make blackjack profits. The type of games that will ultimately make the casinos the most money are the types of games that exist at the Aladdin in which deep dealing and several player options will fatten the casino's bottom line via more rounds dealt and more player mistakes. These games are the same ones that are potentially most vulnerable to the very few good players. Whether the few players or teams of players who pose a financial threat can make a significant impact on the oceans of money made by the casino off of unskilled players is something that is difficult to tell.

Though I do not have access to casinos' account books, I would doubt that their losses to even the most competent blackjack players are anything even remotely approaching what is made from average and poor players.

I can say from my own experience that winning at blackjack is tough. I ended up ahead on my trip, but not by any huge amount. Though I guess it is impossible for me to know, I believe I did not make many non-camouflage mistakes in betting or play decisions. I would also state that I spent a good percentage (maybe not good enough, but good just the same) of my play time in some of the best blackjack games available in Las Vegas. And, still I had to endure two very nasty financial downswings in my eight weeks of play.

I don't think many casino executives realize just how tough it is to win at blackjack. Very few shift supervisors and pit bosses understand phrases like fluctuations and standard deviations and long-range probabilities. If these phrases were understood, I suspect many fewer barrings and hasslings would take place at the blackjack tables.

As I wrote earlier, I don't have access to casino account information. But if I ran a casino, I would bar extremely few, if any, players even if I were allowed to do so. Probably the most drastic action I would take—and this would be to players or teams who pose a serious financial threat—would be to limit the maximum amount that these players could wager as a player or a team. And any pit boss or supervisor in my casino who sweated a game or hassled any player would very quickly become an ex-employee!

The key issue here isn't barring, but education. If most casino executives understood how tough the game of blackjack is and how violent its fluctuations, I suspect that better games for the players would be dealt and that substantially fewer barrings would occur. This would be the best of all possible worlds for both the casinos and the players—even the few competent ones.

**Las Vegas: Las Vegas Hilton, Circus Circus,
Palace Station, Aladdin, Excalibur, San Remo,
Continental, Arizona Charlies**

**Laughlin: Flamingo Hilton, Golden Nugget,
Pioneer, Riverside, Ramada**

April 18

This is the final week of my blackjack trip. Tomorrow, I plan to take a one-day excursion to Laughlin to check out and play blackjack there. On the days I play in Las Vegas, I will hit a number of different casinos. I will try not to overplay any. The only ones that I will not play for sure are the four in which I have been barred (Gold Coast, Plaza, Horseshoe, and Maxim), and the Nugget, Mirage, Treasure Island, the Riviera, the Stardust, the Flamingo Hilton, the Desert Inn and the MGM. I may try out Arizona Charlie's, a small casino on the west side of town. I'll always be looking for the best possible games.

Though it will be almost impossible for me to end up averaging at least $50 per hour in wins (my stated minimum for a successful trip at the start), I do think that this trip has had its plus points.

I've learned a great deal of the realities of playing for serious money inside the casino on this trip. The pit heat, the hassles, the barrings, the help and hindrances given by dealers have all contributed to my education over the seven weeks. If I ever make blackjack a full-time career, this two-month playing period will have been a great help.

I have also come to understand that the huge fluctuations of the game—which are, to an extent caused by hard-to-avoid casino conditions, make a two-month or 200-plus-hour playing test unrealistically short for a "long-run" test.

I have come to understand that a player probably must play at least 40-50,000 hands (play at least 400 hours) before the "long run" is realized. To me, the "long-run" is defined as a period of time in which the skilled player is a significant favorite (about a 95 percent or better favorite—or in the neighborhood of being able to weather two negative standard deviations) to win. Of course, even in this "long-run" playing period, a player must play well in decent games to have the long-range odds in his favor. Good penetration, decent rules, and uncrowded conditions are important. So is being able to get down a decent bet spread for a given game.

But now on to Week Eight.

Session One. Las Vegas Hilton. 9:20-10:05AM. Graveyard shift. 2 decks.

Since I played just once on graveyard last week, I decided to come in today on that shift. I hoped that head-on play would be available. However, I believe that I was recognized by the pit.

The session began very well when I got ahead by almost $1,000 despite never going past two hands of $100. Penetration was just over 50 percent: not good, but I did have head-on play.

Then Mary, an obvious counter catcher, started watching me. Despite my slumping a little and throwing in an intentional mistake (hitting and busting on a 13 versus a three on a -1 true count—under -2 is needed), she continued to watch my play very closely.

When my winnings dropped to around $600, two other players joined the game and I left. As I cashed out, I noticed that Mary left the table and probably went to wait in some hideaway until the pit needed her services again. Good-bye, Hilton! | Won: $597 |

Session Two. Circus Circus. 10:35-11:20AM. Graveyard shift. 2 decks.

I played mostly at the $5 table and got away with varying my bets from $5 to two hands of $100 without any real heat. I was very careful in raising my bets. Four weeks ago it was almost impossible to get up to two hands of $100 at the $25 table! Today, I fell $250 behind, but battled back for a small win. | Won: $198 |

Session Three. Palace Station. 12:00-1:00PM. Day shift. 2 decks.

No $25 tables of any kind were open, so I played at the $5 two-deck game. I fell $500 behind early in the session and came back, though not all the way. Little heat occurred despite a wide bet spread. Maybe my act is getting better.

At the end of the session, several of the players were happy to see the "dumb third baseman" (me) leave. I had hit a 12 and a 15 versus dealer fives (both times in very negative decks). I busted both times and the dealer later made his hand. For this I was loudly criticized by the dealer and the other players. | Lost: $169.50 |

Session Four. Palace Station. 3:25-4:15PM. Day shift. 2 decks.
After eating a comp lunch in the Iron Horse Cafe, I spoke for a
while to some friends (who don't know of my new career in blackjack) in the sports book. With the little heat earlier, I decided to
jump in on an open $25 table.

The deck penetration was fabulous: often over 75 percent! This led
to some great decks and some seemingly strange plays on my part.
In one high-count deck (+10 true count), I stood on a 15 versus a
seven (and lost). In another high-count deck I stood—probably incorrectly though the play did work out—on a 12 versus a seven
(true count was over +30 with about .3 decks and no aces left) and
this time I lucked out on a dealer bust. The high-count plays went
well. I quit when the table filled.

I ended up having my first $1,000 plus win in 11 days. How sweet
it was! | Won: $1,150 |

*Session Five. Aladdin. 5:45-6:50PM. Day and swing shifts. 6
decks.*
I decided to play the Aladdin and try to outfox the sharpest pit
crew in Vegas. Because of the run-down parking lot in the back,
my name for the Aladdin is now The Dump! Today, they dumped
lots of money into my wallet!

I was willing to play at a fairly crowded six-deck table since they
dealt 5-1/2 decks. And, luck and a small fortune came my way!

I not only had a better session than the one I just had at the Palace
Station, but also was very lucky during it. A dumb player made
playing mistakes virtually every time I had big bets on the table.
However, his mistakes almost always worked in my favor! Once,
for example, this player hit a 14 versus a four in a high-count deck
and drew an ace that would have given the dealer a 20 to beat both
my hands. Instead, the dealer drew a seven (to his total of nine) and
then busted with a picture. This stupid play created a plus $600
swing for me (I had two hands of $150 on the table). As I have
written, dumb play by others works both ways.

Despite using a huge spread (with camouflage, naturally) I was not
given heat or asked to leave. The "suits" have only a few days left
to nail me here! | Won: $1,591 |

Session Six. Excalibur. 8:25-9:30PM. Swing shift. 1 and 2 decks.
For this loss I have only myself to blame. On the key hand, I didn't
double down on a soft 15 versus a five with a high-count because
three extra aces (six in all) were still in the deck with .7 decks left.
This ace adjustment made the true count for this decision -4, rather
than the +4 required for this decision, since extra aces left hurt the
player. One should double on the index number, but I did not. I
won less than I should have on the hand, and as a result had less
money to use to parlay onto the next round on which I won both
hands. Penetration continues to be great in this casino: 3/4 in the
double-decks and up to 2/3 in the single decks. | Lost: $252.50 |

After this tough, though small, loss I went by the Palace Station
and thought about playing there again, but decided not to. It was
crowded and I had played there twice at night last week. Though
my blackjack was over for the day, my activities were not.

| April 18 | Won: $3,114 | Time: 5 hr, 30 min |

A couple of more days like this and I still could pass my highwater
mark for the trip. This would be quite an accomplishment considering what I have endured in the last 2-1/2 weeks.

Feeling happy and a little giddy, I decided to make a couple of
calls from a pay phone in the small arcade area. While there, I fell
into a conversation with a woman who also was making some
phone calls. This conversation carried over to a small bar and went
on into other activities.

I could have let the fun last all night, but I did have a scheduled
business trip to Laughlin tomorrow. Later, I remembered the most
fun that I ever had having sex with a woman—a lady I knew well
in Michigan. In that instance, the passion was much more real
(since we'd known each other as friends for a long time before we
unexpectedly became lovers) and lasted all evening and night. The
next day I was driving to New York for Christmas. Despite having
practically no sleep, I was able to make the drive with no help from
my riders. But I was much younger at that time and wasn't scheduled to count cards under casino pressure the next day.

In this instance, the sex was just a welcome relief from my grind.
It fulfilled a need for both of us.

April 19

After last night's fun, I slept in a little later than I originally planned. I didn't start the 100-mile drive to Laughlin until 11:00AM. I had wanted to be playing at the tables by that time or earlier.

I arrived in the city of the casinos by the river by 1:00PM. Using Snyder's *Blackjack Forum* and Wong's *Current Blackjack News* as guides, I decided that five Laughlin casinos were worth my play: the Flamingo Hilton, the Golden Nugget, the Pioneer, the Ramada, and the Riverside.

The Riverside casino presented a unique circumstance. Their six-deck game had terrible rules: the dealer hit soft 17, and the player not only was not permitted to DAS but also could double only on totals of ten or eleven on the first two cards. Normally, if I were to play in such a casino, it would mean I had gone crazy and should be locked up. These rules put the player at about a .92 percent disadvantage off the top, over .3 percent greater than the biggest off-the-top disadvantage I have ever faced in the game of blackjack.

However, the Riverside offered one rule which very much interested me: the bust-out rule. This rule allows the player to bet at 2-1 odds on any amount up to his original bet that the dealer would bust with a ten value card on his first draw on any hand in which his first two cards (up card and hole card) totaled a hard 12-16. The player was permitted to make this bet only if his own hand was not resolved (e.g., he didn't have a blackjack and he hadn't busted). This bust-out rule—a potential gold mine, proven to be eight times more profitable than insurance for card counters—and the great deck penetration (five decks plus) would bring me and my betting bankroll into the Riverside despite the otherwise terrible rules.

Each of the other four casinos in which I would play had downtown Vegas rules: the dealer hit soft 17, no DAS, and the player could double down after any first two cards. Penetration in all games was reported to be excellent, and my type of action would not bring me too much heat. Or so implied Snyder's and Wong's reporters.

Session One. Flamingo Hilton. 1:30-2:25PM. Day shift. 1 and 2 decks.

Early on, I fell behind by about $200, then fought back to get ahead. When the one-deck game got crowded, I switched to the two-deck game. I was getting some mild scrutiny from Judy, a friendly pit boss.

In the less crowded two-deck game, I suspected that Burt, the dealer, knew I was counting. I once stood on a 12 versus a 2 in a fairly plus (over +2 on the true count) situation and won when Burt busted. Burt seemed surprised that I broke basic strategy. I loudly said that "those who wrote the 'book' (basic strategy) never bet their own money." This play and my comment to Burt seemed to help lessen the pit scrutiny. I won and easily got comped to lunch. I varied from $5 (at the end of minus decks off of losses) to as high as two hands of $100 (parlaying wins in high-count decks). Penetration was great—up to 75 percent in both games.   Won: $357

Session Two. Golden Nugget. 3:35-4:20PM. Day shift. 1 deck.
It was spooky coming into the Nugget. It seemed a combination of other Steve Wynn properties: the Golden Nugget and the Mirage of Las Vegas. The rugs and wall colorings seem just like the Vegas Nugget and the "rain forest" in   the center of the casino seemed just like the one at the Mirage. The sportsbook—all the way down to the color of the team markings on the board (green and black)—was a double of the Las Vegas Golden Nugget.

I bounced back and forth between several tables as I tried to play with two or less other players. Penetration was good (2/3 plus) and a late hot streak made the session a winner. Maybe this week will totally make up for my recent disasters.   Won: $452.50

Session Three. Pioneer. 4:50-5:55PM. Day shift. 1 deck.
And, maybe not! I played at my first $15 minimum table in Laughlin and had great conditions there and at every other table I played at in this casino (often head-on play and at least 2/3 penetration). However, in this session, I lost steadily. I did poorly on my biggest bets (two hands of $100).

My losses were joyfully greeted by the bosses (all dressed in Old West cowboy outfits). When one saw me go quickly through two $200 buy-ins, he practically tripped over his boots in his dash to my table to see if I "needed anything". I did get a dinner comp for later.

Even though I used less camouflage (gotta learn to play the act when I'm losing) than usual, I got minimal heat. My losses were assuredly the explanation for that.   Lost: $969

Session Four. Golden Nugget. 6:10-7:10PM. Day shift. 1 deck.
Since this was to be my only day in Laughlin, I decided to go back across the parking lot that the Nugget shares with the Pioneer Club to try to get on track again in a place where I had done well earlier.

I won pretty big, but received my most intense heat of the day. Two pit bosses and a dealer said that they remembered me "from somewhere." My play was also observed by several bosses who pointed at me. Do the Maxim and Steve Wynn share information?

At the very end of the session, I won several $200 rounds (two hands of $100). During this run, I was getting 75 percent deck penetration from Rhene. After one such win at the end of the deck, I heard a pit boss whisper to Rhene to shuffle earlier. Since I had, by now, played for one hour I decided that this was a great time to leave. I left saying that I had a dinner date. | Won: $913.50 |

Instead of dinner, I caught up on NBA action in the sportsbook, going there in a very roundabout way just in case I was being observed. I was very shocked that the Hawks defeated the Knicks in New York. This win just about secures the best record and home edge in the Eastern playoffs for the Hawks. Lenny Wilkins has done a heck of a job coaching a team that was 43-39 last year and made few major personnel additions since then.

However, I don't think I'll ever fully forgive Wilkins for the putrid performance his Cavs had against the Bulls last year in the playoffs. Not only were the Cavs swept (costing me a series bet at nearly 4-1 odds), but they also seemed to give up the series after their first game loss. The Cavs just seemed to expect Michael Jordan to find a way to beat them. And, he did. When I'm in a severe blackjack slump, I feel the same about the dealers! In fact, in my slumps, they seem even tougher to beat than Michael Jordan!

Session Five. Riverside. 9:00-10:00PM. Swing shift. 6 decks.
It was time to play in the bust-out game. Before I did so, I viewed the one-deck games and saw something that made me very uncomfortable. The discards in this game were not put in a discard tray—as in every other game I've seen—but were held by the dealer face up at the bottom of the deck. This is how all games were dealt in the old days. Though I did not see evidence of such here, seconds dealing in such a set-up seems much easier to accomplish. (A view supported by the Steve Forte *Gamblers Protection* tapes.)

This session represented probably the luckiest win in my entire blackjack career. I won even though the shoe never got that positive (I needed a true count of +2-1/2 to justify a bet of $50 because of the .914 percent casino edge against me off the top). My biggest bet of the whole session was two hands of $50. I was able to decrease to as little as $5, however. But, on virtually every hand, I was playing at a disadvantage of over .5 percent.

The table was fairly crowded though the penetration was good with 5-1/4 decks dealt.

My biggest disappointment was that the bust-out was never a correct play (I needed a true count of +3 to play it. The count almost never got that high and never when bust-out was an option). This option was seldom bet by anyone and it also slowed the pace of the game. Oh, well. I guess the bust-out won't be around for much longer.

I joked throughout the session with a couple that sat on either side of me. The wife complained how lucky I was when I hit a 13 versus a three (true count was -4) and drew a seven and won. The dealer didn't seem surprised by my play.

Normally, I never would have played in a crowded game with rules this bad. And the reason I did in this session, the bust-out, never was a correct play! But, I still won a little and left knowing that I had been lucky.

Won: $121

Shortly after I left the Riverside, I started to feel a little sick. I went to get my comped dinner at the Pioneer Club and despite very slow service, felt slightly better. However, now I was also feeling a little tired.

Session Six. Ramada. 12:00-12:10AM. Swing shift. 1 deck.
Almost right after I sat down in the Ramada, I started feeling sick again. At the first $25 table I had played in Laughlin, the conditions (uncrowded and 75 percent penetration) were excellent. This seemed a great place to make money!

However, after ten minutes of play, I had to stop my play. I was feeling increasingly nauseous and was having trouble keeping count with Nick, a fast dealer. I knew that to play when feeling sick and tired took away my advantage. If I lost in such a game, I'd feel really stupid and if I won, I'd be tempted to make that mistake again (playing when sick) and probably lose. So I stopped and managed to drive back to Vegas.

		Won: $24
April 19	Won: $899	Time: 4 hr, 55 min
Week to date	Won: $4,013	Time: 10 hr, 25 min

If I get out West to play more blackjack, Laughlin will be one of my play spots: much more than it was this trip. Reno, with its bad rules (dealer hits soft 17 and double only on 10 and 11), but great penetration, can also probably be exploited.

Though I won for the day, my health suffered. It was a struggle to get back to Vegas and I wondered if I could play the next day or even the rest of the week. I had a win streak going and wanted to exploit it.

April 20 and 21

Wednesdays were usually my half day. This Wednesday I took the entire day off from blackjack play so that I could sleep off my stomach flu. Very late in the day, I left my apartment briefly to play miniature golf in a course by I-15; I had wanted to play there for years and today, totally unforeseen, I did so. The blue skies and warming Vegas weather were good reasons for going out. My health, which drove me back after just nine holes, was not. I went back to my apartment for more soup and drink and tried to get ready for my last two days of play.

With some luck, I might be able to pass my high point of the trip—around plus $7,300. This would provide a little consolation for the recent terrible 2-1/2 week run that prevented me from averaging $50 per hour in winnings for the trip.

I slept and read for the rest of the day. By Thursday morning (April 21) I was ready to play blackjack again.

Session One. Aladdin. 8:30-9:35AM. Graveyard shift. 2 and 6 decks.

I played mostly at the $5 two-deck game. I was given no heat or hassle.

Because of the superb 3/4-plus penetration I was willing to play at close to a full table. This decision cost me on the last hand.

I had two hands of $55 on the table and the dealer had an ace. It was a close call, and I wasn't able to see most of the other players hands. I ended up not taking insurance. The dealer had a blackjack and I lost $110. One of the hands that I couldn't see was a 6-3; this knowledge would have made insurance the correct play. This is why I very seldom play with more than two others in a face-down game. More players than that can badly hurt play decisions (unless one can see all of the cards—very rare at a full table) especially the critical one called insurance.   Lost: $142

Session Two. San Remo. 10:15-11:20AM. Graveyard. 2 decks.
I decided to give this small casino a try, my first in five weeks. I played the $5 (highest limit) two-deck tables and enjoyed great penetration and, surprisingly no real heat. But, I lost.

And, I lost despite unexpected help from a dealer that could have had me barred and had the dealer fired, and have us both arrested. Wouldn't that have been a great way to end the trip?

Robin, my dealer for most of the session, felt sorry for me and was genuinely rooting for me to win (probably because I am not only such a nice guy but because I was also one of those rare losing players who tipped her, which I did because of her 3/4 dealing depth). On one round I had two hands of $80 and faced Robin's dangerous ace. On a true count of +8, I lost the insurance bet, and then played out my hands. I stood on my soft 18 on one and then I tried to double down on the hard ten (on a true count of +4 or higher this is a correct play) on the other. Robin tried to rush me a hit card and practically tried to arm wrestle my chip holding hand to prevent my doubling down. Robin kept saying, "You *don't* want to double down on this hand!" I was dumb enough to believe that Robin wanted to stop me because she felt that doubling a ten against an ace is a foolish play. I was too stupid, dense, and maybe too unhealthy to know what was really going on! I won the arm wrestle with Robin and doubled down. What I lost was the extra bet when Robin turned over (you guessed it) a nine in the hole for 20. I got an eight as the double down card for an 18 total.

I knew right away what had happened, and how dumb I was. I not only felt like a hopeless imbecile, but I was flattered that Robin had risked her career to help me—someone she had not even known an hour earlier—save a lousy $80. Later on, I caught up with Robin outside the gaming area and apologized and told her how grateful I was—the very least I could do. Not everyone in the casino is my enemy. This incident proved that.   Lost: $434.50

Session Three. Continental. 12:30-1:30PM. Day shift. 2 decks.
I continued to play in great two-deck games and I continued to lose. I was harshly criticized by the dealer anytime I made what she considered the wrong play (oh, baby, what you missed in my last session). On one hand Dahlia loudly criticized me for hitting a soft 18 versus a ten because "18 is a winner 75 percent of the time." I'd love to give Dahlia some blackjack betting propositions—assuming I have any money left to bet! | Lost: $809 |

Session Four. Circus Circus. 1:30-2:20PM. Day shift. 2 decks.
I won for the first time in four sessions today and as a reward, I got barred. I should have taken some hints earlier in the session.

I once again played at the $5 two-deck tables and, with what I thought was good camouflage, went as high as two hands of $100. I sometimes started new decks with big bets on the table.

I played at several tables in two different game areas (Circus has three). After a few minutes and some wins, the dealers would start giving me the early shuffle. Instead of dealing out 1-1/3 or 1-1/2 decks out of two, they dealt less than one deck. One dealer, Sophia, would shuffle whenever I would raise my bet anytime after a 1/4 of a deck had been dealt. (A few times I got rid of negative decks, that way but it was still a waste of time.)

The nonsense followed me from one table to the next. At the last table I was just about to leave to end the session (since the hour was up) when a shift supervisor came to the table.

He said, "Hey, you don't have to go find another game. We don't want you to play blackjack here, anymore." My fifth barring (counting the flat-bet ruling at the Horseshoe). Depressed, I went back to my apartment to swim, rest, and think about the less than two days I had left in Las Vegas. | Won: $345.50 |

Session Five. Arizona Charlie's. 7:55-8:55PM. Swing shift. 2 decks.
This is another low-stakes club, with reported good penetration. But, hey, I have less than two days left so what can they do? It would be dumb for me to stop playing now. I'll just use caution.

I used the high-roller shadow approach at Arizona Charlie's. I found a table with just one other player: someone betting more than me. This player bet $100 or more on every hand.

In this high roller's shadow, I was able to spread from one hand of $5 to two of $100 with no real heat. One of the pit bosses, Joseph, was very friendly to me. We had a friendly chat during my small win. Joseph kept his eye on the other player, who actually was a terrible player. Once, for example, he doubled down on a soft 14 versus a ten! The dealer two-card total of 20 showed that this player was not getting hole card info!

Won: $93

Session Six. Continental. 9:35-10:35PM. Swing shift. 2 decks.
When one has been barred three times within a week and a half, paranoia can easily set in. This paranoia may well have cost me some money in this session.

I spread in erratic fashion from one hand of $5 to two hands of $100 and was rewarded—despite the 75 percent penetration—with mostly negative decks. Still, I was a little ahead going into the last deck that I planned to play. In this deck, the count went up.

I had one hand of $25 on the table and lost it as the count jumped up. I wanted to put on a "get even" act and throw out two hands of $50, but saw a pit boss practically sitting on the table and staring at me. At this point I lost my nerve and left and cashed out. Though I won for the session, my cowardly move may have cost me a few hundred dollars. (Of course, I also could have easily lost in the high-counts, but high-counts are what a pro player waits for).

I cursed and second-guessed myself in the parking lot. I know full well that if the Circus barring had not happened today, I never would have left the Continental when I did. Maybe I would not have gone up to two hands of $50, but I never would have left during such a juicy deck.

Won: $137.50

Session Seven. Excalibur. 11:20-11:35PM. Swing shift. 1 deck.
The casino was crowded but I was able to find a few uncrowded single-deck tables. I played until the crowds overwhelmed these tables as well, and then I called it a day. The cards smiled on me in this session.

Won: $346

April 21	Lost: $463.50	Time: 6 hr, 15 min
Week to date	Won: $3,549.50	Time: 16 hr, 40 min

April 22nd

This is the last day of my Las Vegas blackjack venture. My plane east leaves early tomorrow afternoon.

I felt tired and worn down when I awoke. Playing blackjack has really started to wear on me mentally. It's not just the counting and calculating that is draining, it's also the act I need to put on when I play. Trying to play well and win while appearing to be another dumb gambler has started to get to me psychologically.

In addition (as I write more about in the Conclusion) doing this alone is tough. Blackjack, like most other forms of wagering, has severe financial ups and downs. Not really having someone I trust to "bounce" emotions off makes blackjack a wearing experience, emotionally. I now felt very wrung out.

My next eight-week trip, will include a week's break to recharge my batteries after my fourth week. The trip that I took to San Diego after week Five was an excellent idea except that it probably should have been taken sooner and been of longer duration.

"Living blackjack", as opposed to just playing for small stakes or in practice situations, is a learning experience that I imagine all pros go through. And perhaps, it is only the pros who can fully comprehend the emotional roller coaster a player goes through. Survival lessons can't be acted out in practice sessions or even learned from a book; they are learned in a day-to-day, and even a session-to-session process. I will probably be able to take a closer personal inventory on this process when the trip is concluded.

For now, though, the conclusion of my blackjack play:

Session One. Continental. 9:35-10:40AM. Graveyard shift. 2 decks.
The good news was that the heat didn't follow me from last night's shift. The bad news was that I lost in a great penetration game. I battled back near the end winning some high-count bets, but didn't fully make up for some heavy earlier losses. | Lost: $190.50 |

Session Two. Excalibur. 12:05-1:15PM. Day shift. 1 and 2 decks.
Another frustrating session. I not only got great penetration (up to 3/4 on the two-decks) and mostly head-on play, but also pulled off a monster bet spread, going from $5 to as high as two hands of $150! I got dealt stiff after stiff (12's-16's) on the big bets.

Before I played in the two-deck game, I played a little single deck. I won a little in it, but then Lenore started to shuffle up on every bet increase I made. The two-deck action was next.

This session showed how illogical short-term (1 hour, 10 minutes of play) blackjack can be. I win when I get shuffled up on when I am using a small (1-4 or so) spread and I lose when I can get away with a huge (1-60!) spread with super penetration. Another slump appears to be in progress.

| Lost: $708 |

Session Three. Aladdin. 1:45-2:55PM. Day shift. 6 decks.
The penetration again was great (5-1/2 decks out of six). I was willing to play at a crowded table since the game was face up.

But once again, after a decent start, I started losing the high-count bets. I'm getting tired of this!

After I played for about 55 minutes, I told myself that I'd play one more shoe. Not just at the Aladdin, but for the trip. I knew, of course, that I had fallen far short of my financial goals for the trip. I knew now that my trip high was reached in week Five (sometime at Treasure Island in my first session of March 29) and would not be surpassed.

So I played one last shoe. On the very last round, I had two hands of $55 bet—my biggest bet of this shoe. I was dealt an 18 and a 19 versus a dealer six and won on a dealer bust. Though I lost a little money in the session, it was nice to win $110 on the last round. I also escaped barring by the sharp Aladdin crew. Adios, Aladdin and Vegas blackjack. For now, at least!

| Lost: $151.50 |

April 22	Lost: $1,050.50	Time: 3 hr, 25 min
Week 8 Total	Won: $2,499.50	Time: 20 hr, 5 min
Final Trip Totals	Won: $2,303.50	Time: 231 hr, 16 min

Conclusion

My Las Vegas blackjack trip was over. I ended up ahead, but not by nearly as much as I expected I would.

I could be bitter about my experiences in Las Vegas and claim that I was cheated on many occasions, but that would be a foolish, nonsensical response. In reality, there were probably six reasons why my casino performance fell short of expectations.

1) I played too little time to have an accurate gauge of my performance. I was wrong in assuming that 20-25,000 hands would be reaching the long run. A professional card counter probably needs twice as many hands in decent games to have a statistically significant (being down by two standard deviations, or about a 2.5 percent probability), advantage. My results were around one standard deviation south of expectations, something that would occur one run in six, even with perfect play. Not at all statistically significant.

2) Though I am not nearly as bad on this score as many card counters, I played too often in bad games. Two-deck games with around 50 percent penetration like the Stardust, the Flamingo Hilton, and the Las Vegas Hilton should only be played in head-on circumstances. I rationalized my play in these games by saying that I could not overexpose myself in just the good games. That is true, but instead of playing in lousy games, I could have played using wild bet spreads (as first performed on March 2 at the Golden Nugget) in smaller casinos under decent game conditions. I did this in the late stages of my trip. I will do this extensively on my next Vegas blackjack foray.

3) My idea of rotating casinos was good. However, the rotation should have been done in such a way that I would play for two straight weeks in a casino and then not come back again for the rest of my trip. This would make me seem more believable posing as a typical gambler who was "just visiting Vegas to get away from the bad weather" than someone who comes back to play in the same casino a few weeks or a month later. My last three barrings probably could have been prevented if I had done this. Most importantly, I probably could have had better play conditions in a second week of casino play than I did coming back a month (or three weeks) later. That would have meant bigger potential profits.

4) On some occasions when I was not given much heat and was playing under good conditions, I should not have limited myself to

one hour of play. The one hour limit (with the exception of some late trip play at the Nugget) caused me to wear myself down somewhat by extra traveling around Las Vegas, which in turn caused me to take more time to get in my play hours. I am sure that the resulting fatigue cost me money, even if I was not aware of it at the time.

5) Before the trip, I underestimated how mentally wearing playing blackjack can be. The calculations that must be made at casino speed can be draining, but this is only a small part of the mental drain that a professional player faces. Winning in blackjack is tough enough. Winning via skill while appearing to be unskilled to those watching, who are paranoid that you are skilled, takes a lot of energy. Every bet, every play, every word said, every body motion and every eye glance by the skilled player can be critical to his survival. This act of appearing unskilled and a non-threat is the real mental drain created by casino blackjack play.

In virtually all other occupations, people want to be (or appear to be) skilled. They also want outside acknowledgment of their skill. This is a natural and healthy desire. It can be verbal, financial or both. In blackjack, acknowledgment is poisonous because it often leads to barring. Instead of bringing praise to the player, in most casinos large winnings bring suspicion and dislike to the player from bosses who are looking for an excuse to bar. In fact, in sweatjoints like the Barbary Coast and the Gold Coast (where my play career lasted all of 15 minutes on February 28), many clueless blackjack players have been kicked out merely because they have gotten lucky and won a decent amount of money.

All of the above, as I now know, is very mentally draining to any good counter. A player just can't play for long hours at a time without resting. A couple of times that I was aware of—and probably a few times that I was not—I played when I should have been resting. This probably cost me money.

The trip I took to San Diego was a good idea. However, a better idea would have been for me to take it a week sooner, thereby dividing my trip into two four week segments. I should have taken a week away from the game. The resulting mental refreshment probably would have been financially profitable, or would at least figure to be over the long haul.

6) The most successful period of my sports betting career came when I had Sunshine, my ex-girlfriend, living with me. Though we

certainly had our battles and ups and downs, Sunshine brought a sort of stability to my life. Whatever would happen in a game, I felt sure that she loved me just the same and was always on my side— as I tried to be for her. With Sunshine around, wins and losses were less magnified than they've been when I've lived alone. This lack of magnification made the wins occur a higher percentage of the time as compared to when she wasn't part of my life.

As I came to see on my trip, blackjack play is a very lonely, yet turbulent existence. In his book, *Blackjack Secrets*, Stanford Wong mentions in the chapter, "Turning Pro," how professional black-jack play tends to cut off its players from the world. However, having a significant other in one's life can, I am sure, make this existence much less lonely and turbulent regardless of the wild financial fluctuations that exist in the game.

However, the significant other (man or woman) must have special and unique qualities. For me, the woman must be honest about how I am behaving towards her, but also understanding of the turbulence of blackjack (or sports). And I must be honest with her as well. In Las Vegas, I have seen a number of sickening relationships in which the wife of a big bettor is treated as a dependent shadow or trophy of the husband. In my three-year relationship with Sunshine, I was always very aware of that potential trap.

A bunch of one-night stands—one of which I had on April 18— are not the answer in the quest for emotional peace. They often can feel good for the moment, but are not meaningful for long.

Though as yet, I have no basis for comparison, I would predict that having a special woman in my life would make my blackjack play more profitable. My two month Vegas playing experience convinced me of that.

The rules stated are consistent no matter how many decks (one, two, four, six or eight) the game is dealt from.

Blackjack in a casino is played by between one and seven players, who compete not against each other, but against the dealer.

Object of the Game

The object of the game is to get a point total of cards that equals or is as close to 21 as possible without going over that total. A player can win a hand, often called a round, in three ways.

1) He can receive a blackjack (also called a natural) on the first two cards he is dealt. These two cards must be a ten value card—which can be any ten, jack, queen or king—and an ace. The player wins this hand, and is paid at 3:2 odds, unless the dealer also has a ten value card and an ace on his first two cards. In that instance, the hand or round is a tie and no money—or chips—changes hands.

2) His final total is closer to 21 than the dealer's.

3) His final total is any total less than or equal to 21 while the dealer busts (has a final point total that exceeds 21).

A player can lose a round in three ways.

1) The dealer has a blackjack on his first two cards, while the player does not.

2) The dealer—who must keep hitting his hand until he achieves a total of at least 17—ends up with a final total closer to, but not exceeding, 21 than the player.

3) The player busts his hand—exceeds a total of 21. The player still loses his bet on a busted hand even if the dealer later busts on his own hand (when playing out his hand versus other players at the table who have not busted out and have not received a blackjack). This bust "tie," which in effect goes to the dealer, is the basis for the casino edge in blackjack. As will be shown in Player Options on page 176 the player has several options that are not available to the dealer, which can greatly lessen this advantage.

Card Values

Unlike most other card games, the suit of a card is totally insignificant in the game of blackjack. A nine of clubs is, for purposes of blackjack play, the same as the nine of hearts.

Twos through nines are worth their face value: for example, a seven is worth seven points and a five is worth five points.

Tens, jacks, queens, and kings are each worth ten points. Often, these cards are called "picture cards" or "paint" by players.

Aces are unique since they can be valued as either one or 11 points. The player tries to use, and the dealer, by rule, always uses the value of an ace that will most help the hand. For instance, if a player draws a six and a three (total of nine points) on his first two cards and then, on his next card, an ace, he should count the ace as 11 points for a total of 20—a total that he should be satisfied with. (Some beginner players get confused by the ace and hit this 20.) If a player draws a seven and an eight on his first two cards (total of 15 points) and then draws an ace, it counts as one making his total 16. Using the ace as an 11 would bust his hand.

The total of any hand that does not include an ace being used as a point total of 11 is called a "hard" total. A jack (a ten value card) and a nine is a hard 19 total. A seven, a four and an eight is also a hard 19 total. A six, seven, and an ace is a hard 14 total since the ace must count as one point in this hand.

The total of any non-busting hand in which the ace could be used as an 11 is called a "soft" total. For example, a player drawing a five and an ace on the first two cards of a hand has a soft 16 total. Drawing a seven to this hand would now give the player a hard total of 13 since the ace must now count as a one point value. (If it had to count as 11, the hand would be busted.) It is important to remember that a soft total can never be busted by another draw.

How Rounds Are Dealt

Before each round is dealt, each player at the table places a chip or chips (purchased before he started play) in the betting square in front of him. In some casinos—including all in Nevada—a player is allowed to wager cash, which can be placed in the bet box. However, if he wins the wager, the profits are always paid in chips. The chips or cash placed in the betting box is the amount that the player is risking on the round, unless certain options, later discussed, are taken. The amount originally bet by the player must be equal to at least the table minimum, which can be anywhere from $1 to $500. The most frequent table minimum in Las Vegas is $5. The amount originally bet cannot be greater than the table maximum (which can be anywhere from $25 to $10,000!)

The players at the table are each dealt two cards by the dealer. The dealer deals from his left to his right (from right to left from the player's perspective). The dealer actually deals each player one card and then deals himself a face-up card, which can be seen be all the players. A second card is then dealt to each player. The dealer completes the dealing of the round by giving himself a card that is face down (its value is not seen or known by anyone, including the dealer) and placed under his first face up-card. This card is called the dealer's hole card.

The first two player cards can be dealt either face down or face up by the dealer. In almost all Las Vegas blackjack games, the first two player cards in six or eight deck games are dealt face up and can be seen by all, while in one-, two- or four-deck games the first two player cards are dealt face down and can be seen only by the player holding the cards (and occasionally by the alert eyes of others). In face-up games, players are prohibited from ever touching the cards. In face-down games, the players can hold the cards, but only with one hand.

After the first two cards have been dealt, play begins, starting with the first player dealt (at the dealer's left or player's right). This player is often called the first baseman since his position at the blackjack table is analogous to a first baseman in a baseball infield. The player can either take another card—done by scratching his two cards on the table in a face down game or by pointing for a hit in a face up game—or stay if he is satisfied with his total. These hit cards are always dealt face up. Staying at any time during the hand is done by placing the first two cards under the bet chips in a face down game or by a waving off motion (like shooing away a fly) in a face-up game. A player can take as many additional cards—one at a time—as he wishes until he is either satisfied with his point total or has busted. On a bust, the player in a face down game turns over his first two cards, so the dealer can confirm that he has indeed busted. In a face up game, the dealer knows by sight and addition that the player has busted. All cards from a busted hand are immediately placed in the discard tray.

If any player is dealt a blackjack (a natural) on his first two cards in a face down game, he throws the cards over face up to show his blackjack to the dealer. Assuming that the dealer does not have a ten or an ace as his face-up card (thus making a blackjack impossible for him) or as soon as it is confirmed (with a ten or ace card up) that the dealer does not have a blackjack, the player is paid 3:2 for his blackjack win; i.e., he gets $15 for a $10 original bet. (The player should avoid the very few games in which a player blackjack is paid at just even money, since this rule costs the player an astronomical 2.3 percent.)

If the dealer has a blackjack, (usually determined by peeking under the ten or an ace either manually or by using an auto-peek device), he immediately (with no further play) takes away the chips of all players excepting those who also have a blackjack. In some casinos, the dealer does not check for an ace with a ten up-card. This means that he could reveal a blackjack after the players complete their hands.

Assuming that the dealer and some players do not have a blackjack, play continues. After every player—going from right to left or first base to third base—finishes his hand, either by busting or standing (staying on his final total), the dealer then plays out his hand. Unlike the player, whose options we will explore further in a moment, the dealer has no choices in how he plays his hand.

The dealer starts to play out his hand by turning over his hole card. If his first two cards, assuming that a blackjack has been ruled out, total between 17 or 20 (hard or soft), his hand is complete. In some casinos, (notably in downtown Las Vegas and in Northern Nevada) the dealer hits soft 17's (costing the player approximately .2 percent), but we'll assume Strip rules in this discussion. Assuming that the dealer's two card total is 16 or less, he keeps hitting his hand until he either reaches a total of 17-21 (hard or soft) and stands, or he busts. If the dealer busts, he pays out any players at the table who have not busted or drawn a blackjack. If the dealer ends up with a 17-20 total he collects the chips from the players whose final point total is less than his and pays the players whose non-busting totals are greater. If the dealer ends up with a 21 total, the players with unresolved hands all curse as the dealer takes the chips of all the players excepting those who also have a 21 total. On this or any other tie (push), the dealer usually taps the spot next to the tying player's chips to indicate (to the eye upstairs) a tie and no chip exchange.

Player Options

Unlike the dealer, who must play his hands according to preset rules, the player has options in the play of his hand. If used correctly, these options by themselves go a long way towards eliminating the house edge, created by the player having to play first. Let's examine these options.

1) **Stand or hit.** Unlike the dealer, the player can stand or hit on any total. On a total of hard 12-16, a player can stand on his total and hope that the dealer subsequently busts. Against a low (two through a six) dealer up-card, it is often the correct play to play this way. (Of course, some uninformed or beginner players stand on totals like soft 14 even though they can not bust with one draw on this hand and can win only if the dealer does bust. I've even seen a few beginners stand on hard totals of under 12!)

2) **Double Down.** If the player has a strong first two-card total, which he thinks could be greatly improved with one more card, such as an ace or a ten, the player may double his original bet. In a face-down game, the player turns over his first two cards when he wishes to double down; in the face-up game he just says, "double" while sliding over a new stack of chips next to the original bet. In exchange for being allowed to double the original bet, the player receives one and only one more card. He can not draw additional cards. The double down card is usually dealt face down in face down games and face up in face up games. Though the house does allow players to double down for less than the original bet, this is nearly always a sucker play. Some strange and very rare rule exceptions make doubling down for less a very intelligent play. (I did not encounter any of these rules in my Vegas trip.)

Doubling down correctly is an extremely critical option for the player because it allows the player to maximize the financial power of some of his strongest hands. It allows the player to invest more money on hands which he is a favorite to win.

Some casinos, notably most of the ones in Northern Nevada, allow players to double down only on totals of ten or eleven. While these totals are by far the best ones with which to double down, this rule can cost the player over .25 percent. The Excalibur single-deck game allows the player to double down only on totals of nine, ten and eleven: a .132 percent player disadvantage.

3) **Pair Splitting.** If the player has two cards of the same denomination as his first two cards, he can split these cards to form two separate hands. (In every casino I've played in, except one in Michigan, all ten value cards are considered the same for pair

splitting purposes.) To split a pair, the player must fully match his original bet (unlike doubling down when a player can double for less). In a face-down game, the two cards are thrown over face-up, as with doubling down. In a face up game, the player tells the dealer he wants to split the pair. The player then plays each part of the pair face up as a separate hand, ending up by either standing or busting (and losing that part of the bet) before going on to the next part of the split.

In most casinos, a player may resplit a pair. For instance, if a player splits threes and then receives another three as the second card of one of the hands, he may start another hand by matching his original bet yet again. Most casinos do not allow more than four total hands to be played on pair splits. In other words, a player may usually split up to three times.

Some casinos permit players to double down after a split: an option worth .14 percent to the player who uses it correctly. When this option is permitted, a player may double any of the split hands. For example, if a player splits twos and gets a nine card on one of the twos for a total of 11, he may double that part of the split hand (putting out another pile of chips doubling the bet). Exactly one more card is dealt to that hand: the same as for a normal double down. In games in which doubling down is allowed after splits, the player is more likely to split pairs.

In most casinos, aces may be split just once. In addition, in virtually every casino, a player may hit the split ace just once. For instance, if a player splits aces and receives another ace, he is usually stuck on that hand with the lousy total of soft 12 which can only win if the dealer busts.

The reason that most casinos have these rules regarding aces is that starting a hand with a total of 11 is extremely strong for the player. Since a ten-value card is the most likely card to be drawn, a player has an excellent shot at receiving a 21 (or possibly two 21's) on this split: thus the usual restrictive rules on splitting aces.

Pair splitting is one of the most misunderstood and misplayed options in the game of blackjack. As I explained in the Introduction, even most counters don't really understand exactly why it is financially prudent to split when this is the option called for.

4) **Insurance.** When the dealer has an ace as his up card, the player is given the insurance option. (Some casinos, including most in

Canada, do not offer insurance.) The dealer offers this option by asking, "Insurance?"

If a player takes insurance, he is making a side bet that the dealer has a ten value as his hole card, and thus a blackjack. The player can bet up to a maximum of one-half of his original bet on an insurance bet. The player receives 2-1 odds on this bet. If the dealer does have a blackjack—a ten value card in the hole—the player loses his original bet (unless it is also a blackjack in which case his original bet is a tie) but gets paid 2-1 on the insurance bet. A hand like this results in a financial tie for the player. If the dealer does not have a ten in the hole—and thus not a blackjack—all insurance bets are lost. Play then proceeds in the usual fashion.

Insurance is also a very misunderstood option. A common mistake made by players and one that is encouraged by (often well-meaning) dealers is to make an automatic insurance bet on a blackjack. When a player blackjack is insured, it is called an "even-money" play; whether the dealer has blackjack or not, the player collects "even-money" on his original bet. For example, let's say that the player bets $10 originally and gets a blackjack versus a dealer ace. If he bets insurance for $5 (the maximum allowed) and the dealer has a blackjack, the player will collect $10 on the insurance bet (2-1 on a $5 bet) and break even on his original hand for a $10 profit. If the dealer does not have a blackjack, he collects $15 (3-2 odds on $10) on his original hand and loses the $5 insurance bet for a $10 profit. Either way, the profit is $10 or "even-money" on the original bet.

Since "only tying" with a blackjack is a frustrating experience, many players opt for the guaranteed payout at even odds. This is usually a costly mistake. Let's see why.

Let's take a one-deck example. Let's say that off the top of the deck in a head-on game, you have a blackjack versus a dealer ace. The 52-card deck starts out with 16 ten-value cards, which can give the dealer a blackjack; however, you have one of those ten value cards in your hand, leaving just 15 possible blackjack-creating hole cards for the dealer out of the 49 now unknown cards.

Let's say, as above, you have bet $10 on the original hand. Playing out the scenario, the 49 possible ways and always betting insurance, you would make a $490 profit: $10 on every hand. If you never bet insurance, you would make a $510 profit (34 times $15 [which is 1-1/2 times $10]) when the dealer did not have blackjack and break even the 15 times that he did have a blackjack, for a $510 total profit.

A far dumber and usually far worse mistake than insuring a blackjack is insuring a 20. The thinking on this maneuver is that a player wants to "protect" his good hand in case "that damn lucky dealer" has a blackjack. With two tens now in his hand (this assumes that the player has two tens rather than a less likely nine and ace for a soft 20), not only is the dealer less likely to have a blackjack, but also the player now stands the possibility of losing both the insurance bet and the original hand. This will occur if the dealer manages to get a three or more card 21 off his ace up card. This certainly can and has happened! In addition, if the player does manage to win his 20 hand, he profits just half a bet (remember the lost insurance bet?) Thus, the player who insures a 20 is risking 1-1/2 bets while putting himself in a position to win at most 1/2 a bet! In other words, he is risking three times what he can gain! Plus, insurance is more than normally likely to be a bad bet because two of the cards that will win the insurance bet for the player are right in his hand (this again assumes that the 20 is made up of two tens instead of an ace-nine soft 20: a hand that is obviously a better insurance bet possibility [though still a losing bet off the top of the deck] since no tens are in the players hand). Off the top of a single deck game, a player who insures a two-ten 20, has just a 14 in 49 chance of the dealer having a blackjack; this is giving away a 14 percent edge!

Occasionally—since so many normal players do make this error—it can be a good form of advertising for a counter to insure a blackjack (and yell "even money" when doing so) at the wrong time (insurance, as I'll show in the Hi-Opt Count System on page 188, should really be taken only if someone is counting and the count is at a certain level). This makes the pit think he is a "normal" player. I don't recommend insuring blackjacks all the time, but doing so at the right time can add greatly to career longevity.

Also, the smart card counter can use the stupidity of other players who insure 20's in face-down games to his advantage. (I would not recommend this play, especially a two-ten 20, for cover because I feel that it is too costly an error.) When a player insures and places his cards underneath his chips (meaning he won't want a hit if the hand continues) in a face-down game, I have found that it signals a 20 (which is, again, usually two tens) a very high percentage of the time. This unseen card knowledge helps me to make my own insurance decision, usually leading me towards not taking it.

5) **Surrender.** Most casinos do not offer this player option. However, those that do so are giving the player—especially a card counter—an important weapon.

When a player surrenders his hand, he does so, with very rare casino exceptions, immediately after receiving his first two cards. When he takes this option, he is giving up the hand (almost always a stiff hand, like a 15 or a 16 versus a dealer ten), but getting half of his money returned. The house takes the other half of the bet. However, if the dealer has a blackjack, the player loses the whole bet. A very few casinos in the world offer early surrender; which gives the player half of his bet back even if the dealer does have a blackjack.

When used properly, the surrender option can be used to cut losses. For a counter using a wide bet spread, cutting down losses on his big bets can make a significant difference in his long-range bottom line.

Appendix B: Basic Strategy

The basic strategy for making decisions on how to play black-jack hands was first developed in the late 1950's and early 1960's. Using only the knowledge of a player's own cards plus the dealer up-card, basic strategy shows the best way to play every conceivable blackjack hand. Perfect use of basic strategy will reduce the edge of the casino to usually no more than .5 percent over the player. This rate of player loss is far less than in any other available casino game. A player who just plays perfect basic strategy will, at worst, be losing money at one-fourth the rate of the normal blackjack player (who loses at about a 2 percent rate). With rarely-found good rules in a single-deck game, a non-counting basic strategist can even be playing with a small long-range advantage (as much as .16 percent) over the casino!

Even when a player has an edge over the casino by card counting, he still uses basic strategy to determine the play of his hand over 80 percent of the time. Before learning card counting, a player must know, *without any hesitation, whatsoever*, basic strategy. There are several differences between one-deck and multi-deck basic strategy: thus I will show tables for both.

Table 1: Multi-Deck Basic Strategy
Hard Total Standing and Hitting

Player Total	Dealer Up Card									
	2	3	4	5	6	7	8	9	10	A
17-21	Always Stand									
13-16	S	S	S	S	S	H	H	H	H	H
12	H	H	S	S	S	H	H	H	H	H
11 or less	Always Hit									

Notes: H = Hit, S = Stand. Player should stand on three card or more total of 16 versus a dealer 10.

Table 2: Multi-Deck Basic Strategy
Soft Total Standing and Hitting

Player Total	Dealer Up Card									
	2	3	4	5	6	7	8	9	10	A
19-21	Always Stand									
18	S	S	S	S	S	S	S	H	H	H
17 or less	Always Hit									

182

Table 3: Multi-Deck Basic Strategy
Hard Doubling Down: Two Card Totals

Player Total	Dealer Up Card									
	2	3	4	5	6	7	8	9	10	A
11	D	D	D	D	D	D	D	D	D	H
10	D	D	D	D	D	D	D	D	H	H
9	H	D	D	D	D	H	H	H	H	H
8 or less	Always Hit									

Note: D = Double Down.

Table 4: Multi-Deck Basic Strategy
Soft Doubling: Two Card Totals

Player Total	Dealer Up Card									
	2	3	4	5	6	7	8	9	10	A
19-20	Always Stand									
18	S	D	D	D	D	S	S	H	H	H
17	H	D	D	D	D	H	H	H	H	H
15-16	H	H	D	D	D	H	H	H	H	H
13-14	H	H	H	D	D	H	H	H	H	H

Table 5: Multi-Deck Basic Strategy
Pair Splitting: No Double After Split Allowed

Player Pair	Dealer Up Card									
	2	3	4	5	6	7	8	9	10	A
10,10	Never Split									
9,9	P	P	P	P	P	S	P	P	S	S
8,8	Always Split									
7,7	P	P	P	P	P	P	H	H	H	H
6,6	H	P	P	P	P	H	H	H	H	H
5,5	Never Split (treat as 10)									
4,4	Never Split (treat as 8)									
2,2 and 3,3	H	H	P	P	P	P	H	H	H	H
Ace,Ace	Always Split									

Note: P = Split.

Table 6: Multi-Deck Basic Strategy
Pair Splitting: Double After Split Allowed
(only differences shown)

Player Pair	2	3	4	5	6	7	8	9	10	A
				Dealer Up Card						
6,6	P	P	P	P	P	H	H	H	H	H
4,4	H	H	H	P	P	H	H	H	H	H
2,2 and 3,3	P	P	P	P	P	P	H	H	H	H

Surrender

Multi-deck surrender is called for on the following hands: all 16's except 8,8 (which is to be split) versus a dealer nine, ten or ace and all 15's, except the 8,7 combination, versus 10's. There are no single deck games of which I am aware that offer surrender.

Insurance

Never bet insurance in single or multiple deck games.

Single-Deck Basic Strategy

The hard standing and hitting table for single-deck basic strategy is exactly the same for single-deck as for multi-deck with a few exceptions.

- When the player has a total of 12 versus a dealer four, the player should hit if he has a two card 12 consisting of a ten value card and a two.

- Versus a dealer six, a player should also hit a two card 12 consisting of a ten and a two. Otherwise, the player should stand on these hands.

- If a player has a 12 versus a dealer three, he should stand on a 7,5 or 8,4. Otherwise, he should hit.

- If the player has a two-card 13 versus a dealer two, the player should hit if he has a two-card 13 consisting of a ten value card and a three. Otherwise, the player should stand on this hand.

- On a two-card 14 versus a ten, the player should stand if he has a pair of sevens in his hand. He stands in this instance because two of the four cards in the deck that can help him the most on his hand (sevens) are already in his hand. The player hits on all other 14's versus 10's.

The soft standing and hitting table has only one small basic strategy change for single-deck versus multi-deck. The player should stand on soft 18 versus a dealer ace rather than hit (as in multi-deck). However, in a single-deck game in which the dealer hits on soft 17, the player should hit his soft 18 versus a dealer ace: as in all multi-deck play.

Table 7: Single-Deck Basic Strategy
Hard Doubling Down: Two Card Totals

	Dealer Up Card									
Player Total	2	3	4	5	6	7	8	9	10	A
11	Always Double									
10	D	D	D	D	D	D	D	D	H	H
9	H	D	D	D	D	H	H	H	H	H
8	H	H	H	D*	D*	H	H	H	H	H
7 or less	Never Double									

Note: D* = Special Case (see below)

Doubling down on an eight is a single-deck basic strategy special case in which the correct play depends on the cards that make up the player's two card total of eight. The player should not double down on an eight versus a dealer five or six if his two cards are a six and a two. He should merely hit. A player should double down versus a dealer five or six if he holds a five and a three. If the player holds two fours, he should double down versus a dealer five or six only if doubles after splits are not permitted (which is mostly the case in single-deck play). If doubles after a pair split are allowed, the player should split fours versus a dealer five or six (as well as against a four).

Table 8: Single-Deck Basic Strategy
Soft Doubling: Two Card Totals

	Dealer Up Card									
Player Total	2	3	4	5	6	7	8	9	10	A
20	Always Stand									
19	S	S	S	S	D	S	S	S	S	S
18	S	D	D	D	D	S	S	H	H	S*
17	D	D	D	D	D	H	H	H	H	H
13-16	H	H	D	D	D	H	H	H	H	H

* Hit if dealer hits soft 17.

Table 9: Single-Deck Basic Strategy
Pair Splitting: No Double After Split Allowed

Player Pair	Dealer Up Card									
	2	3	4	5	6	7	8	9	10	A
10,10	Never Split									
9,9	P	P	P	P	P	S	P	P	S	S
8,8	Always Split									
7,7	P	P	P	P	P	P	H	H	S	H
6,6	H	P	P	P	P	H	H	H	H	H
5,5	Never Split (treat as 10)									
4,4	H	H	H	D	D	H	H	H	H	H
3,3	H	H	P	P	P	P	H	H	H	H
2,2	H	P	P	P	P	P	H	H	H	H
Ace,Ace	Always Split									

Table 10: Single-Deck Basic Strategy
Pair Splitting: Double After Split Allowed
(only differences shown)

Player Pair	Dealer Up Card									
	2	3	4	5	6	7	8	9	10	A
7,7	P	P	P	P	P	P	P	H	S	H
6,6	P	P	P	P	P	P	H	H	H	H
4,4	H	H	P	P	P	H	H	H	H	H
3,3	P	P	P	P	P	P	P	H	H	H
2,2	P	P	P	P	P	P	H	H	H	H

Even if a player plans to become a professional blackjack card counter, he must learn the basic strategy first. When known instinctively—and this should take no more than a week's practice for both multiple and single-deck games—the player will know—without hesitation, the usual (basic strategy) way to play any hand that he'll ever come across in a blackjack game. Only when basic strategy is known without needing any thought is the player ready to begin card counting. As the player learns card counting, he will learn how, according to the composition of the remaining deck, he will occasionally play his hands differently than according to basic strategy.

Even if a player does not graduate into card counting after he learns perfect basic strategy, he will still be a better blackjack player than virtually any other player he will come across in the casino. I would estimate that no more than one blackjack player in 50 is capable of playing perfect basic strategy for the game he is involved with. And, as I've already written, a perfect basic strategist will play with a smaller disadvantage in virtually any blackjack game than he will in any other casino game. In virtually all Las Vegas single-deck games, the perfect basic strategist will be playing with no more than a .2 percent disadvantage and, often, with virtually no disadvantage at all. This small house percentage edge means that the perfect basic strategist would expect to lose just $2 for every $1,000 that he wagers over the long run. In multi-deck games, the basic strategist usually faces a .5 percent or less disadvantage; this player in the long run will lose just $5 (or less) for every $1,000 he wagers. Though the perfect use of basic strategy in blackjack is certainly not a way in which to make money or play for the long haul, a perfect basic strategist, who is a recreational gambler (who has brought along only money that he can afford to lose), can—with a modicum of good luck—make money at the blackjack tables over a short run, such as a two or three-day vacation. His probabilities of a short term win in blackjack are certainly far better than in any other casino wagering proposition.

Appendix C: Hi-Opt Count System

A Brief Explanation of Card Counting

The premise of basic strategy is that the only cards taken into consideration on a given hand are the cards in a player's hand and the dealer's up card. Whatever cards have been dealt earlier in the deck or the shoe are irrelevant in terms of a player's play decisions on the present hand. The cards of the other players at the table are also irrelevant in terms of basic strategy.

In the 1950's and very early 1960's, as ancient computers and hard-working mathematicians were figuring out an optimal basic play strategy for blackjack, a few smart bettors had already come to realize through their own blackjack playing experiences that when the remaining cards in the deck—and all blackjack games were one-deck games in those days—contained a disproportionately high number of tens, good events for the player tended to happen more frequently than usual. The player was more likely to receive a blackjack (and its 3-2 payoff); the ten and eleven double downs—and in those days virtually no one doubled down on other totals—often tended to become 20 and 21 totals and usual winners; the dealers seemed to bust more often, especially when they had two through six up cards.

These alert bettors, though not having access to very good play strategy, came to understand instinctively that if more money was bet when the deck was rich in tens (and a few of these alert bettors realized the strength of aces because of their place in the player blackjack), a player could make blackjack a game in which the player and not the casino would have the edge! Though probably not being aware of mathematical terms like dependent sequential events, which is what blackjack is, these early counters were able to turn the tables on the casinos by betting much more heavily in ten and ace rich situations than when the deck did not have this composition. The optimal betting strategy for blackjack (as opposed to its playing strategy, which lagged far behind) was known by the early counters and is basically the same today.

For over ten years (I have even heard of one bettor, now deceased, who was perhaps the very first known card counter; he began his casino blackjack assaults in the late 1940's), these few bettors enjoyed advantages over the casinos, which never before and probably never again will exist. These early counters used tremendous bet ratios, like $1-$500, to take advantage of the betting strategy of counting. The big bets were placed in ten (or ten and ace) rich decks. The tiny bets were made when the deck was lean in tens (and aces). These giant bet ratios and the 100 percent deck penetration (virtually every game was dealt to the last card until the 1960's) won tremendous sums of money for these few early counters despite fairly poor, by today's standards, play strategies and a fair amount of dealer and house cheating, which existed at that time, but now, at least in Nevada and Atlantic City, is probably very rare. Ed Thorp, in his classic blackjack book, *Beat the Dealer,* writes of the success of some of these first counters, which included himself, in the late part of this era. Thorp's (and other) mathematical and computer work on the game of blackjack confirmed what the early counters had known for as long as 15 years: extra tens and aces in the deck benefit the player while surpluses of low cards, especially fives, hurt the player. These facts were also used to help put the final touches on basic strategy.

From the later 1960's through today, play strategies for various counts have been developed. These strategies were developed to help the player know the best time to vary his play from basic strategy, according to the composition of the deck. This play strategy, unlike basic strategy, is based on dependent sequential events. To use one quick example, basic strategy says to hit a 12 versus a dealer three. However, most count play systems say that if the count is slightly positive (+1 true count, or more, in Hi-Opt I), the player should stand because the chances of a player bust as well as a subsequent dealer bust are greater than normal (because of the greater than normal number of tens left in the deck or shoe.)

Thus was born card counting. Though the blackjack games and the casinos awareness of card counting have changed greatly since the early 1960's, the principle of card counting and the reasons for its success (which I have written about in more detail in the chapter on card counting myths) have basically remained the same. When the composition of the remaining cards is rich enough in tens and aces (different games and rules require different amounts of richness), the financial edge in the game of blackjack goes over to the player's side of the table. This earthshaking event never occurs in independent event (which means that the odds of an event's occurring always stay the same, regardless of the events that proceeded it) games such as craps, keno, roulette or slot machines.

The Hi-Opt I Count System

A running argument that exists among card counters is which blackjack count system is the best. For over 20 years, computer simulations have been used to "prove" that one count system is better than another.

To me computer simulations are just that: simulations. The real world of the casino of the mid-1990's is very tough to simulate on a computer. A computer simulation does not have a pit boss or shift supervisor glaring at and putting mental pressure on a suspected card counter. A computer simulation does not have a shift supervisor starting a conversation with a suspected counter in order to see if his eyes avoid his to look at and count the cards. A computer simulation does not have a stupid player doubling down on a 12 (a play I've seen) and busting with the ten which would have gone very well with your big-bet eleven double down (and instead you get an ace) and its possible brief mental distraction. A computer simulation does not have a perfect basic strategy player and/or dealer very loudly second guessing a losing "strange" play by a professional card counter (such as busting on a 13 hit versus a three in a very negative deck). A computer simulation does not have a cocktail waitress yelling out, "Drinks, anyone?" while the card counter is deciding whether to bet insurance on an important play. In other words, no computer simulation can put into its program the thousand-and-one possible distractions that a counter will face when he plays in the real world of the casino, at casino speed. Casino distractions, by the way, are why my casino win expectations are always less than how I perform in my home play.

Now, the above is not to say that computer simulations of the game of blackjack are worthless. Thirty years ago, as stated, computers were the instruments used by Dr. Ed Thorp to make blackjack a potential winning game for the card count player. Computers were also a big aid in developing the perfect basic strategy. Computers have been an absolute necessity in creating play strategies (or when to vary from the basic strategy) for every count system. Today, computer runs are excellent at showing the profitability of games when certain rules and conditions—such as deck penetration and a certain number of other players at the table—are imposed. To an extent, computer software can be used to show the long-range financial effects of bet camouflage. However, virtually none that I have seen or read of can fully imitate what a good counter playing for decent money must do to mask his betting style in the real world of the casino—though my east coast computer friend and blackjack player, Norm Young (mentioned in the acknowledgments), may have come closest in his software.

One reality of casino play, that can not be simulated by a computer, is that all card counters make mistakes in casino play. I mentioned some of mine in the diary. And, these were just the mistakes that I caught. I am positive I made others. The counter who says that he always plays perfectly with his only "mistakes" being intentional ones for the benefit of the pit bosses is either a liar or an ignorant fool. What a card counter needs is an efficient count system that is simple enough to use at casino speed with a minimum amount of mistakes.

Thus, for me, a balance of simplicity and effectiveness was needed when I decided which blackjack count system to use in the casino. The count that satisfied these qualifications for me was the Hi-Opt I. Early in my blackjack play, I started using a side count of aces for bet decisions. This factor, as I wrote in the Introduction, I believe is underestimated by Lance Humble in his *World's Greatest Blackjack Book*. Later I expanded the ace side count for play decisions. The betting efficiency of this count system (which tells the counter the optimal time to raise his bets) is .96 and its playing efficiency (which tells the counter how to play his hands) is .635. The play and efficiency level of the Hi-Opt I is very competitive with other count systems. Most of the few that score higher are much more sophisticated and thus much more difficult to use under casino pressure and speed. Accordingly, they may cause their users to make many more mistakes than I do.

The Hi-Opt I user counts threes through sixes as low cards (adding one to the running count each time he sees one of these cards) and counts all ten value cards as high value cards (subtracting one from the running count each time he sees one of these cards). The running count, again, is the calculation in which the user subtracts the number of high cards (tens) that have come out of the deck or shoe from the number of low cards (threes, fours, fives and sixes) that have come out. For example, if on the first round of a deck or a shoe, four low cards (threes, fours, fives, or sixes) and two high cards (ten-value cards) were dealt, the running count for the deck or shoe would now be +2 (four low cards less two high cards). There are two more high cards left in the deck or shoe than low cards (as I'll show, the significance of this difference in differing conditions is shown in the true count).

I keep a side count of aces because of the uniqueness of the ace in blackjack, and, especially because the Hi-Opt I does not count the ace. Rounding out to the nearest 1/4 deck, since there is normally one ace per quarter deck, I add one to the running count for each "extra" ace left in the deck (or shoe) and I subtract one from the running count for each ace the deck (or shoe) is lean for betting purposes. An ace should be treated as a high card (i.e., as a ten-value card) for betting purposes because of its placement in a black-jack—the winning hand that pays the player at 3:2 odds. For example, if I am playing in a two-deck game and there are five aces left in the deck with 3/4 of a deck left to be dealt, I raise my running count by two since a "normal" 3/4 deck has three aces. In such a game, I am more likely to be making a larger than normal bet since I am more likely than normal to be dealt a blackjack on the next hand.

The side count of aces is also important for play decisions. Let's say I want to double down on an eleven: the most likely time I would be doubling down. If the remaining deck is ace rich, I would be less likely to double down because an ace on my eleven would be disastrous; I would be left with a 12 total and could only win my double down if the dealer busts. For this play decision, the ace has the value of a low card.

A very critical decision in which the ace should be treated as a low card is the insurance decision—the most important strategy variation for a counter in a single-deck game (and still a very important variation in multiple deck games). Extra aces still in the deck make it less likely that the dealer will turn over a blackjack when checking under the ace up card. When the remaining deck is ace poor, a dealer blackjack becomes more of a possibility. The most frequent decision a blackjack player is faced with is the 16 versus 10 decision. A player faces this decision about once every 30 or so hands. In this play decision, the ace—one of the five cards that won't bust the player—should be treated as a low card. On this play, the more aces left to be dealt, the more likely that hitting is the right decision—even though aces make the count rise for betting decisions. For players using the High-Low count (in which twos through sixes are low and tens and aces are high cards)—the 11 double down, the 16 versus the ten and the insurance bet all have great potential to be played incorrectly because the ace is always treated like a ten: a high-value card.

The nine and ten, as well as the infrequent eight double downs are other occasions in which the ace should be counted as a high card. The more of them left in the deck, the better the deck is for the player and the more likely a player will double down.

Largely because of its importance as a low card for the insurance and the 16-versus-ten decisions, I decided to keep a separate side count of the aces for play decisions. The other play decisions are also important, but the insurance and the 16-versus-10 decisions were what led me to keeping an ace side count for play decisions.

Most counters are poor at calculating the true count: the count obtained at by dividing the running count by the number of decks remaining. The reason that a true count is so critical is that the number of extra high or low cards left in the deck or shoe has a very different significance (for both playing and betting decisions) at different times. As an example, two extra high cards (a running count of +2) being in the shoe at the very beginning of a six-deck game is equal to about 1/3 of an extra high card per deck: no real advantage (see "True Count Advantages in Various Games" beginning on page 29). However, two extra high cards with just one-deck left to deal is significant. Two divided by six (decks remaining) equals 1/3, while two divided by one (deck remaining) equals two: or six times 1/3rd! Thus, the necessity of using the true count.

Some counters claim they get the true count by "eyeballing" the cards left in the discard tray to figure out how many decks have been dealt and subtract this number from the total number of decks in the game. The running count is then divided by this number. However, I have known very few counters who eyeball very successfully. Virtually none can accurately estimate the discards within 1/4 of a deck in shoe games. When I started practicing the true count, I came up with another way of figuring out how many cards have been dealt; my method virtually always has me within 1/10 of a deck accuracy in one- and two-deck games and more often than not within that accuracy in shoe games (in which I'm virtually always within a 1/4 of a deck accuracy).

In my deck count down system, I count every participant at the table, including the dealer, as one player. For each player on a round, I subtract 1/20 of a deck dealt (or .05 decks). Let's say that I open up a six-deck shoe with two other players at the table. If we all play one hand, there will be 5.8 decks left after the first round (1/20 deck times four equals .2 decks, which is subtracted from six decks). If I decide to play two hands on the next round and the other two players stay at the table each playing one hand, there will be 5.55 decks left in the shoe after the second round.

There are two modifications I use to sharpen the accuracy of this countdown system. One is subtracting another 1/20 of a deck whenever a player splits a pair. And another is subtracting an extra tenth of a deck once every two decks. For example, in the six-deck shoe game mentioned above, let's say there are now 4.3 decks left in the shoe. Let's say that the same two players and I are still at the table and that we each play one spot. After this round, assuming no splits, I would calculate four decks to be left in the shoe since I would be subtracting an extra tenth of a deck at this point. I'll subtract another extra tenth of a deck when the two-deck-to-go level is reached. One can also subtract an extra 1/20 of a deck each deck, as I do in two-deck games after the first deck is dealt, instead. In single-deck games, I subtract an extra 1/20 of a deck after, and if, the 1/2 deck level is reached and dealt from.

My deck counting method is easier to use than you might think. Try it! Keeping an accurate track of decks to deal and thus a true count is necessary to win in blackjack.

I will now show the table indexes for the Hi-Opt I count system. All index numbers are true count numbers. All index numbers take into account all of the cards seen up to the time that the player makes his decision, including the ones in his present hand.

How To Read the Hi-Opt I Count Charts

The tables should be read this way: the Hard and Soft Hitting and Standing Tables tell the player when to stand. When the true count is equal to or greater than the index number, the player stands. When less, he hits. In the Hard and Soft Double Down Tables, the index number tells the player when to double down in the same way. The pair splitting tables are the same—split the pair when the true count is equal to or greater than the index number—with one major and minor exception. The major exception is splitting eights against a ten. In this case, when the true count is greater than +5 in a non-DAS game, or greater than seven in a DAS game the player does not split the eights. He splits eights only when the true count is lower than or equal to the index in this case. The reason for this exception is that a high true count makes a dealer 20 and two player 18's much more likely than usual. In this case, the player should stand—or surrender the hand if the game permits—on the two eights and accept the probable loss of one hand rather than split and have a very possible loss of two hands. In this instance, not splitting is a defensive move that cuts down losses. The minor exception is splitting threes against a seven in a non-DAS game. One should not split the threes if the true count is over +7.

The true count numbers used below were obtained by using Stanford Wong's *Blackjack Count Analyzer*. True counts from -10 to +10 are used in these tables. These tables are for multi-deck games, the pre-dominant blackjack games available. These tables also assume that the dealer will stand on all 17's. While some indexes are *slightly* different in single-deck and dealer hit soft 17 games, the reader will be getting virtually the full-gain of the Hi-Opt I count system by using these charts.

Table 1: Multi-Deck Hi Opt I Strategy
Hard Total Standing and Hitting

Player Total	Dealer Up Card									
	2	3	4	5	6	7	8	9	10	A
18-21	Always Stand									
17	S	S	S	S	S	S	S	S	S	-4
16	-7	-7	-8	-10	-10	+7	+6	+4	0	+7
15	-4	-5	-6	-7	-7	+8	+8	+6	+3	+8
14	-2	-3	-4	-5	-5	H	H	H	H	H
13	0	-1	-2	-3	-3	H	H	H	H	H
12	+2	+1	0	0	0	H	H	H	H	H

Note: Stand if the true count ≥ index number, otherwise hit.

Soft Total: Standing and Hitting

The play for soft total hitting and standing is exactly the same as shown in Basic Strategy with just one count play to remember. With a soft 18 against an ace, the player stands if the true count is +1 or greater. In a single-deck game, stand if the count is zero or greater on this hand. Always hit this hand if the dealer hits soft 17. Outside of this play, always hit or stand according to the Basic Strategy Chart.

Table 2: Multi-Deck Hi Opt I Strategy
Hard Doubling Down: Two Card Totals

Player Total	Dealer Up Card									
	2	3	4	5	6	7	8	9	10	A
11	-8	-0	-9	D	D	-7	-5	-3	-3	+1
10	-7	-8	-9	-10	D	-5	-3	-1	+5	+4
9	+1	0	-2	-3	-5	+3	+8	H	H	H
8	H	+8	+5	+3	+2	H	H	H	H	H
7	H	H	H	+9	+9	H	H	H	H	H

Note: Double down if the true count ≥ index number,
otherwise hit.

Table 3: Multi-Deck Hi Opt I Strategy
Soft Doubling Down: Two Card Totals

Player Total	Dealer Up Card									
	2	3	4	5	6	7	8	9	10	A
20	+10	+8	+6	+5	+4	S	S	S	S	S
19	+6	+4	+3	+1	+1	S	S	S	S	S
18	0	-1	-3	-5	-5	S	S*	H	H	H*
17	-1	-1	-4	-6	-9	H	H	H	H	H
16	+10	+3	-1	-4	-7	H	H	H	H	H
15	H	+5	0	-2	-6	H	H	H	H	H
14	H	+5	+2	0	-2	H	H	H	H	H
13	+10	+6	+3	0	0	H	H	H	H	H

Note: If the true count ≥ index number, double down. *
= On soft 18 versus an eight, hit if the true count < -10,
otherwise stand. On soft 18 versus an ace, stand if the
true count ≥ +1.

Table 4: Multi-Deck High Opt I Strategy
Pair Splitting: No Double After Split Allowed

Player Pair	Dealer Up Card									
	2	3	4	5	6	7	8	9	10	A
10,10	-10	-8	-6	-5	-4	S	S	S	S	S
9,9	0	-1	-2	-4	-3	-6	-10	P	S	S
8,8	P	P	P	P	P	P	P	P	+5	P
7,7	-6	-7	-8	-10	P	P	H	H	H	H
6,6	+1	0	-2	-4	-5	H	H	H	H	H
5,5	Never Split (treat as 10)									
4,4	Never Split (treat as 8)									
3,3	+6	+3	0	-2	P	+7*	H	H	H	H
2,2	+5	+2	0	-3	P	P	H	H	H	H
Ace,Ace	-8	-8	-9	-10	-10	-6	-6	-5	-6	-2

Note: Split if the true count ≥ index number, otherwise treat the same as in the standing and hitting charts. * = Split if the true count ≤ index.

Table 5: Multi-Deck High Opt I Strategy
Pair Splitting: Double After Split Allowed

Player Pair	Dealer Up Card									
	2	3	4	5	6	7	8	9	10	A
9,9	-2	-3	-4	-5	-5	+2	-10	P	S	S
8,8	P	P	P	P	P	P	P	P	+7	P
7,7	-7	-8	-9	-10	-10	P	-9	H	H	H
6,6	-1	-2	-4	-6	-8	H	H	H	H	H
4,4	H	+7	+3	0	0	H	H	H	H	H
3,3	0	-3	-6	-8	P	P	H	H	H	H
2,2	-2	-4	-6	-7	P	P	+5	H	H	H

Note: Aces, tens, and fives (which are never split) are treated the same as in the non-DAS game.

Table 6: Multi-Deck High Opt I Strategy
Late Surrender: First Two Cards

Player Cards	Dealer Up Card			
	8	9	10	Ace
10,6	+4	-1	-2	0
9,7	+4	-1	-2	0
8,8	P	P	+1	P
10,5	+5	+2	-1	+1
9,6	+6	+2	0	+2
8,7	+6	+2	0	+2
10,4	NS	+6	+3	+5
9,5	NS	+6	+3	+6
8,6	NS	+5	+3	+5
7,7	NS	+4	+2	+4
All 13's	NS	NS	+8	NS

Note: NS = No surrender, play this hand according to the previous tables. Otherwise, surrender the hand if the true count is ≥ than the index number.

Ace Side-Count Adjustment

In my opinion, there are five playing decisions in which the ace side count adjustment has the most importance.

1) Insurance. In this critical decision, the Hi-Opt I player should consider the ace a low card. This is because the more aces that are left in the deck, the less likely the dealer is to have a ten underneath his ace for a blackjack. For each extra ace left in the deck—rounding out to a 1/4 deck—the player should subtract one from his running count. For each ace that the deck is lean, the player should add one to his running count. In this case, the less aces (and other non-tens) left to be dealt, the more likely the dealer is to have a blackjack (or a ten under his ace).

2) **16 versus 10.** This decision comes up more frequently than any other in the game of blackjack. For this decision, the player should again consider the ace a low card since these are the Hi-Opt I low cards—with the six being the exception—that a player needs to make (get a 17-21) his hand. For each extra ace left in the deck, the player should subtract one from his running count; for each ace that the deck is lean, he should add one to the running count.

3) **Doubling down on 11.** Again, the player should count the ace as a low card. This is because an ace dealt on a double down will give the player a 12, a poor total, as are the other totals (13-17) that would result from a Hi Opt I low card being dealt in this instance. The running count should be adjusted as in cases 1) and 2).

4) **Doubling down on 8-10.** For these decisions, extra aces in the deck help the player. Having one dealt on a doubling down of an eight, nine, or ten would give the player the best possible total that he could achieve using the double down option. For each ace that the deck is rich, add one to the running count. For each ace that the deck is lean, subtract one from the running count.

5) **Doubling down on soft 18-20.** As in case 4), an ace dealt to these totals would give the player his best possible double down total. The running count should be adjusted as in case 4).

Insurance Decision

I have saved the insurance play for last since it is such a critical decision. The numbers that should be used for the insurance decision in the Hi-Opt I are +2.2 in the single deck and +3 in the multideck games. I tend to use +3 as the index in all games for the following reason: in my deck count down method (see Page 146) I use the same deck(s) amount left for the play decision on one round as I do for the betting decision on the following round. However, insurance is a decision that usually must be made before the play of the hand (assuming no dealer blackjack). Thus, there tends to be more of a deck or decks remaining which the running count is divided by. Because of this, I use the index of +3 (insure at this number or more; don't insure at less) for this play. This stops possible confusion for me as I might be playing both single and multi-deck games in the same casino and it also possibly saves me from losses since the larger number I am using stops me from making possible incorrect calculations based on more cards remaining than I usually would calculate for the single-deck insurance decision.

To make my decision a little more accurate, I keep a side count of aces and count them, as stated previously, as a low card. I add one to the running count for each ace the deck is short or I subtract one from the running count for each extra ace left in the deck.

In my single deck play, I sometimes make potential adjustments off the top of the deck. In this situation, I try to see as many cards as possible at the table. The problem doing this, especially on the insurance bet (so critical in one-deck games and important in two-deck games, which are also dealt face down), is the major reason that I almost have never played with more than two others in a single-deck, and now, most face-down games. If I am alone at the table and playing just one hand, I'll never insure off the top of the deck (unless I decide to insure a blackjack to "advertise" my "stupidity" to the pit as I did in my very first round of play at the Horseshoe on March 7). With at most 16 ten cards left in the deck out of 49 unknown cards, insurance can never be a right play for a solo player playing one hand off the top of the deck. If I see no ten cards in two hands off the top, I know that insurance is a slightly profitable play (16 tens out of 47 cards is a little better than a 1:3 ratio). If a player can see three hands off the top, he shouldn't bet insurance unless he sees no ten cards. In four hands seen off the top, one or no tens seen would make insurance a profitable bet. In five or six hands seen off the top, two or fewer tens seen makes insurance the right wager. In seven hands—if one is at a full table and can somehow see every card—three or fewer tens seen makes insurance the right play off the top.

Because insurance is such a key play—largely because it allows counters to cut losses on big bets when the dealer is likely to have blackjack in high-count decks—I try to make my calculations for this play as precise as possible, especially in single deck play.

Even before I began to play blackjack in the casinos (in February 1993), I had heard of shuffle tracking. A late 1994 and early 1995 series by Arnold Snyder in *Blackjack Forum* made shuffle tracking well known to any blackjack player who hadn't been aware of it before. Though I have much personal skepticism about shuffle tracking, I believe that this is a serious subject that deserves discussion in any blackjack book.

Readers should not make the mistake of confusing shuffle tracking—a method that, in theory, has extraordinary money-making potential in blackjack play—with systems such as New Blackjack in which "card clumping" is discussed in terms of how to play hands based on how various cards are "running." Blackjack experts have shown that these systems simply have no mathematical basis. Advocates of these systems claim that by playing the hands "correctly" according to how the cards are "running," a player can perform miracles such as winning the majority of his 15 and 16 hands. (I'd love to offer anyone who actually believes that some betting propositions.) From what I have read about New Blackjack, its advocates also recommend a Martingale (progressive) type betting style, a style in which players try to win one unit via a progression (doubling up). The Martingale and all wagering "systems" that limit winnings to the minimum but have much higher limits on losses, have made casinos, gambling houses, and bookmakers all over the world billions, if not trillions of dollars in the history of gambling. Stanford Wong and Arnold Snyder have already totally discredited the New Blackjack System in their publications, so I will not discuss it here any further.

Shuffle tracking is a method of tracking large clumps or slugs of low or high cards in shoe games and having them put, via the cut, in known and advantageous positions for the card counter. Let's look at two examples of how shuffle tracking can be very helpful to a card counter. First, let's say that a counter is playing by himself in a shoe game and is able to note a one and a half deck clump of low cards that have a running count value of plus ten (true count value of almost plus seven). If these cards are kept together in the shuffle, the counter can cut them out of play (especially if it is a six-deck game with over 1-1/2 decks cut off) and have a shoe to play in, which has a true count value of over plus two (ten extra high cards divided by 4-1/2 decks). The counter would have over a .5 percent edge (closer to one percent with good game rules) by just flat betting this shoe. And with count and bet adjustments during play, we would have perhaps as much as a two percent edge in such a shoe. The bigger the amount of cards—if they are the plus-value cards—cut out of play, the better. This type of counter shuffle tracker would want shallow, not deep, deck penetration—exactly the opposite desire of a normal counter.

Second, let's say that the tracker has located a one-deck or so shuffle-preserved clump of high cards (tens and aces) that has a count value of minus ten. The shuffle tracker can cut these cards right to the top of the shoe and have a very strong deck off the top. Best yet, this shuffle tracker can bet very big (maximum bets) off the top with a strong (probably over 6 percent!) edge and not appear at all like a normal card counter, who usually makes his big bets late in the shoe. After the high-card clump passes, the counter would make small bets and then would try to follow the high clump through the next shuffle when he can again cut it to the top of the shoe. And as in the other example, this counter would want a shallow cut. In fact, one deck dealt out of every shoe would be just fine, so long as it is highly plus (and also assuming that this tracker can always follow the unbroken ten and ace clump through shuffle after shuffle).

In theory, shuffle tracking is a brilliant idea for playing casino blackjack. The card counter who can shuffle-track perfectly could not only win at a higher rate than the normal card counter, but he could also do so with a smaller bet spread. And if the tracker so desires, he can use a large betting spread with less pit scrutiny than a "normal" counter would endure. He would make his big bets when the pit least expects a counter to make them—off the top or wherever the rich parts of the shoe are located. Casino counter catchers would figure to be frustrated by shuffle trackers since their betting and decision patterns do not follow the normal count pattern of the shoe. And, in fact, some of the big bets would be made when the true count of the whole remaining shoe (the count that normal counters and counter catchers use) would be very negative. Plus, in many cases, trackers love shallow cuts. This is very unlike normal card counters. Shuffle tracking thus has the potential to make shoe-playing card counters with tracking ability much more money with much less casino heat than regular card counting methods. Most likely, good shuffle trackers wouldn't be hassled or barred, but would be comped to the absolute hilt by the casino bosses who would be licking their chops over the inevitable "breaking" of a prime "sucker, who has just been lucky". But, the casino, not the tracker, would be playing the role of the sucker in this example!

As I wrote in the section on player barrings, what should happen theoretically and what happens in reality are often two different worlds. Usually, such is also the case with shuffle tracking.

For a shuffle tracker to have a chance to be successful, one of two events must occur. Either the casino shoe shuffle must be an extremely simple one in which a few different sections of the shoe are kept apart from each other in the shuffle (and hopefully one is a high or low value section) or the shuffle tracker must have a way to remember the value of every segment of the shoe and keep track of the value of the segments each is shuffled then reshuffled into.

There may have been very simple shuffles 15 or 20 years ago in the casino shoe games; I can't say for sure because I wasn't a blackjack player at that time. But, I do know that when I practiced dealing myself six-decks at home, I shuffled pretty thoroughly just so that the new shoe would feel "fresh." And, I would imagine that most players, especially normal players, always have wanted the cards to be well-shuffled and fresh, though not wanting the dealer to take too long to do so (I did my home, thorough six-deck shuffle in three or four minutes).

Since I have played blackjack in the casinos, I have not seen any simple shuffles and this makes shuffle tracking really tough. There are four major reasons why I believe shuffle tracking has at best limited value in the real world of casino blackjack today.

1) A shuffle track player not only has to locate and note the exact value of a good clump (preferably a high one that he can put into play) that is unbroken by the shuffle—very unlikely—or he must know the exact value of the segments this high clump is being mixed with. This exactness is vital for two reasons.

First, in high-count decks, a large part of the player's gain comes from correct play decisions (this is why depth charging—betting more money further into the deck no matter what the count is—can beat some single-deck games; play variation is critical for a counter in the volatile count game of single-deck). To make correct play decisions, one must know the correct true count! After, all, even in the best deck clump, a player won't be getting blackjacks, for which no thinking is required, on every hand! I became suspicious of one allegedly successful shuffle tracker when he told me that he never split tens in his shuffle-tracking play. Ten splitting not only would be a frequent possibility in rich decks, but would be an important and correct option to take. (In my single-deck play, which shuffle tracking has been compared to, ten splits are a correct play about once every eight hours of play.) Even better, ten splitting would bring a shuffle tracker less heat than it would a traditional card counter. This person's explanation that he was afraid of losing his casino RFB comps if he split tens really did not stop my skepticism! Other important plays like insurance can be made correctly only if the tracker not only evaluates the clump's original value correctly, but also keeps track of its current count value.

The second reason for knowing the exact segments of the rich clump and any clump it has been mixed into is that if the rich clump is mixed with a clump of low cards (which is more normal than likely since other parts of the shoe have an excess of low cards), the potential edge of knowing about the rich clump is very possibly gone. If the tracker is satisfied with just finding a rich clump and ignores the clump it is mixed into, he will often be betting big and also making wrong play decisions in situations in which he actually has a disadvantage. A fair number of such bet and play mistakes and such a tracker will go broke. I have serious doubts that very many players can keep track of all shoe segments through a shuffle, know the newly shuffled shoe's new segment values, and make correct bet and playing decisions in the "good" sections of the new shoe at casino speed without the aid of a computer (a felony).

2) When I wrote about the true count and the problems most counters have keeping and calculating it, I mentioned that one of the biggest roadblocks that frustrates counters with their true count calculations is estimating how many decks have already been dealt by "eyeballing" the discards. Virtually no counter that I know is consistently accurate within a 1/4 of a deck in "eyeball" estimations—particularly late in the shoe when the discards are piled highest and the true count calculation is usually most important for both bet and play decisions.

To be a good shuffle tracker, a player has to be not just a good "eyeballer," he must be a perfect one. Being off by 1/4 of a deck in the attempt of cutting the good cards to the top can easily spell disaster. And, if a player hasn't cut the good cards to the top—but still thinks he knows their location—he can't be off even by one round—especially if other players are at the table. If the tracker has discovered a high card one-deck clump (let's say a minus eight true count deck) in the previous shoe and is off by even one round as to when it comes out, it is a good probability that he will either: a) Bet too high one round too soon in a negative part of the shoe or b) Bet too small for one round too long as aces and tens fill the table. I can't speak for other players, but I can say for myself that trying to be that perfect in gauging where the good cards are and exactly when they will be coming out of the shoe (even assuming that all my segment math was perfect) is like trying to climb up the outside of the Empire State Building while wearing a blindfold and having my hands tied behind me!

3) A shuffle tracker must be able to get the cut card or must be a member of a tracking team that has taken over a table. If he does not, it may be difficult to have a strong clump (if one exists) cut to an advantageous part of the shoe. If the shuffle tracker is at a table with other players who do not know his act, he has a major problem. Either he has to get the cut card an inordinate percentage of the time—and the dealer usually rotates it amongst all players—or he has a much tougher job of tracking. And though pit bosses may not be Einsteins, they know enough by now to know why one person would always be demanding the cut card from the other players!

4) Most casinos are now aware of shuffle tracking and with typical overreaction have put in very complicated shuffles and methods of plugging the unplayed cards into the discards. These more-complicated-than-necessary shuffles slow down the game and make the casinos less money. (And, as with card counting, the casinos are reacting to a lone threat out of a huge herd of players. Except with shuffle tracking, I would estimate that instead of inconveniencing and making less money from most of the 999 non-threatening players out of 1,000, they are now inconveniencing and making less money from 9,999 non-threatening out of 10,000 players because of the one accurate shuffle tracker, who poses a real financial threat to the casino.) As an example of the toughness of shuffle tracking, my East Coast computer friend, Norm Young, has analyzed on his software a "step-ladder" shuffle that a casino he plays in uses. He has thus far concluded that at best, a player can get a good and accurate count read on 3/4 of a deck of this six-

deck game: 1/8 of the total cards in the shoe. How often will these cards have a good value which a player can use for good bet and play decisions in the next shoe (assuming that the tracker has the cut card at the key moment)? Probably not that often!

Do the four problems I just brought up mean that shuffle tracking is totally worthless? No, it does not. The theoretical concept of shuffle tracking is sound. No question. However, performing it accurately any decent percentage of the time seems unrealistic.

If a lone player is occasionally able to track, accurately, a slug of high or low cards, he should definitely try to use it to his advantage. The best and most realistic scenario seems to be if a player can somehow cut some rich cards to the top of the shoe. However, being able to do so will turn out to be the exception and not the rule of his play. Shuffle tracking, in virtually all cases, should be considered a bonus: not something that a player should rely on to win in today's casino blackjack.

Probably, the most viable method of shuffling tracking shoes would be by team play. A team of players could conceivably take over a table and have each member track different parts of the shoe. Obviously, elaborate signals would have to be used at the table to convey information to keep the casino bosses in the dark. And, even with team play such as I just described, there would still be very little room for error. In addition, having the same players at the same table for any length of time (unless the team has about 20 or 30 members who rotate tables, pits and casinos) would throw up a huge red flag for the paranoid casino pit bosses.

Appendix E: Final Casino Record

Table 1: Final Casino Record

Casino	Win-Loss Session Record	Time (Hrs:min)	$ Record
Aladdin	4-4	7:35	Won: $570
Arizona Charlies	1-0	1:00	Won: $93
"Cheat" Casino (see March 10)	0-1	:05	Lost: $25
Circus Circus	4-3	5:55	Won: $598.50
Continental	2-2	4:00	Lost: $825
Desert Inn	8-3	11:00	Won: $3,111
Excalibur	4-3	6:30	Won: $1,796.50
Fitzgeralds	1-1	1:20	Won: $165.50
Flamingo Hilton (Laughlin)	1-0	:55	Won: $357
Flamingo Hilton (Vegas)	2-4	5:10	Lost: $1,277
Four Queens	1-1	:20	Won: $154.50
Fremont	1-2	2:40	Won: $332.50
Gold Coast	1-0	:15	Won: $698
Golden Nugget (Laughlin)	2-0	1:45	Won: $1,366
Golden Nugget (Vegas)	19-14	33:15	Lost: $2,039
Harrahs	3-10	11:25	Lost: $2,535.50
Horseshoe	9-4	7:20	Won: $156
Imperial Palace	6-4	8:50	Lost: $464.50
Lady Luck	2-3	2:20	Lost: $126.50
Las Vegas Hilton	5-4	7:15	Lost: $187.50
Luxor	1-2	2:45	Lost: $588.50
Maxim	5-3	7:05	Won: $2,450.50
MGM	4-5	9:40	Won: $812
Mirage	10-14	21:55	Lost: $1,075
Palace Station	8-4	8:30	Won: $537
Pioneer (Laughlin)	0-1	1:05	Lost: $969

Casino	Win-Loss Session Record	Time (Hrs:min)	$ Record
Plaza	3-1	1:16	Won: $366
Ramada (Laughlin)	1-0	:10	Won: $24
Rio	8-3	8:10	Won: $1,490.50
Riverside (Laughlin)	1-0	1:00	Won: $121
Riviera	8-7	14:35	Won: $2,003
San Remo	2-2	3:10	Lost: $446
Sands	4-5	7:00	Lost: $1,749.50
Stardust	4-6	8:10	Lost: $2,500.50
Treasure Island	7-11	17:50	Lost: $90.50
Final Totals	142-127	231:16	Won: $2,303.50

Appendix F: Recommended Resources

The reader wishing to explore the game of blackjack in more detail will find the following books, and computer software to be of interest.

Basic Blackjack, Stanford Wong, Pi Yee Press.

Beat the Dealer, Edward O. Thorp, Vintage Books.

Beat the X Deck Game, Arnold Snyder, RGE Publishing.

Blackbelt in Blackjack, Arnold Snyder, RGE Publishing.

Blackjack Count Analyzer (software), Pi Yee Press.

Blackjack for Profit, Arnold Snyder, RGE Publishing.

Blackjack Forum (magazine), RGE Publishing.

Blackjack Secrets, Stanford Wong, Pi Yee Press.

Blackjack Trainer (Windows or Macintosh software), ConJelCo.

Card Counting for the Casino Executive, Bill Zender.

Current Blackjack News (newsletter), Pi Yee Press.

Playing Blackjack as a Business, Lawrence Revere, Lyle Stuart.

Professional Blackjack, Stanford Wong, Pi Yee Press.

The Theory of Blackjack, Peter Griffin, Huntington Press.

The World's Greatest Blackjack Book, Lance Humble and Carl Cooper, Doubleday.

Index

About the Author

Stuart Perry was born in 1953 and graduated from Oakland University in Michigan with a degree in psychology. He has always had an intense interest in the gaming and statistics fields. For a good number of years Stuart made a living betting and writing about sports, especially pro football. He is currently a consultant on sports betting in the NFL and NBA.

In late 1992, Stuart discovered blackjack. For about a year, he studied and practiced the game very seriously before embarking on the two month Las Vegas odyssey, chronicled in this volume. Stuart says that his knowledge of statistics was very helpful to him in learning about the expectations of blackjack.

Stuart resides in Yonkers, NY.

About the Publisher

ConJelCo is a publisher based in Pittsburgh, Pennsylvania that specializes in books and software for the serious gambler. In addition to this book, ConJelCo publishes the book *Winning Low-Limit Hold'em* by Lee Jones and several software products including *Blackjack Trainer* for the Macintosh and Windows, *Ken Elliott's CrapSim* for DOS, *Percentage Hold'em* for DOS, and *Sozobon Poker* for Windows.

ConJelCo periodically publishes a newsletter, *The Intelligent Gambler*, sent free to our customers. *The Intelligent Gambler* carries articles by our authors as well as other respected authors in the gambling community. In addition, it is the source of information about new ConJelCo products and special offers.

ConJelCo also sells books, software and videos from other publishers. If you'd like a free catalog or to be put on the mailing list for *The Intelligent Gambler* you can write to us at:

> ConJelCo
> 132 Radcliff Dr.
> Pittsburgh, PA 15237

Our phone number is 800-492-9210 (412-492-9210 outside of the U.S.), and our fax number is 412-492-9031.

ConJelCo is on the Internet. You can send electronic mail to us at *orders@conjelco.com*. From the World Wide Web you can reach us at URL *http://www.conjelco.com*. On our web server you'll find a complete, annotated, ConJelCo catalog, demos of software by ConJelCo and others, and lots of other goodies for the serious gambler.